Blough, Jenna,
Moon Palm Springs &
Joshua Tree /
2016.
33305236778019
la   10/12/16

D0179239

PALM SPRINGS
& JOSHUA TREE

JENNA BLOUGH

© AVALON TRAVEL

PALM SPRINGS AND JOSHUA TREE

Cleghorn Lakes Wilderness

Sheephole Valley Wilderness

Twentynine Palms

62

Cholla Cactus
Garden

*Joshua Tree
National Park*

Lost Palms
Oasis

177

Desert Center

10

Mecca Hills Wilderness

Orocopia Mountains Wilderness

0	10 mi

0	10 km

Salton Sea

111

To Bombay Beach
and Slab City

*Chocolate Mountain
Naval Aerial Gunnery Range*

Contents

DISCOVER

Palm Springs &
Joshua Tree

Despite being such near neighbors, the sleek urban chic of Palm Springs and the spiky swath of Joshua Tree National Park appear to have little in common. Their link is the California desert, where relentless sunshine and rocky landscapes evoke a sense of the unknown.

The resort town of Palm Springs got its start in the 1920s and its popularity escalated as a getaway for the Hollywood Rat Pack. Today, it's a stylish time capsule with impeccable mid-century architecture, luxury resorts, boutique hotels, and retro gems tucked away against the rocky foothills. In a landscape of drama and leisure, the gleaming blue of its plentiful swimming pools competes with the crystal blue sky.

Joshua Tree is wild, eroded, and fantastical; its surreal rock formations cooked up through millions of years of erosion, sedimentation, and continental collisions to form hulking, toothy piles of granite. The namesake Joshua trees, with their jagged silhouettes, run rampant among the jumbled piles of boulders. This is the high desert—gorgeous in spring and fall, searing hot in summer, and cold enough in winter that snow sometimes dusts the agave.

Clockwise from top left: rusting jalopy in Joshua Tree; cholla cactus; the 29 Palms Inn; wind farms against the San Jacinto Mountains; rappelling in Joshua Tree; a desert garden.

Joshua Tree was my first experience with the California desert, and I could hardly believe something so magical existed—the right blend of rustic, funky, and chic. I went to Palm Springs that same summer and navigated my way to a classic mid-century boutique hotel where all the guests in the pool knew each other and welcomed us with Bloody Marys.

It's these contrasts that shape Palm Springs and Joshua Tree: the confluence of nearly perpetual sun, well-watered canyons, and bubbling hot springs backdropped by snowcapped mountains and a scoured desert make any visit here unique.

Clockwise from top left: yucca in the Mojave Desert; rock arch in Joshua Tree; giant saguaro cactus; rock climbing in Joshua Tree.

Planning Your Trip

Where to Go

Palm Springs

Palm Springs is a charmed escape. Filled with preserved **mid-century architecture**, nonstop **pool parties**, and lounges to release your inner **Rat Pack**, it was Hollywood's playground in the 1920s through the 1960s—and it still delivers retro pleasures in a modernist time capsule. Take a whirlwind flight up the **Palm Springs Aerial Tramway**, wander amid Picassos and Warhols at the **Palm Springs Art Museum**, or simply park yourself **poolside** and soak in the rays.

Idyllwild

Idyllwild is an **artsy, rustic mountain town** set one-mile high in the forests of the **San Jacinto Mountains**. In under an hour, you can **escape the desert heat** of the searing valley floor with a quick tram ride or a short drive to hike

cool mountain trails or spend the night in a picturesque cabin.

The Coachella Valley

Surrounding Palm Springs is the **Coachella Valley**, with day trips to **date farms, desert museums, hot springs**, and lush canyons. **Desert Hot Springs, Thousand Palms, Palm Desert**, and **Indio** comprise the constellation of towns, but the region is perhaps best known for its popular outdoor music festival: the **Coachella Valley Music and Arts Festival**.

Joshua Tree National Park

Dusty desert roads, jagged **boulder piles**, and spiky **Joshua trees** draw droves of **hikers, rock climbers**, and day-trippers to this otherworldly, geologic landscape. Tour the **historic mines**

views from the South Ridge Trail to Tahquitz Peak

and **ranches** of desert dreamers, wander amid strange cacti and colorful **wildflowers,** and take in the views from **scenic peaks.**

The Yucca Valley

Peppered along the northern border of Joshua Tree National Park are the gateway towns of **Yucca Valley, Joshua Tree,** and **Twentynine Palms.** All offer **unique accommodations** and alternatives to camping in the park, as well as **local saloons, live music,** and **epic desert art** worthy of exploration.

Know Before You Go

High Season (Oct.-Apr.)

October-April is the on-season for both Palms Springs and Joshua Tree National Park, with spring the busiest time of year. Advance reservations for hotels in Palm Springs and campsites in Joshua Tree are a good idea during big events like **Modernism Week** and the **Coachella Valley Music and Arts Festival.**

At only 479 feet above sea level, Palm Springs's low elevation means that temperatures are fairly mild in **winter.** The months of October through April are the most temperate, with temperatures ranging from the high 60s to the low 90s during the day.

Low Season (May-Sept.)

Summer is the low season, with **brutally hot temperatures** holding fast in the triple digits for much of **June, July, August,** and **September.** Some businesses have **limited hours** or close altogether. Joshua Tree National Park remains open, with average highs in the 100s and temperatures not dipping lower than the high 70s at night. Recreational activities are extremely limited, and can even be dangerous.

The San Jacinto Mountains and the town of **Idyllwild** offer a cool retreat during these searing months.

Transportation

The **Palm Springs Airport** (PSP, 3400 E Tahquitz Canyon Way, 760/318-3800, www.palmspringsca.gov) services the resort town and can otherwise save you the 3-4-hour drive from Los Angeles. Prices tend to be high, however, and there are only a few airlines. International travelers should fly into **Los Angeles International Airport** (LAX, 1 World Way, Los Angeles, 424/646-5252, www.lawa.org) and spend a few days in LA before renting a car for the drive east along I-10.

Further exploration of the Coachella Valley and Joshua Tree National Park will require **your own vehicle.** There is no public transportation in Joshua Tree National Park.

Entrance Stations

Joshua Tree National Park (www.nps.gov/jotr) has three entrance stations open year-round. The entrance fee is **$20 per vehicle** ($10 per motorcycle, bike, or on foot), which is good for seven days. The Annual Park Pass is $30, and season pass-holders are often offered a shorter line at entrance stations.

- **West Entrance** (Hwy. 62 and Park Blvd.) is accessed from the gateway town of Joshua Tree and sees the heaviest visitation.
- **North Entrance** (Hwy. 62 and Utah Trail) is located in the gateway town of Twentynine Palms.
- **South Entrance** (off I-10) accesses Cottonwood Spring and sees the fewest visitors.

Visitors Centers

The **Palm Springs Visitor Center** (2901 N Palm Canyon Dr., 760/778-8414, 9am-5pm daily) is housed in the 1965 Tramway Gas Station, near the entrance to the aerial tramway.

The **Joshua Tree Visitor Center** (6554 Park

Palm Canyon fan palms

Blvd., 760/366-1855, 8am-5pm daily) is in the town of Joshua Tree on Park Boulevard before the park's West Entrance with a bookstore, restrooms, and a café.

The **Oasis Visitor Center** (74485 National Park Dr., 760/367-5500, 8:30am-5pm daily) is at the North Entrance in the town of Twentynine Palms with a bookstore, drinking water, restrooms, and picnic tables.

Reservations

In **Palm Springs,** you'll want to book accommodations in advance during spring events **(February-April).**

Camping reservations (877/444-6777, www.recreation.gov, $20) in Joshua Tree National Park are only accepted at two campgrounds—**Black Rock** and **Indian Cove**—and only **October-May**; demand is especially high in spring. If you're planning a weekend camping trip in the park, plan to arrive by **Thursday afternoon** to score a spot. All other campgrounds are first come, first served. Only three campgrounds—Black Rock, Indian Cove, and Cottonwood—have **drinking water.**

Visiting the historic **Keys Ranch** in Joshua Tree is by **reservation only.** Book your tour at any visitors center at least one day in advance.

Palm Springs Weekend

Palm Springs is a hipper Las Vegas, a more restrained and stylish resort destination that's perfect for a weekend getaway. Whether you're lounging poolside at a mid-century resort, partying at a ladies' weekend, or relaxing at a couples' spa getaway, Palm Springs has got your weekend wonderland squared away.

Friday

Fly into Palm Springs airport. Or, if you're driving from LA, hop in the car Thursday night to avoid rush hour and start the weekend early. Spend the afternoon visiting the Palm Springs Art Museum and riding the Palm Springs Aerial Tramway to the top, where you can take in the refreshing view of the valley below.

Back on the desert floor check in to a stylish mid-century hotel, such as the Del Marcos Hotel or the Desert Hills and enjoy some time poolside. For dinner, dine on Pacific Rim plates at retro throwback Tropicale Restaurant and Coral Seas Lounge. At night, opt for tropical drinks at Bootlegger Tiki, retro-chic cocktails at Melvyn's, or stay put on the buzzing patio bar at Coral Seas.

Saturday

After a breakfast with Bloody Marys at Cheeky's, head to the Uptown Design District for vintage shopping. Browse the wares at The Shops at Thirteen Forty-Five, where the stunning architecture matches the vintage and accessories inside, then pick up some Bakelite adornments at Dazzles.

One of the best sights in Palm Springs is the area's stunning mid-century architecture. Pick up a driving tour map at the Palm Springs Visitor Center, itself housed in the Albert Frey-designed Tramway Gas Station, and discover the works of Donald Wexler, William F. Cody, and Richard Neutra, among others. For a sneak peek inside, sign up for a tour of Elvis's Honeymoon Hideaway or historic Sunnylands, which has hosted everyone from British royalty to Hollywood icons.

Tramway Gas Station

Best Pool Scenes

Looking for a buzzing pool scene? Following are a few of Palm Springs' best. Some of these hotel pools are only open to guests, while others allow day-use visitors for events.

- **Ace Hotel & Swim Club** (page 32): Dive into one of Palm Springs' biggest pool scenes at one of this hotel's weekend events.

- **Hard Rock Palm Springs** (page 33): With a poolside cocktail bar, cabanas, and day beds, this pool can turn into a party at any time.

- **Saguaro** (page 33): It's notorious for its lively pool scene.

- **The Parker Hotel** (page 33): Choose from three outdoor pools: one with drink service, one for families, and one for adults only.

- **Sparrows Lodge** (page 33): Rejuvenate in the guest-only pool or party at the bar in the communal barn.

Around dinnertime, enjoy the steamed, grilled, or fried seafood at **Shanghai Red's Bar & Grill** (you'll want the Anthony Bourdain-lauded fish tacos), then take in a drag show before dancing the night away at **Toucan's Tiki Lounge** or mingling with the cool kids at the **Ace Hotel's** pool party.

Sunday

Continue the Saturday party vibe with brunch at **Pinocchio in the Desert** where the bottomless mimosas draw a packed patio crowd. For more calm with your morning, head to Palm Springs mainstay **Spencer's** for upscale resort dining.

Palm Springs and the Coachella Valley are surrounded by epic desert beauty. Nowhere is this more evident than with a hike through **Indian Canyons.** The **Lower Palm Canyon Trail** visits the world's largest fan palm oasis, while **Tahquitz Canyon** offers a short but scenic stroll to a rare desert waterfall.

After your hike, work out the kinks of mind and body with a massage at one of Palm Springs' many **day spas** before packing your bags for the flight or long drive back to reality.

The Best of Joshua Tree

The landscape of Joshua Tree National Park is mesmerizing—from the spiky trees to the scoured desert and jumbled boulders, begging to be climbed. A visit here typically means **camping,** with extra time spent exploring the funky sights of the surrounding desert towns. **Bring water** and **your own vehicle** and plan a week to visit this desert wonderland **October-May.**

Day 1

Start the day off in the town of Joshua Tree at the nouveau diner **Crossroads Café** for a creative take on diner classics, including plenty of veggie options. The laid-back vibe and fresh plates ranging from grilled herbed polenta and eggs to buttermilk hotcakes will set you up for a day of exploring in the park.

After breakfast, follow Park Boulevard to the **West Entrance,** stopping at the **Joshua Tree Visitors Center** to pick up maps, load up on water, and make reservations for the Keys Ranch Tour (Fri.-Sun. Oct.-May) before entering the park.

Enjoy a scenic drive along Park Boulevard into the popular **Hidden Valley** region of the park, stopping off to explore the short nature trails at

A visit to Palm Springs is a trip back in time. Don't miss these Rat Pack-era abodes, whimsical desert structures, and modernist design examples from noted architects.

- **Colony Palms Hotel** once drew glitterati like Frank Sinatra, Zsa Zsa Gabor, Kirk Douglas, Howard Hughes, and Ronald Reagan (page 62).
- **Del Marcos Hotel** was designed by William F. Cody in 1947 and still welcomes hotel guests (page 64).
- **Elvis Honeymoon Hideaway** was the site of Elvis and Priscilla Presley's 1967 honeymoon (page 26).
- **Frey House II,** the second home of famed architect Albert Frey, perches 220 feet above the desert floor (page 26).
- **The Integratron** is a spherical all-wood dome, built by a self-proclaimed alien contactee. It offers sound baths designed to rejuvenate the spirit (page 132).
- **Kaufmann House** was designed by Richard Neutra in 1946-1947 (page 38).
- **McCallum Adobe** was the first Palm Springs homestead. Still standing, it is now home to the Palm Springs Historical Society (page 29).
- **Melvyn's** is where Frank Sinatra once held court (page 34).
- **Pioneertown,** a former Wild West movie set, is open for strolling, shopping, and live music at popular Pappy & Harriet's (page 135).

The Integratron in Landers

- **The Palm Springs Visitor Center** is housed inside the mid-century Tramway Gas Station, with an iconic soaring roofline designed by Albert Frey with Robson Chambers (page 38).
- **The Purple Room** is one of the last holdouts of the Rat Pack nightlife (page 34).
- **The Tropics Hotel,** a 1964 Polynesian-themed resort, still retains its kitschy tiki elements (page 65).

Barker Dam, Cap Rock, and Skull Rock. If you haven't reserved a **campsite** in advance at Black Rock, Indian Cove, or Cottonwood, keep your eyes peeled for available sites at **Hidden Valley Campground** or **Jumbo Rocks.** Try to time your arrival for a Thursday, before campsites have filled for the weekend.

After staking your campsite, check the park calendar for an **evening stargazing tour.**

Day 2

Today, plan your activities around your reservations for the guided 90-minute tour of the **Keys Ranch,** a preserved historic homestead near the Hidden Valley Campground. After the tour, you're perfectly positioned for a hike to the remains of the **Wall Street Mill,** another legacy of rancher Bill Keys.

Finish your exploration with a scenic drive to

Fan Palm Oases

As the San Andreas fault runs through the Coachella Valley, native California fan palms cluster around surface pools, forming shaded oases worth seeking out for their natural beauty—and their relief from the desert heat.

- **Lower Palm Canyon:** The world's largest fan palm oasis lies at the bottom of a rocky gorge in Palm Springs' Indian Canyons (page 48).

- **Coachella Valley Preserve:** Across the preserve, clusters of native California fan palms flash in the glaring sun, protecting hidden pools (page 83).

- **Oasis of Mara:** A short interpretive trail leads from the Oasis Visitor Center to this lush palm grove (page 101).

- **49 Palms Oasis:** Hike to this mirage-like fan palm oasis (page 121).

- **Lost Palms Oasis:** From lush Cottonwood Spring, this trail crosses desert ridges to the largest collection of fan palms in the park (page 124).

the trail to Lost Palms Oasis

his **Keys View,** a 20-minute detour from Park Boulevard along Keys View Road. Stay and watch the sun set over the Coachella Valley below.

Day 3

Enough of these easy natural trails! Today, it's time to get those lungs pumping a more rigorous hike. For epic views, climb **Ryan Mountain** to its 5,457-foot summit. If you just can't get enough of the parks' numerous mining ruins, opt instead for a steep climb to the **Lost Horse Mine.** And for those irresistible boulder piles, the **Willow Hole Trail** offers a scenic out-and-back ramble.

If it's too hot to hit the trail today, hit the road instead on a backcountry drive. The **Geology Tour Road** is accessible to all vehicles for the first 5 of its 18 miles through the park's unique geologic formations. Those with four-wheel drive have more options, such as **Berdoo Canyon**

Road or several backcountry roads in the park's southern **Cottonwood Spring** region.

Take a night off from campfire cooking to grab a burger with other hikers, rock climbers, and locals at the lively **Joshua Tree Saloon,** a 20-minute drive west from the Willow Hole Trailhead.

Day 4

It's your last day in the park proper, so break camp and head east on Park Boulevard, with stops along Pinto Basin Road to check out **Arch Rock** and the **Cholla Cactus Garden.** Continue south along **Pinto Basin Road** to soak in the stark landscape of the Sonoran Desert, a contrast to those iconic boulder piles. Pinto Basin Road ends at scenic **Cottonwood Spring,** where you can take a short hike around the spring or a longer hike to the **Mastodon Mine** or **Lost Palms Oasis.**

Pappy & Harriet's in Pioneertown

After your hike, return north on Pinto Basin Road to Park Boulevard and exit the park at **Twentynine Palms,** where you've booked a room at the **29 Palms Inn.** Spend the evening wandering the lush grounds and dining at the on-site restaurant. For more music and company, see what's on at **The Palms** in Wonder Valley.

Day 5

From **Twentynine Palms,** the wonders of the Yucca Valley await today's exploration. After breakfast, drive west on Highway 62 to the town of Joshua Tree and wander amid the outsider art at the **Noah Purifoy Outdoor Desert Art Museum,** where the artists' large-scale creations sweep across the Mojave Desert floor.

Arrive in Landers, just north, in time for your sound bath at **The Integratron** (reserve in advance) where the domed structure hums and chimes with the sounds of crystal bowl harmonies.

Dinner is at the saloon and restaurant **Pappy & Harriet's** (reserve one of their seatings up to two weeks in advance), a former Wild West movie set in aptly named Pioneertown. Debrief your day, people-watch, and enjoy the funky surroundings while digging into the hearty Tex-Mex menu at this one-of-a-kind spot. If the excellent live music keeps you up late, you can always bed down at the **Pioneertown Motel** out back.

sweeping views from the top of Lost Horse Mine

Best Hikes

The Palm Springs and Joshua Tree region are host to hidden waterfalls, fan palm oases, stunning canyons, and twisted boulder piles all begging to be explored. The best season to hit the trail is **October-April;** in the hotter months, plan to start from the trailhead early, in order to miss the heat of the day. Or if it's too hot, opt instead for the lofty and much cooler San Jacintos, just a short drive (or tram ride) away.

Indian Canyons

Andreas Canyon (page 48) is an easy—and popular—loop in the scenic **Indian Canyons** near Palm Springs. The shaded trail follows a permanent creek for **2 miles round-trip** through stands of leafy fan palms.

Tahquitz Peak

This steep, **7.6-mile round-trip** trail switchbacks through the manzanita, Jeffrey pine, and white fir forests of the **San Jacinto Wilderness** to reward

with breathtaking views from the historic lookout tower at the top of **Tahquitz Peak** (page 71).

McCallum Grove

A **2-mile round-trip** stroll leads across open desert to a series of shaded pools hidden under an impressive cluster of fan palms in the **Coachella Valley Preserve** (page 83).

Red Dome

In **Whitewater Preserve** (page 84), a **4-mile out-and-back** scenic walk through a wide canyon ends at the **Whitewater River,** which maintains a surprising and brisk presence across the open desert floor for much of the year.

Ryan Mountain

This **3-mile round-trip** hike climbs more than 1,000 feet in elevation to panoramic **views** from the 5,457-foot wind-scoured vantage point atop **Ryan Mountain** (page 115).

Lost Palms Oasis in Cottonwood Spring

Lost Horse Mine

This moderate loop hike scales **Lost Horse Mountain** (page 115) in about **4-7.4 miles round-trip** to visit one of the best-preserved **mining sites** in Joshua Tree National Park.

Willow Hole Trail

Admire the spiky **Joshua trees** and **boulder piles** on this **7-mile round-trip** flat track into the heart of the **Wonderland of Rocks** (page 117).

49 Palms Oasis

This easy-to-follow trail is only **3 miles round-trip,** yet offers no hint to the secret oasis of **native fan palms** (page 121) that awaits.

Lost Palms Oasis

As the south entrance to Joshua Tree, this exposed trail wanders **7.5 miles round-trip** through **desert gardens** to the **Lost Palm Oasis** (page 124), a watering hole for bighorn sheep and other wildlife.

Palm Springs and the Coachella Valley

When considering its 300 days of annual sun, well-watered canyons, and natural hot springs, it's hard to imagine what could make Palm Springs more charmed...

...until you see its impeccable mid-century architecture preserved like a time capsule. After the town's initial heyday for the Hollywood set from the 1920s through the 1960s, it was somehow left alone in its former glory. Lucky for us. Today, you can stay in a retro boutique hotel, lounge by a gleaming pool, shop the design district, and live like you're on permanent vacation in this timeless hot spot.

The western border to this desert oasis, the San Jacinto Mountains offer a quick place to cool off from the valley heat. The charming mountain town of Idyllwild provides a good jumping-off point for camping, hiking, and skiing.

The Coachella Valley sprawls eastward, stretching all the way to the barren Salton Sea and encompassing the mostly residential towns of Palm Desert, Desert Hot Springs, and Coachella. Today, it's best known as the home of the popular Coachella Valley Music and Arts Festival.

PLANNING YOUR TIME

Los Angeles residents have a special relationship with Palm Springs; being so close, it's easy for them to pop out here for a **weekend** or enjoy a couples' spa getaway.

October-May tends to be high season in Palm Springs, with Christmas week, spring break, and big events like Modernism Week and the Coachella Valley Music and Arts Festival packing in the crowds (and raising the prices). Advanced hotel reservations during these peak times are always a good idea. In **summer,** tourism slows and many places shutter for the season as the heat escalates.

Previous: Living Desert Zoo and Gardens; Coachella Valley Preserve. **Above:** Palm Canyon.

Look for ★ to find recommended sights, activities, dining, and lodging.

Highlights

★ **Palm Springs Aerial Tramway:** This dizzying feat of engineering whisks you nearly 6,000 feet from the desert floor to the San Jacinto Mountains (page 24).

★ **Palm Springs Art Museum:** This highly acclaimed art museum houses contemporary and Western American art in its sleek, lofty space (page 26).

★ **Poolside:** Choose between lively party scenes and quiet oases—poolside is the place to be (page 32).

★ **Vintage Shopping:** The walkable and chic Uptown Design District offers vintage couture clothing, pristine mid-century antiques, and reproduction housewares and furnishings (page 40).

★ **Indian Canyons:** Hike through the world's largest fan palm oasis and explore miles of hiking

trails through sacred land, scenic streams, and dramatic canyons (page 47).

★ **Mount San Jacinto State Park:** Escape the heat of the desert at this 14,000-acre state park in the San Jacinto Mountains (page 49).

★ **Tahquitz Peak:** If you're going to do only one hike in the Idyllwild area and are up for a challenge, hike Tahquitz Peak (page 71).

★ **Cabot's Pueblo Museum:** This Hopi-inspired pueblo is an artistic masterpiece (page 80).

★ **Coachella Valley Music and Arts Festival:** This annual music festival draws big names and huge numbers of people to the desert valley south of Palm Springs (page 81).

★ **Coachella Valley Preserve:** This diversely beautiful desert habitat features rocky, barren ridges and lush oases with clusters of native California fan palms (page 83).

Palm Springs and the Coachella Valley

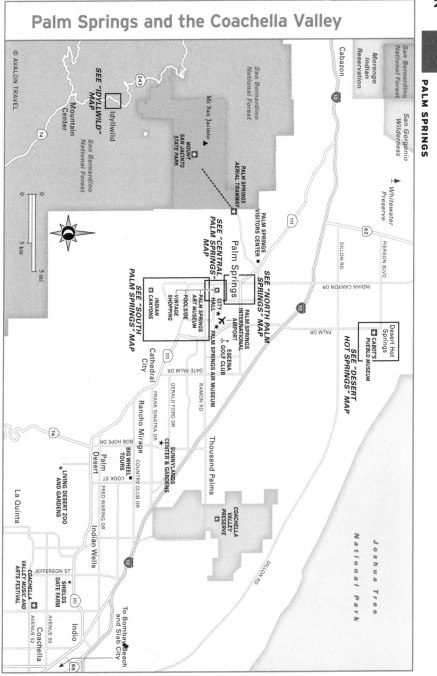

© AVALON TRAVEL

Sights

Palm Springs may be on the small side, but the town sprawls widely across the valley floor. The North Palm Springs and Uptown Design District runs along North Palm Canyon Drive from East Vista Chino (north) to Alejo Road (south). The Central Palm Springs and Downtown neighborhood encompasses the blocks south of Alejo Road all the way to Ramon Road. A bit farther off the beaten path, Ramon Road forms the northern boundary of South Palm Springs, which stretches south to Indian Canyons and east past the "curve."

Palm Springs is a vibrant resort city that is continually reinventing itself. New businesses are constantly being added as old ones are refreshed and made contemporary. Call to confirm operating hours in advance of planning a trip.

NORTH PALM SPRINGS AND UPTOWN DESIGN DISTRICT
★ Palm Springs Aerial Tramway
One of the paradoxes of California's dramatic

geography is that at times, stark desert and green alpine push up against each other as strange neighbors, separated only by a few thousand feet of rocky elevation. The **Palm Springs Aerial Tramway** (1 Tram Way, 760/325-1391, www.pstramway.com, every half hour, 10am-8pm Mon.-Fri., 8am-8pm Sat.-Sun., $24.95) allows you to marvel at just how startling this transition can be. The tramway consists of suspended cable cars that zip visitors from Valley Station on the desert floor (elevation 2,643 feet) to Mountain Station in the lofty San Jacinto Mountains (elevation 8,516 feet) over the course of a 2.5-mile, 10-minute ride traversing rugged Chino Canyon. As you dangle from the cable, the cars rotate, offering dizzying views of the rocky canyon below, salt-crusted desert, and pine-studded mountain peaks.

Frances Crocker, a young electrical engineer living in the heat-stoked town of Banning, dreamed up the project in 1935 as a way to get to the cooler temperatures that were within sight but out of reach. After a series

The tram ascends rugged Chino Canyon with views of the Coachella Valley.

North Palm Springs and Uptown Design District

© AVALON TRAVEL

of interruptions and political roadblocks, the project was finally completed in 1963.

When the sun is blazing in the desert, the tram provides swift relief as temperatures average about 40 degrees cooler at the top. In summer, most visitors buy day passes and spend the day picnicking and hiking the San Jacintos, which offer a range of options from easy interpretive trails like the 1.5-mile Desert View Trail to the more difficult 11-mile round-trip trek to San Jacinto Peak.

Wilderness permits are required for day hikes and can be obtained at the Long Valley Ranger Station at the top of the tramway. Mountain Station also provides a jumping-off point for many well-established backpacking routes.

The mountains are often crusted with snow in winter months when visitors enjoy snowshoeing, cross-country skiing, snow camping, or just good, old-fashioned snow frolicking. A **Winter Adventure Center** (10am-4pm Mon. and Thurs.-Fri.,

9am-4pm Sat.-Sun.) is open seasonally and rents snowshoe and ski equipment.

Mountain Station has year-round amenities including restrooms, a gift shop, lockers, and the **Pines Café** (11am-8:30pm daily) with cafeteria-style dining and snacks. The **Lookout Lounge** provides cocktails, while the **Peaks Restaurant** (760/325-4537) offers fine dining and spectacular views from its perch at the top of Mountain Station.

For guests with disabilities, the Valley Station has designated parking, and the tramcars are handicap-accessible. Mountain Station has accessible dining and a viewing platform.

Frank Sinatra Home

Located in the historic Movie Colony district, the original Palm Springs estate owned by **Frank Sinatra** (877/318-2090, www.sinatrahouse.com) was designed by E. Stewart Williams in 1947 as Sinatra's weekend house. It was Williams' first residential commission. Sinatra originally wanted a Georgian-style mansion with columns and a brick facade, but Williams was able to lure him into a more desert-appropriate modernist style. The 4,500-square-foot residence features four bedrooms, seven bathrooms, and a piano-shaped swimming pool. The house is now available for private vacation rental, private events, dinner parties, and tours.

Elvis Honeymoon Hideaway

Originally christened the House of Tomorrow for its iconic shape (three stories of four concentric circles), this estate was built by well-known Palm Springs developer Robert Alexander for his family. It was leased for Elvis and Priscilla Presley in 1966, and they retreated here for their honeymoon on May 1, 1967. The **Elvis Honeymoon Hideaway** (1350 Ladera Cir., 760/322-1192, www. elvishoneymoon.com, tours 1pm and 3:30pm daily by advance reservation, $30 pp) is now available for daily tours.

Tours are geared toward Elvis Presley

fans. Knowledgeable docents share a wealth of information about the home's architecture and Elvis's history. Tours include the home's interior, where visitors are allowed to touch all of the furniture—including sitting on the honeymoon bed.

CENTRAL PALM SPRINGS AND DOWNTOWN

★ Palm Springs Art Museum

With its three lofty floors kept at a cool 75 degrees, the sophisticated **Palm Springs Art Museum** (101 N Museum Dr., 760/322-4800, www.psmuseum.org, 10am-5pm Tues.-Wed. and Fri.-Sun., noon-8pm Thurs., $12.50) is a refreshing oasis of art. Spread across three lofty floors, 28 galleries, and two outdoor sculpture gardens, the museum showcases collections of international modern and contemporary painting and sculpture, architecture and design, Native American and Western art, photography, and glass. The midsize collection approaches those of metropolitan museums with works by such well-known artists as Marc Chagall, Ansel Adams, Roy Lichtenstein, Pablo Picasso, and Andy Warhol. The museum was originally established in 1938 as the Palm Springs Desert Museum, specializing in Native American artifacts and the natural history of the Coachella Valley. The current museum, designed by architect E. Stewart Williams in 1974, has expanded as a cultural center with an Architecture and Design Center and Annenberg Theater. The museum also houses a café and a museum store. Admission is free every Thursday evening 4pm-8pm and the second Sunday of each month.

Frey House II

Up the road from the Palm Springs Art Museum, the 1963 **Frey House II** (686 Palisades Dr.) sits tucked on a hillside 220 feet above the desert floor. The tiny, rectangular glass box is the second home of famed architect Albert Frey, with an interior that

The Hollywood Rat Pack

In the 1930s, the arrival of Hollywood celebrities put Palm Springs on the map. By the 1950s and '60s, the scene was in full swing. Hollywood A-listers fled to Los Angeles to "winter" in Palm Springs, kicking off with a party at the now-gone Racquet Club presided over by Frank Sinatra, Sammy Davis Jr., Bing Crosby, and Bob Hope.

Sinatra and Hope settled in Palm Springs permanently, while celebrities like Elvis Presley, Dean Martin, Dinah Shore, and Lucille Ball continued to winter here. Today, you can still experience the nostalgia of the Rat Pack era in a few of the old hangouts and homes.

- **Bob Hope Residence:** Hike the Araby Trail for views of the entertainment icon's former home, a massive, orbital glass and concrete structure designed by John Lautner.

- **Colony Palms Hotel:** In the late 1950s, this former underground casino, speakeasy, and brothel drew the glitterati (including Frank Sinatra, Zsa Zsa Gabor, Kirk Douglas, Howard Hughes, and Ronald Reagan), who reveled at its poolside supper club featuring Las Vegas acts.

- **Copley's Restaurant:** Experience a piece of Cary Grant's former 1940s estate (the guesthouse, to be specific), located in the historic Movie Colony neighborhood.

- **Elvis Honeymoon Hideaway:** Tour the site of Elvis and Priscilla Presley's May 1, 1967, honeymoon.

- **Frank Sinatra Home:** Designed by E. Stewart Williams, Sinatra's former Palm Springs estate set the standard for Hollywood glamour post-World War II.

- **Melvyn's:** At this time capsule where Frank Sinatra once held court, you're as likely to see longtime regulars swanning around in matching pantsuits as you are young hipsters yearning for a glimpse of the old days.

- **The Purple Room:** It's one of the last holdouts of the Rat Pack nightlife. The usual suspects—Frank Sinatra, Sammy Davis Jr., and Dean Martin—graced the place with their presence, and you can too.

- **Riviera Palm Springs:** Back in the day, the Riveria hosted movie stars, entertainers, and presidents. It was featured in the 1963 film *Palm Springs Weekend* about a group of college students on a spring weekend romp.

- **The Willows:** Throughout the 1930s, this glamorous mansion was the occasional home of superstar lawyer Samuel Untermyer, who entertained luminaries like Hollywood child star Shirley Temple and scientist Albert Einstein.

comes in at less than 1,000 square feet—much of that being taken up by the giant boulder that the house was built around. Frey House II is owned and managed by the Palm Springs Art Museum Architecture and Design Center and **tours** (760/322-4878, bransom@psmuseum.org, $75) are available by special request.

Palm Springs Art Museum Architecture and Design Center

The **Palm Springs Art Museum** **Architecture and Design Center** (300 S Palm Canyon Dr., 760/423-5260, www.ps-museum.org, 10am-5pm Tues.-Wed. and Fri.-Sun., noon-8pm Thurs., $12.50 adults, $10.50 seniors, children under 12 free) is the hub of Palm Spring Art Museum's growing collection of architecture and design holdings including drawings, photography, and models. The center is intended as a space for architects, scholars, and the general public. Docent-guided **tours** are available (11am and 2pm Wed. and Fri.-Sun. and 1pm Thurs.). Docents will also answer questions on Thursday (4pm-8pm).

Central Palm Springs and Downtown

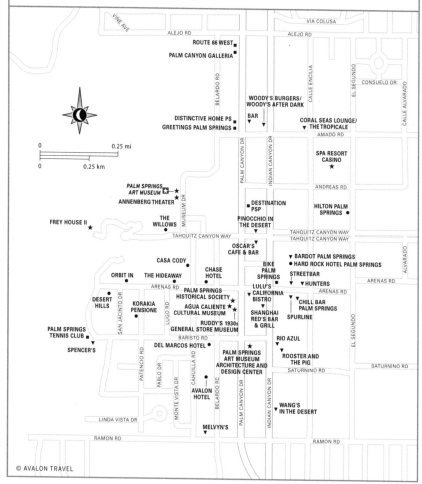

Most exciting, the center offers **guided tours** (760/904-0904, info@themoderntour.com, tours 2.5 hours, $150-200) of some of Palm Springs legendary homes and stellar examples of mid-century modern architecture and design. Noted architects featured on the tour include Richard Neutra, John Lautner, Albert Frey, William Cody, E. Stewart Williams, Donald Wexler, and William Krisel. It's also your chance to peek at homes owned by Elvis Presley, Elizabeth Taylor, Frank Sinatra, William Holden, Peter Lawford, and other celebrities.

Agua Caliente Cultural Museum

Native American ties to the Coachella Valley are strong. The ancestral lands of the Agua Caliente Band of Cahuilla Indians span the scenic, water and palm-filled Indian Canyons (open to visitors for hiking) at the base of the San Jacinto Mountains. Learn more about the history and culture of the Agua Caliente Band and the Cahuilla peoples of the Coachella Valley at the Agua Caliente Cultural Museum (219 S Palm Canyon Dr., 760/323-0151, www.accmuseum.org, 10am-5pm Wed.-Sun. Sept.-May; 10am-5pm Fri.-Sun. June-Aug., free). The nonprofit tribal museum features core exhibits on Agua Caliente and Cahuilla history and culture as well as a new feature exhibit each year. Past exhibits have included a focus on Section 14, a historic tract of land that underwent social, cultural, and economic upheaval in the 1940s through 1960s. Other exhibits focus on Cahuilla culture through the perspective of women and traditional baskets, and a deeper look at Native American history is told through street names. The museum also offers a calendar of events including Native film festivals.

Palm Springs Historical Society

The Palm Springs Historical Society (PSHS, 221 S Palm Canyon Dr., 760/323-8297, www.pshistoricalsociety.org, 10am-4pm Wed.-Sat., noon-3pm Sun., summer hours vary) keeps the history of Palm Springs alive through exhibits and historical walking tours of Palm Springs' historic neighborhoods. The historical society is based in the two oldest remaining buildings in Palm Springs, both open to the public. The McCallum Adobe was built in 1884 as a home for Palm Springs' first pioneer family. It now houses varying exhibits focusing on Palm Springs history, architecture, and culture. In addition, the museum houses hundreds of photographs documenting Palm Springs' history dating from the 1880s to the 1980s.

Stroll next door to the Cornelia White House (built in 1893) to see an example of a turn-of-the-last-century Palm Springs residence. The house was originally part of The Palm Springs Hotel, Palm Springs first hotel, and is named for the pioneer Cornelia White who later called the residence home.

Docent-led walking tours (reserve at 760/323-8297 or www.pshistoricalsociety. org, $20) give visitors a chance to see Palm Springs' charming neighborhoods through the lens of architecture, celebrity, and pioneering efforts. Explore historic neighborhoods, including old La Plaza and Palm Springs' resort beginnings with Spanish stucco and red tile roofs; the Tennis Club neighborhood featuring futuristic atomic age modernist architecture and inns; the avant-garde modernist tract homes of Vista

Palm Springs Art Museum

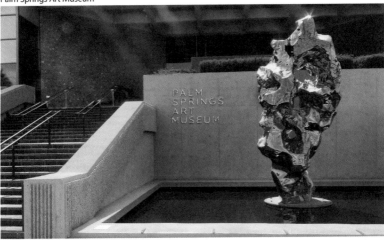

Las Palmas; a Rat Pack playground; and the Movie Colony neighborhood designed for Hollywood royalty with its Spanish Colonial Revival and mid-century modern style. The tours range 1-2.5 hours and must be reserved ahead of time through the Palm Springs Historical Society or the Welwood Murray Memorial Library (100 S Palm Canyon Dr.). The PSHS is also a local partner of **Modernism Week** and offers tours ($35) during the February event.

Ruddy's 1930s General Store Museum

Stepping through the doors of **Ruddy's 1930s General Store Museum** (221 S Palm Canyon Dr., 760/327-2156, www.palmsprings.com, 10am-4pm Thurs.-Sun., $0.95) is a nostalgic trip to a simpler time. The recreated general store is stocked with an extensive collection of unused packaged goods from the 1930s and 1940s. It is chock-full of more than 6,000 unused goods from hardware and clothing to groceries, medicines, and beauty aids.

Palm Springs Air Museum

The fact that most of the aircraft are still flyable at the **Palm Springs Air Museum**

(745 N Gene Autry Trail, 760/778-6262, www.palmspringsairmuseum.org, 10am-5pm daily, $16) makes their larger-than-life exhibits even more impressive. This living history aviation museum features 40 flyable static aircraft from World War II, the Korean War, and the Vietnam War as well as permanent and temporary exhibits and artwork across three climate-controlled hangars and outside tarmac. Docents give added depth to the experience since many are veterans. A small **café** (10am-4pm daily Nov.-May; 10am-4pm Tues.-Sun. June-Oct.) and gift shop are on-site.

SOUTH PALM SPRINGS
Moorten Botanical Garden

The **Moorten Botanical Garden** (1701 S Palm Canyon Dr., 760/327-6555, www.moortenbotanicalgarden.com, 10am-4pm Thurs.-Tues., 10am-4pm Fri.-Sun. in summer) has been introducing visitors to the wonders of cacti and other desert plants since 1938. Chester "Cactus Slim" Moorten and his wife, Patricia, established the landmark on their own one-acre property, and the gardens have remained in the family, operated today by their son, Clark Moorten. You'll glimpse the Moorten's Mediterranean-style home,

Moorten Botanical Garden

South Palm Springs

"Cactus Castle," as you wander the sinewy pathways.

The private desert garden was established just two years after Joshua Tree National Park became a National Monument when appreciation for desert life was less widespread. Seeing the homespun sign for Moorten Botanical Gardens, it's easy to imagine motoring along a dusty road in a different era to stop for this curious roadside attraction. The minimal entrance fee allows you to wander the wide trails among the jagged lattice formed by the more than 3,000 varieties of plants that make up this natural habitat. It's a peaceful place despite the spiky shapes and the rattling screech of desert insects that have made the habitat their home. The hushed green of the place quickly transports visitors from the street to a microcosm of desert trees, cacti, and plants from around the world. Hand-painted rocks provide labels for the myriad fuzzy, spiky, leafy, jaunty, and snaky plants. A small nursery offers desert plants and pottery for sale. It's a feel-good place—educational, relaxing, and filled with nature—and it offers a novel break from the dining, shopping, and pool lounging that make up much of the Palm Springs experience. The hotel pool will feel that much more refreshing when you return.

Sunnylands

In its history as private residence and high-level retreat center, Sunnylands has seen a host of distinguished guests including U.S. presidents, British royalty, and Hollywood icons. The historic, modernist estate now known as **Sunnylands Center and Gardens** (37977 Bob Hope Dr., Rancho Mirage, www.sunnylands.org, gardens 9am-4pm Thurs.-Sun., gardens free, house $40) was designed for media tycoon Walter Annenberg and his wife, Leonore, in the mid-1960s by Los Angeles-based architect A. Quincy Jones. The architect's signature style is apparent in the statement roof (a pink pyramid), overhangs to shield the sun, and glass walls for brightness.

Outside, nine acres of sustainable landscape design transcend politics to create a serene setting designed to change with the seasons. When drought-mandated water restrictions put an end to the era of the estate's traditional green lawns, landscape architect James Burnett created a canvas of native and drought-resistant plants, with inspiration from the Annenbergs' large collection of Impressionist and Post-Impressionist art (including Cézannes and Van Goghs). Garden paths wander through arid species and more than 53,000 individual plants. The center and gardens are open to the public with no reservation.

Tours of the historic house are available by reservation only. The 90-minute guided house tour takes guests to key areas of the home and features information about the estate's history and architecture and interior design. Tickets must be purchased two weeks in advance. They are released in blocks on the first and 15th of each month at 9am PST for the following two-week block. They often sell out, so getting them the morning of release is advisable. No children under 10 years old are allowed. Wheelchairs can be accommodated with advance notice.

The Sunnylands Center and Gardens offers a gift shop and café on-site. The café (Thurs.-Sun. 9am-3:30pm) serves a variety of light breakfast and lunch items including pastries, salads, wraps, coffee, and tea.

Entertainment and Events

★ POOLSIDE

I have yet to hear of a hotel in Palm Springs that does not have a pool. If it exists, no one goes there. Chances are you'll never need to leave the confines of your hotel to put in the poolside lounge time that may very well form the backbone of your vacation.

Some of Palm Springs' best pool scenes are only open to hotel guests; others may allow day-use visitors (usually for events). Choose your hotel wisely: some pools are known for their serene relaxation, while others have a party vibe. Some are BYOB, while others have a full-service bar. Some skew young, while others…you get the picture.

The pool scene in Palm Springs tends to be relaxed compared to, say, Las Vegas. But if you're looking for a pool party, a handful of hotels book deejays and sling poolside cocktails. Events are open to both hotel guests and the public. Check individual hotel websites for event information. The pool party season runs **March–September.**

Ace Hotel & Swim Club

The stylish, sprawling **Ace Hotel & Swim**

Club (701 E Palm Canyon Dr., 760/325-9900, www.acehotel.com/palmsprings) is home to some of the biggest weekend pool parties in town with poolside drink service, outdoor bar, and deejays. The enthusiastic crowds are carefree and cool (some might say "too cool for school").

The Amigo Bar is open to the public, so you can enter through the lobby and enjoy the bar's poolside offerings. For hotel guests, a second pool on the grounds, the Commune Pool, is much quieter.

Non-hotel guests can pay for a Swim Club Membership ($350) or a Day-Use pass ($30). The yearly Swim Club Membership gets you a lot for that price including daily pool and hot tub access (7am-2pm), admittance to pool parties and events, the use of the hotel spa and gym, and discounts on spa services and restaurant. Day passes will gain you a full day's entrance to the pool or pool event. Blackout dates apply.

Hard Rock Hotel Palm Springs

The pool at the Hard Rock Hotel Palm Springs (150 S Indian Canyon Dr., www.hrhpalmsprings.com, 11am-5pm Mon.-Thurs., 10am-6pm Fri., 10am-5pm Sat.-Sun.) features a poolside cocktail bar with cabanas and daybeds available for rent. Pool passes (11am-4pm Sat.-Sun., $10-20) for nonguests are available for weekend pool parties (11am-4pm Sat.-Sun., $10-20).

Saguaro

The trendy Saguaro (1800 E Palm Canyon Dr., 760/323-1711, www.thesaguaro.com) has a lively pool scene. An outdoor Olympic pool with two hot tubs and lounge seating (8am-noon) offers a great place to relax and party against the Technicolor hotel backdrop. The hotel also hosts pool parties during Coachella weekend (Apr.) and Splash House (June and Aug.), with international deejays and high-profile art, music, and fashion influencers catering to a young, dance-loving crowd. The hotel pool is open to guests only; day passes (around $20) are available for non-hotel guests and for pool party events.

The Parker Palm Springs

The Parker Palm Springs (4200 E Palm Canyon Dr., 760/770-5000, www.theparkerpalmsprings.com) offers three outdoor pools for hotel guests on 13 acres of tropical landscaped grounds. The main pool has poolside drink service. A family-friendly pool offers an adjacent whirlpool. The Gene Autry pool is open 24 hours and adults only.

Sparrows Lodge

The pool and hot tub scene at the rustic-chic Sparrows Lodge (1330 E Palm Canyon Dr., 760/327-2300, http://sparrowslodge.com) strikes a perfect balance between relaxation and fun. This guests-only pool provides a stylish setting for rejuvenation, while the bar in the communal barn adds the party with refreshing white sangria, beer, wine, and specialty sodas.

NIGHTLIFE

Despite being a resort and party destination, Palm Springs has only a moderate number of bars. They range from well-styled watering holes to Rat-Pack era piano lounges to gay dance clubs. Depending on the type of scene you're looking for, you might want to get creative and check out some of Palm Springs' restaurants, which also have a festive cocktail scene.

Cocktail Lounges

NORTH PALM SPRINGS AND UPTOWN DESIGN DISTRICT

Trio (707 N Palm Canyon Dr., 760/864-8746, www.triopalmsprings.com, 11am-10pm Mon.-Thurs., 11am-11pm Fri., 10am-11pm Sat., 10am-10pm Sun.) in the Uptown Design District is a sleekly styled destination for celebrations (bachelorette parties love this place). Its side bar can be lively.

Eight4Nine Restaurant and Lounge (849 N Palm Canyon Dr., 760/325-8490, www.eight4nine.com, 11am-10pm Mon.-Thurs.,

11am-11pm Fri., 9am-11pm Sat., 9am-10pm Sun.) offers a crisp white decor for its restaurant and lounge set in the building that was home to the Palm Springs Post Office in 1954. Its swanky lounge with backlit onyx bar is a fun place to linger over cocktails. The lounge stays open all day offering a bar menu every day from 11am to close.

CENTRAL PALM SPRINGS AND DOWNTOWN

Lulu's California Bistro (200 S Palm Canyon Dr., 760/327-5858, www.lulupalmsprings. com, 8am-10pm Sun.-Thurs., 8am-midnight Fri.-Sat.), right on the main downtown strip, has a central bar located in its bright open-design space with good views of Palm Canyon Drive.

The retro-tropical Tropicale Restaurant features the swanky, neon-lit **Coral Seas Lounge** (330 E Amado Rd., 760/866-1952, www.thetropicale.com, 4pm-10pm Sun.-Thurs., 4pm-11pm Fri.-Sat., 11am-3pm Sat.-Sun.), as well as an oasis-like patio bar.

Wang's in the Desert (424 S Indian Canyon Dr., www.wangsinthedesert.com, 3pm-close daily) has a popular happy hour that is especially happy on Friday with locals and weekend visitors.

Melvyn's (Ingleside Inn, 200 W Ramon Rd., 760/325-2323, www.inglesideinn.com, 6pm-2am daily), the iconic Palm Springs lounge, is still going as strong as its popular Rat Pack days. Nestled in the historic Tennis Club District's Ingleside Inn, it sports an old Hollywood Regency decor, chandeliers, and decadently upholstered booths. The white tuxedoed maître d's run a tight ship, directing diners and dancers. The lounge gets going most nights, fueled by live piano music and martinis that often inspire dancing on the tiny dance floor. Order a gimlet and enjoy the people watching.

It's a diner up front and party in the back at **Woody's Burgers** (317 N Canyon Dr., 760/230-0188, http://woodysburgersps.com, 11am-close daily). The low-key storefront lunch counter serves up burgers, fries, and milk shakes. The back room has a completely different vibe, serving up live jazz and blues and beer, wine, and cocktails seven nights a week at **Woody's After Dark** (7pm nightly).

SOUTH PALM SPRINGS

One of the last remaining Rat Pack hangouts in Palm Springs, the **Purple Room Supper Club** (1900 E Palm Canyon Dr., www.purpleroompalmsprings.com, 4pm-close Tues.-Sun.) is an old-school supper club and lounge that opened in 1960 in the Club Trinidad Resort. Nightly music and comedy shows accompany a surf and turf menu. Happy hour and late-night drinks are available in the 1960s-era lounge.

Bars and Clubs
NORTH PALM SPRINGS AND UPTOWN DESIGN DISTRICT

Bootlegger Tiki (1101 N Palm Canyon Dr., 760/318-4154, www.bootleggertiki.com, 4pm-2am) took on the legacy of tiki bar royalty when it opened on the site of the original Don the Beachcomber, Palm Springs (established 1953). Velvet paintings, flocked wallpaper, red lighting, and guarded secret recipes impress with dramatic style, and the layered drinks earn their place in tiki history. Grab a friend and grab a booth. Pro tip: If you're not up for a heavily laced rum drink, the gin-based Tom Collins is sprucey and refreshing.

Bardot Palm Springs (150 S Indian Canyon Dr., 760/325-9676, www. hrhpalmsprings.com, 9pm-2am Fri.-Sat., $10 pp after 11pm) is a lounge and dance club inside the Hard Rock Hotel. The club goes for a disco vibe with deejays spinning danceable tracks on Friday and Saturday nights.

CENTRAL PALM SPRINGS AND DOWNTOWN

The name **BAR** (340 N Palm Canyon Dr., 760/537-7337, www.barwastaken.com, 5pm-midnight Sun.-Thurs., 5pm-2am Fri.-Sat.) reflects the stripped-down style of this place that attracts a youngish hip party set without being pretentious. They combine a lot of great

Bootlegger Tiki is on the site of Don the Beachcomber, the grandfather of tiki bars.

things: craft cocktails, beers, whiskey list, and pizza. The best part is the huge outdoor patio with Ping-Pong, full wall murals, and picnic tables out back. Live bands can give this place a rock-club feel.

The dark-wood, galley-style hole-in-the-wall **Shanghai Red's Bar & Grill** (233 S Indian Canyon Dr., 760/322-9293, www.fishermans.com, 4pm-10pm Mon.-Thurs., 4pm-11:30pm Fri., 11am-11:30pm Sat., 11am-10pm Sun.) is the unlikely home to some of the best fish tacos known to man. It's a great, low-key place to pair said tacos with an icy beer (with a full seafood menu available as well). Happy hour specials and live music on the patio on weekends make this a fun hang for locals and visitors.

SOUTH PALM SPRINGS
Located in the Ace Hotel, the **Amigo Room** (701 E Palm Canyon Dr., 760/325-9900, www.acehotel.com/palmsprings, 9am-2am daily) is the perfect purveyor of the Ace Hotel's brand of cool with a retro dark styling. The bar is

open day and night. Daytime it also serves the packed outdoor pool scene. Nighttime brings deejays and theme nights. The crowd skews young and über-hip, but don't be put off. If you like karaoke, live music, trivia, or a dark bar with a good soundtrack, you might end up here at some point.

Dead or Alive Bar (150 E Palm Canyon Dr., www.deadoralivebar.com, 5pm-2am daily) filled in a big gap in the Palm Springs bar offerings when it opened its well-designed beer and wine bar in February 2016. They offer a highly curated beer and wine list in a chic, inviting space. Sip a beer from one of their stylish ceramic beer mugs from the comfort of a handwoven bar stool. The bar is also conveniently located next to **El Mirasol** (140 E Palm Canyon Dr., 760/323-0721) Mexican restaurant, if you're hungry.

LGBT
All bars and nightlife venues in Palm Springs are gay-friendly; however, there are a range of bars geared specifically toward a gay clientele. Choose from dance clubs, cafés with cabaret performances, and divey neighborhood watering holes.

NORTH PALM SPRINGS AND UPTOWN DESIGN DISTRICT
Located in North Palm Springs, **Toucan's Tiki Lounge** (2100 N Palm Canyon Dr., 760/416-7584, www.toucanstikilounge.com, 2pm-2am Mon.-Tues., 2pm-midnight Wed., 2pm-2am Thurs.-Fri., noon-2am Sat.-Sun.) is a fun and friendly gay cocktail bar adorned with tropical tiki touches and a round bar that slings sugary drinks to fuel a lively dance floor. Drag shows and other special events offer plenty of entertainment.

CENTRAL PALM SPRINGS AND DOWNTOWN
The long-running **Hunters** (302 E Arenas Rd., 760/323-0700, www.hunterspalmsprings.com, 10am-2am daily, happy hour 10am-7pm daily) is a gay club that draws a mostly male

crowd for drink specials, deejays, dancing, and weekly entertainment.

A recent addition to downtown, **Chill Bar Palm Springs** (217 E Arenas Rd., 760/327-1079, www.chillbarpalmsprings.com, 10am-2am daily) is a gay cocktail bar and nightclub in an open, designed contemporary space with an outdoor patio. The adjoining Scorpion Room has karaoke, deejays, dancing, and themed nights.

Spurline (200 S Indian Canyon Dr., www.spurline.com, 2:30pm-2am Mon.-Thurs., noon-2am Fri.-Sun.) is a popular neighborhood sing-along spot with strong drinks and theme nights, including show tunes, retro, cowboy country, and karaoke cabaret. The low-key bar draws a primarily male crowd, but all are welcome.

Oscar's Café and Bar (125 E Tahquitz Canyon Way, #108, 760/325-1188, www.oscarspalmsprings.com, 11am-9pm Mon.-Thurs., 11am-10pm Fri., 9am-10pm Sat., 9am-3pm Sun.) has a casual patio for drinking and dining; the spot is open for breakfast, lunch, and dinner, as well as brunch on Saturday and Sunday. They offer a daily happy hour (3pm-7pm) and a popular Sunday tea dance (4pm-close), as well as cabaret and live music.

Streetbar (224 E Arenas Rd., 760/320-1266, www.psstreetbar.com, 10am-2am Mon.-Sat., 6am-2am Sun.) is a Palm Springs fixture that caters to a male clientele. The central bar is accented by a chandelier and club lighting. In addition to daily drink specials, there's something going on every night of the week—from karaoke to deejay nights and live performances.

At the **Tool Shed** (600 E Sunny Dunes Rd., 760/320-3299, www.toolshed-ps.com, 10am-2am daily), pool tables, go-go dancers, drink specials, and events cater to the mostly male Levi's and leather neighborhood crowd.

Casino

Palm Springs' proximity to tribal lands (Morongo Band of Mission Indians and the Agua Caliente Band of Cahuilla Indians) means that there are several deluxe casino

BAR serves up craft beer, cocktails, pizza, and live music.

resorts in the Coachella Valley. The **Spa Resort Casino** (401 E Amado Rd., 888/999-1995, www.sparesortcasino.com, 24 hours) is the only casino in downtown Palm Springs. It only partially lives up to its name—the casino is open, but the spa and hotel closed in July 2015. The casino offers slots and table games, a 24-hour deli, lounge, and steakhouse (dinner only 5pm-10pm Sun.-Thurs., 5pm-11pm Fri.-Sat.). Casino resort lodging is available at their sister resort in Rancho Mirage (www.hotwatercasino.com).

THE ARTS

The **Annenberg Theater** (101 N Museum Dr., www.psmuseum.org/annenberg-theater), housed within the Palm Springs Art Museum, hosts live professional performances in its 433-seat state-of-the-art theater. The Annenberg Theater combines the visual and performing arts to feature a yearly series showcasing theater, dance, music, and mixed media works. Order tickets online on the website or call the **box office** (760/325-4490,

Modernism Architecture

TRAMWAY
GAS STATION
★

111

PALM CANYON DR

SAN RAFAEL DR

INDIAN CANYON DR

★
ALEXANDER STEEL
HOUSES

RACQUET CLUB RD

VIA ESCUELA

KAUFMANN HOUSE ★ VISTA CHINO

VISTA CHINO 111

PALM CANYON DR

INDIAN CANYON DR

TACHEVAH DR

TAMARISK RD

CHINO DR

ALEJO RD

PALM CANYON DR

INDIAN CANYON DR

FREY HOUSE II ★

BELARDO RD

TAHQUITZ CANYON WAY

DEL MARCOS HOTEL ★

★
PALM SPRINGS
ART MUSEUM
ARCHITECTURE AND
DESIGN CENTER

COACHELLA VALLEY ★
SAVINGS AND LOAN

RAMON RD

★ CITY NATIONAL BANK

MESQUITE AVE

0   0.5 mi

0   0.5 km

E PALM CANYON DR

PALM CANYON DR

★
TROPICS HOTEL/
CALIENTE TROPICS

CAMINO CARMELITA
SHIP OF THE DESERT ★

LA VERNE WAY

© AVALON TRAVEL

10am-4pm Wed.-Fri., hours vary based on performance schedules).

FESTIVALS AND EVENTS

Modernism Week

Modernism Week (www.modernismweek. com, Feb.) is Palm Springs' signature annual event, celebrating mid-century modern architecture, design, and culture over two nonstop weekends every February. Modernism Week fosters appreciation for Palm Springs' shining modernist history while encouraging a fresh approach and thinking about design, art, fashion, and sustainable modern living. The festival features more than 250 events, including signature home tours with a chance to peek into some of Palm Springs' fabulous historic houses, a modernism show and sale, modern garden tours, architectural double-decker bus tours (including sunset tours of illuminated mid-century classic buildings), nightly parties (soiree at Frank Sinatra's estate, anyone?), walking and bike tours, lectures and cocktail hour discussions, fashion events, a vintage travel trailer exhibition, films, music, and more. Modernism Week hosts a **Fall Preview** (Oct.), a mini Modernism Week to kick off Palm Springs' social and recreation season. Check online for highlights, recommendations, and ongoing news.

Tickets (up to $150) for Modernism Week (on sale Nov. 1) and the Fall Preview (on sale Aug. 1) are sold online for individual events. Tickets sell out quickly, especially for the popular house tours.

Splash House

The pool party to end all pool parties is the annual **Splash House** (www.splashhouse. com, June and Aug.), a three-day electronic dance music and pool party held in Palm Springs two weekends a year. Two host hotels form ground zero for Splash House with deejays and daytime events; shuttles run between the host hotels. A general admission wristband (from $95) gets you access to the

Mid-Century Modernism

In the 1930s, celebrities streamed from Los Angeles to Palm Springs, acquiring second homes to hide in and party away the winter season. This laid-back desert lifestyle allowed architects the creative freedom to explore modernist materials, designing structures inspired by the clean lines of the desert. The 1950s and 1960s were the height of modernist design. Throughout the city are design examples from noted architects Albert Frey, E. Stewart Williams, William Cody, Donald Wexler, John Lautner, and Richard Neutra.

The Palm Springs Visitors center sells a mid-century modern map ($5), highlighting civic buildings, inns and hotels, celebrity homes, and other exceptional residences. Interior tours of some gems are available during **Modernism Week** (www.modernismweek.com, Feb.). The following are listed from north to south; see the map on page 37 for a walking tour:

- **Tramway Gas Station** (2901 N Palm Canyon Dr.): This 1965 gas station once serviced the Palm Springs Aerial Tramway. Now the **Palm Springs Visitors Center,** it features iconic lines and a soaring roofline designed by Albert Frey with Robson Chambers.

- **Kaufmann House** (470 W Vista Chino): Designed by Richard Neutra in 1946-1947 for Edgar Kaufmann Sr. (who had also commissioned Frank Lloyd Wright to design Fallingwater), this private residence has been impeccably restored.

- **Alexander Steel Houses** (btw. E Molino Rd. and N Sunnyview Dr.): Designed by Donald Wexler and Richard Harrison and built in 1960-1962 by the George Alexander Construction company, these seven prefabricated homes use light-gauge steel to frame glass walls that afford striking mountain views.

- **Frey House II** (686 Palisades Dr.): This 1963 rectangular glass box sits tucked on a hillside 220 feet above the desert floor and was constructed around a giant boulder.

- **Del Marcos Hotel** (225 W Baristo Rd.): Designed by William F. Cody in 1947, the Del Marcos was ahead of its time, featuring a post-and-beam construction with organic, natural materials including redwood and stone. The angular lines highlight interior garden rooms that form a U-shape around the pool, all complete with mountain views.

pools and events at both hotels as well as the shuttle. General admission tickets can be purchased separately or as a package with hotel rooms. Late-night parties are held off-site at unique Palm Springs locations, such as the Palm Springs Air Museum. Tickets for the off-site parties are sold separately (from $30).

Palm Springs International Film Festival

The prestigious **Palm Springs International Film Festival** (www.psfilmfest.org, Jan.) is a well-established, destination film festival that draws more than 100,000 filmgoers every January. The festival features more than 180 films from 70 countries. In addition, screenings, planned presentations, tributes, and nightly parties are all set against Palm Springs' dramatic backdrop.

Advance **tickets** go on sale in December and can be purchased online, by phone (800/898-7256, 9am-5pm Mon.-Fri.), and in person at Festival Ticket and Information Center (Courtyard Plaza, 777 E Tahquitz Canyon Way), Camelot Theatres (2300 E Baristo Rd.), Regal Cinemas Palm Springs, Palm Canyon Theatre (789 E Tahquitz Canyon Way), and Annenberg Theater (101 Museum Dr.) during business hours. The **Palm Springs International ShortFest** (www.psfilmfest.org) also happens every June.

American Documentary Film Festival

American Documentary Film Festival (www.americandocumentaryfilmfestival. com, Apr.) showcases films from around the globe that focus on making an impact through

- **Santa Fe Federal Savings and Loan** (300 S Palm Canyon Dr.): Now the **Palm Springs Art Museum Architecture and Design Center,** this iconic 1961 structure has been impeccably restored; note the elevated concrete foundation and aluminum solar screens.

- **Coachella Valley Savings and Loan** (499 S Palm Canyon Dr.): Designed by architect E. Stewart Williams in 1960, the structure (now Chase Bank) stands out with its arched facade and vertical bronze siding.

- **City National Bank** (588 S Palm Canyon Dr.): Designed in 1959 by Rudi Baumfeld of Victor Gruen Associates, this current Bank of America is striking for its curved exterior and blue mosaic tile.

- **Palm Springs City Hall** (3200 E Tahquitz Canyon Way): Built in 1952-1957 with diverse architectural elements, the building represents a stylistic collaboration between architects John Porter Clark, Albert Frey, Robson C. Chambers, and E. Stewart Williams. Noted features include a portico with a circular cutout encompassing two palm trees.

- **Ship of the Desert** (1995 S Camino Monte): Designed in 1936 by Los Angeles architects Eric Webster and Adrian Wilson, this streamlined, nautical house gets its name from the prow-front living room. Bedroom suites can only be accessed by an exterior redwood deck. (The home is currently owned by fashion designer Trina Turk and her husband, photographer Jonathan Skow.)

- **Tropics Hotel** (411 E Palm Canyon Dr.): Now the **Caliente Tropics,** the 1964 Polynesian-themed resort still retains some of its fun and kitschy tiki elements.

- **Elrod House** (2175 Southridge Dr.): The 1968 residence of interior designer Arthur Elrod features bold, concrete circles, movable walls, a fully retracting glass living room wall, and infinity pool. Designed by architect John Lautner, it was featured in the 1971 James Bond thriller *Diamonds Are Forever.*

real stories with real issues. First held in 2012, the nonprofit festival screens more than 100 documentaries during its five-day annual run. Tickets to individual screenings, many with Q&As, as well as tickets to the opening night gala and festival passes are available online ($10). Films are screened in venues in Palm Springs, Rancho Mirage, and Palm Desert.

AGUA CALIENTE CULTURAL MUSEUM NATIVE FILMFEST

Agua Caliente Cultural Museum Native FilmFest (219 S Palm Canyon Dr., 760/778-1079, www.accmuseum.org, Mar.) features films by Native American filmmakers as well as those about and starring Native Americans and other indigenous people from around the world. The FilmFest includes feature, short, and documentary films. Other activities

include Q&A sessions, discussion panels, and receptions.

CINEMA DIVERSE

Started in 2008, **Cinema Diverse** (www.cinemadiverse.org, Sept.) is a Palm Springs gay and lesbian film festival that is on the upswing. Held annually in September, the festival showcases feature films, short films, and new media as well as a series of after-parties in popular Palm Springs bars and restaurants. Tickets are available online (individual tickets $13, all-access pass $159).

ARTHUR LYONS FILM NOIR FESTIVAL

The **Arthur Lyons Film Noir Festival** (www.arthurlyonsfilmnoir.ning.com, May) showcases a mix of black and white, film noir

B classics and obscure vintage gems. The festival was founded in 2000 by Arthur Lyons, the late mystery author and Palm Springs community leader. Screenings take place in Palm Springs at the **Camelot Theatres** (2300 E Baristo Rd.). Other activities include post-screening Q&As and book signings.

LGBT

Palm Springs is a year-round LGBT vacation destination with hotels and nightlife that cater exclusively to the LGBT community. The two biggest parties are held annually in **April.**

THE DINAH

Established in 1991, **The Dinah** (locations vary, www.thedinah.com, Apr.) is the self-proclaimed largest girl party music festival in the world. This four-day, four-night annual getaway catering to the lesbian community takes Palm Springs by storm every April. It kicks off with a massive opening party on Thursday night and continues its deluge of celebrity-studded events and parties throughout the weekend. The event features deejays including celebrity guest deejays, dancers, daytime pool parties, live concerts, comedy, and nightclub parties throughout the weekend.

The festival is based in a few of the larger Palm Springs hotels and is where the daytime pool parties take place. Stay at one of these featured hotel sponsors to make sure you are at the center of the action. Tickets are available on The Dinah website with **weekend package deals** ($259-269) or tickets to **individual events** ($40-90).

WHITE PARTY

The **White Party** (locations vary, www.jeffreysanker.com, Apr.) is a massive gay dance party for male couples and singles. The three-day, three-night festival is held annually every April (not the same weekend as The Dinah). It kicks off Friday at noon and goes strong until 7am Monday morning with daytime pool parties, deejays, live performances, and themed nighttime events. White Party festival's main event happens on Saturday night—a 10-hour dance party with multiple levels, dancers, special effects, and huge sound system. The White Party Ferris Wheel and fireworks display choreographed to a deejay music remix add even more spark to the event. White Party is centered in several host hotels in Palm Springs. **Weekend passes** ($385-465) are available on the White Party website, or you can buy tickets to **individual events** ($50-150).

Shopping

Palm Springs is known for its mid-century antiquing and stylish desert home furnishings.

NORTH PALM SPRINGS AND UPTOWN DESIGN DISTRICT

The sleek Uptown Design District has the highest concentration of modern shopping in Palm Springs. Stroll colorful North Palm Canyon Drive between Vista Chino (north end) and Alejo (south end) to find pristine vintage furnishings and housewares, clothing and gift boutiques, mid-century reproductions, and high-end concept interiors.

★ Vintage

Fully outfit the lanai in time for your retro cocktail party with vintage household items from **Dazzles** (1035 N Palm Canyon Dr., 760/327-1446, call for hours), a cheerful treasure trove stuffed into a defunct mid-century hotel. Oh, and be sure to outfit yourself too—the collection of Bakelite and colorful costume jewelry is unparalleled.

Drool over fine vintage furnishings at **Christopher Anthony** (800 N Palm Canyon Dr., 760/322-0600, www.christopheranthonyltd.com, 10:30am-6pm Tues.-Sat., noon-5pm Sun.). From sleek, 1960s lounge chairs to abstract paintings, it's everything you need to seriously step up your household game.

The elegant building that now houses **The Shops at Thirteen Forty-Five** (1345 N Palm Canyon Dr., 760/464-0480, www.towneps. com, 11am-5pm Thurs.-Sun.) was originally commissioned in 1955 by Harold Hicks, the Palm Springs real estate developer. Renowned designer E. Stewart Williams planned the real estate and insurance building, which has seen an expansion and some alterations, but maintains a striking architectural integrity. The commitment to high-quality design continues inside with this collective of 12 unique shops featuring vintage and modern furniture and accessories. **Soukie Modern** (www.soukiemodern.com) offers Moroccan-inspired, handcrafted home goods including rugs, home accessories, furniture, wedding blankets, and bags, while the curated vintage shop **Lindy California** (www.lindycalifornia. com) sells pedigreed finds. And **Towne Palm Springs** (www.towneps.com) features vintage and modern furniture, accessories, and art.

Flow Modern Design (768 N Palm Canyon Dr., 760/322-0768, www.flowmodern. com, 10:30am-5:30pm Mon. and Wed.-Sat., noon-5pm Sun.) is both a shop and gallery, specializing in carefully selected mid-century

modern fine furniture, art, jewelry, and accessories including silver and brass pieces. Favorites include Milo Baughman, Arthur Elrod, and Scandinavian Glass and Rosenthal Studio Pieces. Flow Modern is a 1st Dibs dealer, a leading marketplace for globally selected rare and beautiful objects. The gallery features rotating exhibits of photography, painting, and sculpture.

Modernway (745 N Palm Canyon Dr., 760/320-5455, www.psmodernway.com, noon-4pm Sun.-Mon. and Thurs., noon-5pm Fri.-Sat.) is a well-established and well-regarded Palm Springs vintage retail outlet specializing in mid-century modern furnishings from the 1950s, '60s, and '70s.

After visiting **A La MOD** (844 N Palm Canyon Dr., 760/327-0707, www.alamodps. com, 10am-6pm Mon.-Sat., noon-5pm Sun.) with its room after groovy room of impeccable vintage furnishings, you might just wish you could move in here instead of trying to update your own place to be this stylish. Couches, lamps, tables, chairs, bookends—one of each, please.

Vintage cuff links? Check. Chunky necklaces? Check. Animal curios, curvy lamps, and massive multicolored glassware collection? Check, check, and check. Find it

Shop for stylish furniture in the Uptown Design District.

all at **Bon Vivant** (766 N Palm Canyon Dr., 760/534-3197, www.gmcb.comshop, 10am-5pm Thurs.-Mon.) and have a heck of a good time doing it.

Boulevard (800 N Palm Canyon Dr., 760/832-9011, www.boulevardps.com, 11am-4pm Sun., 10am-5pm Tues.-Sat.) is devoted to offering a discerning mix of cool, classic, and iconic mid-century modern vintage items in pristine condition, as well as contemporary new furniture, lighting, art, and accessories.

Gift and Home

Stock up on gifts for yourself or others at **Pelago** (901 N Palm Canyon Dr., #105, 760/322-3999, www.pelagopalmsprings.com, 10am-5pm Mon.-Fri., 10am-6pm Sat., 11am-5pm Sun.). This contemporary boutique offers a tempting and stylish array of home and fashion accessories that manage to make place, floor, and table mats cool.

Vintage reproductions that you can actually afford, as well as a colorful arsenal of household gifts, make **Just Modern** (901 N Palm Canyon Dr., #101, 760/322-5600, www.justmoderndecor.com, 10am-5pm Sun.-Fri., 10am-6pm Sat.) a fun place to shop for stylish goods from couches to lighting and from rugs to candles.

Find retro-style original art, prints, books, and other merchandise evocative of atomic-era Palm Springs by the artist Shag at **Shag: The Store** (725 N Palm Canyon Dr., 760/322-3400, www.shagthestore.com, 10am-5pm Mon.-Thurs., 10am-8pm Fri.-Sat.).

Fashion

Local fashion design star Trina Turk has come to be synonymous with California chic. Her flagship store, **Trina Turk** (891 and 895-897 N Palm Canyon Dr., 760/416-2856, www.trinaturk.com, 10am-6pm Mon.-Sat., 11am-5pm Sun.) occupies a luxurious glass-walled corner space originally designed by Albert Frey. The revamped modernist bohemian location features women's apparel, accessories, and Mr. Turk menswear.

Ignore the feeling that you're entering grandma's mothball closet because there are some serious fashion finds to be had in the **Déjà vu Room** (664 N Palm Canyon Dr., 760/699-5365, www.dejavuroom.com, 10am-5pm Wed.-Sun.). Browse vintage and couture clothes and accessories, for men and women, from the 1950s, '60s, '70s, and '80s.

CENTRAL PALM SPRINGS AND DOWNTOWN

While most of the high-design and mid-century shopping is concentrated in the Uptown Design District, some of it filters into downtown where a few shops showcase contemporary home decor as well as vintage finds. However, the main downtown drag, which runs along Palm Canyon Drive from Alejo Road to Ramon Road, tends to be much more touristy than the Design District.

While downtown doesn't constitute a shopping destination, some of the stores are fun to browse and you can find gifts, ice cream, bathing suits, fast fashion, and skin products that may also come in handy for your vacation emergency.

Every Thursday, the downtown blocks of Palm Canyon Drive close to vehicles and open to **Villagefest** (6pm-10pm Thurs. Oct.-May, 7pm-10pm Thurs. June-Sept.). Vendors display art, sell handcrafted items, and set up food booths and many shops, galleries, and restaurants stay open late.

Vintage

Palm Canyon Galleria (457 N Palm Canyon Dr., 760/323-4576, www.gmcb.com, 11am-5pm daily) is an antiques collective that brings together six shops to feature 20th-century home furnishings, ceramics, metal craft, art, and international design.

Route 66 West (465 N Palm Canyon Dr., 518/281-2517, www.rubylane.com, 11am-5pm Thurs.-Mon.) boasts an astounding collection of retro costume, designer, mid-century, and Bakelite jewelry as well as Lucite handbags, vintage sunglasses, pottery, glass, sculpture, chrome, and more.

Gift and Home

Destination PSP (170 N Palm Canyon Dr., 760/354-9154, www.destinationpsp.com, 9am-6pm Sun.-Wed., 9am-10pm Thurs., 9am-8pm Fri.-Sat.) offers a colorful and wide-ranging array of originally designed merchandise for the Palm Springs lifestyle including swim apparel, towels, and housewares such as serving trays and coasters, decor, and gifts. This is a great place to pick up souvenirs and contemporary, mid-century-inspired pieces for gift giving and living.

Distinctive Home PS (301 N Palm Canyon Dr., 760/864-1250, www.distinctivehomeps.com, 10am-6pm Mon.-Wed.,

10am-7pm Thurs.-Sat., 10am-5pm Sun.) is a colorful and design-forward store focusing on furniture and accessories for the home—from bar and cocktail pieces to mid-century modern and Hollywood Regency artwork. Upscale gift boutique **Just Fabulous** (515 N Palm Canyon Dr., 760/864-1300, www.bjustfabulous.com, 9am-6pm daily) features a wide selection of glitzy coffee table books, cards, and gifts. **Greetings Palm Springs** (301 N Palm Canyon Dr., 760/322-5049, www.sohopalmsprings.com, 9am-6pm Sun.-Wed., 9am-9pm Thurs.-Sat.) is a pop culture emporium with loads of greeting cards, gifts, glassware, art, and books.

Sports and Recreation

DAY SPAS

Several of Palm Springs' resort and spa hotels offer day spa services including massage and skin and body treatments. If you are interested in the type of day spa that is more about relaxing in a pool or Jacuzzi, the town of Desert Hot Springs 12 miles north (a 20-minute drive) is your best bet.

The hotel spa at the trendy Technicolor **Saguaro Palm Springs** (1800 E Palm Canyon Dr., www.thesaguaro.com, 760/969-6483, 10am-3pm Sun., by appointment only Mon., 10am-6pm Tues.-Sat.) offers massage and signature facial and body treatments for rejuvenation, hydration, and detox.

Estrella Spa (415 S Belardo Rd., www.avalonpalmsprings.com, 877/760-0846), in the classic, luxurious Avalon Hotel, offers massages, facials, scrubs, nails, waxings, and holistic health treatments by appointment. The spa also offers seasonally based specials including romance packages.

The Hard Rock Hotel Palm Springs offers signature treatments in its **Rock Spa** (150 S Indian Canyon Dr., 760/969-6665, www.hrhpalmsprings.com, by appointment: 10am-4pm Mon.-Thurs., 10am-6pm Fri.-Sun.), including a massage with a soundtrack and

therapeutic sound vibration as well as wraps, facials, and skin treatments. Treatment packages are available for couples … or for you and your entourage.

The Hilton Palm Springs offers an assortment of services in its **Elements Spa** (400 E Tahquitz Canyon Way, 760/318-8528, elements.spa@hiltonpalmsprings.com), including Swedish and deep-tissue massage, exfoliating and rejuvenating skin treatments, manicures, pedicures, and aromatherapy. Day guests also enjoy hotel amenities such as a pool, hot tub, and fitness facilities, as well as access to a full restaurant menu and poolside bar. Spa and couples packages are also available.

The hip Ace Hotel features organic treatments with raw botanical products in its **Feel Good Spa** (701 E Palm Canyon Dr., 760/866-6188, www.acehotel.com/palmsprings, feelgoodspa@acehotel.com, by appointment 9am-6pm Sun.-Thurs., 9am-8pm Fri.-Sat.). Body treatments range from body masks and reflexology to massage and facials.

WATER PARK

Wet & Wild (1500 S Gene Autry Trail, 760/327-0499, www.wetnwildpalmsprings.

com, hours and days vary Mar.-Oct., $39 adults, $28 children 3-11 and seniors 62 and older) is a family-friendly water park offering slide rides, raft rides, and family rides. On Friday night in July the park offers its Dive-in Movie series where family-friendly movies are shown poolside after dusk with limited park attractions until 10pm, weather permitting.

GOLF

With moderate winter temperatures and spectacular mountain views, Palm Springs is a golfing destination. Several golf courses are located within Palm Springs, including municipal as well as semiprivate golf clubs and resorts open to the public. There are many more located in surrounding towns throughout the Coachella Valley, which boasts more than 100 golf courses.

Despite the idyllic setting, drought-mandated water enforcement is in effect throughout Southern California. Golf courses have been asked to limit water use by 25 percent, so some courses may not be as lush and green as in wetter periods. Courses vary widely for a range of skill levels and price points, from basic courses for casual practice to PGA Classic Courses. Many courses require dress codes.

Most golf courses maintain online booking for tee times on their website. Pricing is dynamic, reflecting real-time conditions including weather, demand, and other market factors.

Booking Resources

Stand-By Golf (760/321-2665, www.standbygolf.com, 7am-7pm daily) is a comprehensive booking site that is able to search for tee times in all Coachella Valley communities including Palm Springs, Cathedral City, Rancho Mirage, Palm Desert, Indian Wells, La Quinta, and Indio. You can search by desired tee time, price range, and course. Book directly through their website.

Golf Now (800/752-9020, 5am-5pm) offers an online tee time retail service for Palm Springs and other international golfing

destinations. Search for daily available tee times to book online through their website (www.golfnow.com) or by phone.

Public Courses

Within Palm Springs the **Escena Golf Club** (1100 Clubhouse View Dr., 760/778-2737, www.escenagolf.com, 6:30am-9pm daily, $34-109) is a public, 18-hole, par 72 championship golf course that spans 172 acres with multiple heavily landscaped native areas and water features. Golf club rentals are available ($65 pp), and there are an on-site **bar and grill** (6:30am-9pm daily) and pro shop. Tee times can book quickly on weekends.

The **Indian Canyons Golf Resort** (1097 Murray Canyon Dr., 760/833-8700, www.indiancanyonsgolf.com, $45-125) maintains two distinct golf courses set on 550 acres of Native American tribal property; both are 18-hole championship courses. The classic par 72 North Course plays 6,943 yards set in the canyon district and is surrounded on three sides by the San Jacinto Mountains. The course, designed by noted architect William F. Bell, dates to 1961 and winds through historic, mid-century properties including some originally owned by Walt Disney. The famous Walt Disney fountain acts as a water hazard and visual centerpiece, shooting water jets more than 100 feet high.

The par 72 South Course was redesigned in 2004. The 6,582-yard championship course features four large lakes, 5 par holes, rolling mounds, fairways, and hundreds of native palm trees important to the Agua Caliente tribe. There are on-site club rentals, a pro shop, and restaurant.

The **Mesquite Country Club** (2700 E Mesquite Ave., 760/323-9377, www.mesquitegolf.com, $39-64) is a traditional, par 72 regulation, 18-hole championship course featuring fairways lined with mature trees. A classic, Spanish-style clubhouse offers a casual restaurant for breakfast and lunch, a cocktail lounge, and pro shop. Rental clubs are available.

Tahquitz Creek Golf Course (1885 Golf

Club Dr., 760/328-1005, www.tahquitzgol-fresort.com) offers a pro shop, bar and grill, and two courses. The Legend Course was designed in 1957 and offers a traditional country club-style golf experience. The 18-hole regulation golf course plays more than 6,800 yards and meanders through historic neighborhoods with undulating "push up" greens. The Resort Course is a par 36 regulation course designed in 1995. It features environmentally friendly design elements including the use of drought-tolerant native landscaping, reclaimed irrigation, and reclaimed materials for mounding. The Resort plays more than 6,700 yards and offers tees for various handicaps to create a fair playing field. Rental clubs are available ($55 before twilight; $30 after twilight).

HIKING

Although it may be difficult to tear yourself away from the hotel swimming pool, Palm Springs offers some good hiking opportunities in its surrounding canyons and mountains. A few trails leave directly from near the Palm Springs Art Museum, climbing into the foothills and offering views of Palm Springs and the Coachella Valley.

Palm Springs

Trails in Palm Springs are exposed and are best hiked **October-March** when temperatures are more moderate. If hiking other times of the year, start very early (plan to finish by 9am-10am during summer) and make sure you are off the trail before the heat of the day. Carry plenty of water, sunscreen, and a hat for shade.

PALM SPRINGS MUSEUM TRAIL

Distance: 2 miles round-trip
Duration: 1.5-2 hours
Elevation gain: 1,000 feet
Effort: Moderate
Trailhead: North parking lot of the Palm Springs Art Museum Architecture and Design Center
Directions: From the Palm Springs Visitors center, head south on N Palm Canyon Drive for 2.9 miles.

Turn right on Tahquitz Canyon Drive. Drive one block, then turn right on North Museum Drive. Pass the Palm Springs Art Museum on your left and make a left into the north parking lot. The signed trailhead begins from the parking lot.

Don't let the two-mile round-trip distance or the quaint trail name fool you. This is an intensely steep hike. The payoff is the bird's-eye view of downtown Palm Springs.

From the **Palm Springs Art Museum** (101 N. Museum Dr.), the trail starts with a bang in a series of tightly wound switchbacks that navigate the rocky hillside and never let up until the summit. (Stick to the main trail, and avoid social trails that cut switchbacks and cause erosion.) The summit is marked by a picnic table where you can have a triumphant slug of water or a snack as you look out over the modernist lines of Palm Springs below. Just beyond the summit, the trail intersects with the five-mile **North Lykken Trail** that continues north and south above Palm Springs. The Museum Trail also links up with the Skyline Trail, the backbone of the infamous Cactus to Clouds Hike that takes intrepid hikers a grueling 22 miles up to 10,400 feet in elevation from the desert floor to the peak of Mount San Jacinto in one day.

SOUTH CARL LYKKEN TRAIL

Distance: 6 miles round-trip to Tahquitz Canyon overlook (out-and-back along same route)
Duration: 2-3 hours
Elevation gain: 1,000 feet
Effort: Moderate
Trailhead: S Palm Canyon Drive
Directions: From the Palm Springs Visitors center, take N Palm Canyon Drive south for 6.4 miles; continue straight when it turns into S Palm Canyon Drive. The signed trailhead is on the west (right) side of S Palm Canyon Drive just south of Canyon Heights Road.

This exposed hike into the toothy hills outlining the west side of Palm Springs offers excellent views of Palm Springs with a bonus peek into Tahquitz Canyon. The trail is in a neighborhood and is used by locals during the early morning hours and cooler winter months. There is a good reason—rewarding climbs give way to expansive city views as the trail levels out and winds along a north and east-facing ridge.

The trail begins at a **signed trailhead** near the road at 550 feet in elevation. It heads west before beginning a series of switchbacks up to a lookout point, checking in at 1,170 feet. From here the trail levels out, winding along the rocky hillside before climbing again to top out at 1,550 feet above **Tahquitz Canyon.** This is a good turnaround point, marked by picnic tables, and you can return the way you came.

It is also possible to continue the trail down a steep drop to street level where it intersects with a second trailhead at the end of W Mesquite Avenue. You can arrange for a car shuttle from here or, as one enterprising hiker suggested, call a cab to get back to your hotel.

This trail is completely exposed. Carry enough **water** and make sure you start early and are off the trail no later than mid-morning in summer months. The good news is that even if you are not able to make it to the final turnaround point, the continuous views mean that hiking almost any length of the trail will be a satisfying experience.

ARABY TRAIL

Distance: 3 miles round-trip
Duration: 2 hours
Elevation gain: 800 feet
Effort: Moderate
Trailhead: South Palm Springs at Rim Road/ Southridge Road. Parking area is on the right, past the turnoff from Highway 111.

The Araby Trail reaches excellent heights above the city of Palm Springs, winding past celebrity homes and offering excellent views of the town and the windmills to the north. This is a popular neighborhood exercise trail, and it does provide a great workout while rewarding with interesting views and architecture.

From the parking area, the trail cuts switchbacks steeply up the rocky hillside to the south, passing famed architect John Lautner's dramatic **Elrod House** with its circular bladed rooftop. (This is where part of the 1971 James Bond thriller *Diamonds Are Forever* was filmed.) Next door is the groovy bachelor pad of actor **Steve McQueen.** Continuing climbing the steep switchbacks and you'll pass the crowning rooflines of yet another celebrity house and architectural wonder: The **Bob Hope Residence,** a massive domed structure designed by John Lautner that sits perched on the hillside. It is

views of Palm Springs from the South Carl Lykken Trail

The Indian Canyons are a refreshing place to hike.

establishing villages and irrigating and planting crops. The Agua Caliente own 32,000 acres spread across desert and mountains in the Palm Springs area. Tahquitz and three other canyons are listed on the National Register of Historic Places, while Palm Canyon boasts the world's largest California fan palm oasis.

These trails are best hiked **October-March** due to soaring temperatures. You have the best chance of encountering the seasonal snowmelt streams that feed these canyons in early spring. However, since the canyons offer short hikes with some shade, visiting the canyons at other times of the year is also worthwhile. When it is hot, start early (the canyons open at 8am year-round). Seasonal **ranger talks** are open to the public and are held at Palm Canyon (10am Mon.-Thurs.) and at Andreas Canyon (1pm).

GETTING THERE

A **Trading Post** and ranger station on South Palm Canyon Drive is the hub for exploring Andreas, Murray, and Palm Canyons. The Trading Post has hiking maps, drinks and snacks, books, jewelry, and Indian pottery, baskets, and weaving. Restrooms and parking are available. To get there from the Palm Springs Visitors center (2901 N Palm Canyon Dr.), head south on Palm Canyon Drive for nine miles until the road ends at the Trading Post and Palm Canyon overlook. Visitors will pass through a toll gate to pay the entrance fee prior to reaching the Trading Post.

The entrance to **Tahquitz Canyon** (www. tahquitzcanyon.com) is from the Tahquitz Visitors center, where water, maps, parking, and restrooms are available. From the Palm Springs Visitors center (2901 N Palm Canyon Dr.), head south on Palm Canyon Drive for 3.8 miles and turn right on Mesquite Avenue. The road ends at the **Tahquitz Canyon Visitors center** (500 W Mesquite Ave.) in 0.4 mile.

TAHQUITZ CANYON

Distance: 2 miles round-trip
Duration: 1 hour

the highest structure in Palm Springs. The trail winds to a ridge above his house, a good place to turn around and return.

★ Indian Canyons

The **Indian Canyons** (760/323-6018, www. indian-canyons.com, 8am-5pm daily Oct.-June; 8am-5pm Fri.-Sun. July-Sept., day use $9-11) refer to the rugged, scenic canyons that burrow into the flanks of the San Jacinto Mountains in the southwest corner of Palm Springs. The steep, often snowcapped San Jacintos feed the seasonal streams that transform the rocky canyons in spring. Natural fan palm oases and groundwater feed perennial pools and streams year-round, making the canyons a haven from the surrounding arid landscape and a delight for hikers.

The Indian Canyons are sacred to the Agua Caliente Band of Cahuilla Indians who own and manage the land. Ancestors of the Agua Caliente Cahuilla settled Tahquitz, Andreas, Murray, Palm, and Chino Canyons,

Elevation gain: 240 feet

Effort: Easy

Trailhead: Tahquitz Canyon Visitors center

Tahquitz Canyon is the most popular trail in the Indian Canyons, and for good reason. This moderate two-mile loop winds through a scenic, rocky canyon full of native vegetation across an ancient **Cahuilla village site** to end at Tahquitz Falls, a rare **desert waterfall.** At the visitors center, pay your fee and pick up a Tahquitz Canyon trail guide for interpretive descriptions of historic and scenic points along the trail. (Water is also available for purchase.)

The trail follows a seasonal creek dependent on snowmelt from the San Jacinto Mountains. The best time to hike is **February-April** for more moderate canyon temperatures and the highest chance of water in the canyon. On the way back you'll have wide views of Palm Springs and the Coachella Valley to the east. Seasonal **ranger-led hikes** (10am and 1pm Fri.-Sun.) are also available.

Tahquitz Canyon

LOWER PALM CANYON TRAIL

Distance: 2.2 miles round-trip

Duration: 1 hour

Elevation gain: 100 feet

Effort: Easy

Trailhead: Trading Post and scenic overlook for Palm Canyon

Directions: From the Palm Springs Visitors center (2901 N Palm Canyon Dr.), head south for nine miles until Palm Canyon Drive ends at the Trading Post and Palm Canyon overlook.

You'll catch the views of the world's largest fan palm oasis, hundreds of green palms clustered improbably at the bottom of a rocky gorge, before strolling down to the canyon floor to be dwarfed by their primordial trunks. Fifteen miles long, Palm Canyon marks the divide between the Santa Rosa and San Jacinto Mountains. It offers stunning contrasts—the lush proliferation of palms set against the craggy canyon walls and arid desert.

A graded trail winds down into the canyon from the **Palm Canyon overlook.** The trail wanders through mammoth palms offering shaggy seclusion and shade. Depending on the season and snowmelt, you'll come across secret pools and intermittent streams studded with boulders. The canyon feels mysterious and Jurassic—it wouldn't seem out of place to catch a glimpse of a dinosaur strolling along. You'll follow a trail on the right side of the canyon above the level of the streambed for about 0.7 mile, continuing through spectacular palm groves. At 0.7 mile the trail crosses to the left side of the canyon, an easy or more difficult task depending on water flow in the canyon. Soon (after a mile total), the palms become less dense, and the trail becomes exposed, forking with the **East Fork** and **Victor Trails.** This is a good turnaround point if your goal was to experience the palm oasis. Return the way you came (the full trail travels 15 miles one-way).

ANDREAS CANYON LOOP

Distance: 2 miles round-trip

Duration: 1 hour

Elevation gain: 50 feet

well-watered Murray Canyon in the Indian Canyons

A clubhouse was built in 1925. Prior to procuring the land, members camped in the canyon's streambed in rock caches. The return route on the left side of the canyon follows a high ridge south of the stream.

MURRAY CANYON

Distance: 4 miles round-trip
Duration: 2 hours
Elevation gain: 500 feet
Effort: Moderate
Trailhead: a picnic area and trailheads for Andreas and Murray Canyons
Directions: From the intersection of S Palm Canyon Drive and Highway 111, continue south for under 3 miles, following signs for Indian Canyons. After the toll, take the road to the right for 0.7 mile until it ends.

The winding trail through Murray Canyon offers a longer chance to explore a palm-filled canyon than its scenic neighbor Andreas.

The trail begins at the parking area for Andreas and Murray Canyons and heads south before entering **Murray Canyon** proper. It delves into the lower edges of the San Jacinto Mountains, providing views of its soaring cliffs as you meander through the palm-enclosed, stream-crossed canyon. The second half of the trail requires hopping back and forth across a picturesque stream that varies in intensity depending on the season. California fan palms are abundant and mixed in with a scattering of cacti, desert willow, and cottonwood. A series of gentle cascades (**Seven Sisters Waterfall**) marks the end of the hike. Return the way you came.

★ Mount San Jacinto State Park

The granite peaks of the San Jacinto Mountains may be a world away from the sunbaked desert floor, but the miracle of engineering that is the **Palm Springs Aerial Tramway** (1 Tram Way, 760/325-1391, www. pstramway.com, every half hour 10am-8pm Mon.-Fri., 8am-8pm Sat.-Sun., $24.95) allows visitors to reach the cool mountain air in about 10 minutes. The tramway leaves from Valley Station on the desert floor (elevation

Effort: Easy
Trailhead: a picnic area and trailheads for Andreas and Murray Canyons
Directions: From the intersection of S Palm Canyon Drive and Highway 111, continue south for under 3 miles, following signs for Indian Canyons. After the toll, take the road to the right for 0.7 mile until it ends. Start by hiking the right (north) side of the canyon to follow the creek.

The trail through lovely Andreas Canyon follows a permanent creek through hundreds of native California fan palms. Secluded pools and striking rock formations make this well worth the small amount of effort the hike requires. Until the late 1800s, the Cahuilla used the creek to irrigate crops of melons, corn, and pumpkins. The turnaround point for this scenic desert stroll is a fence blocking off land for the **Andreas Canyon Club**. The secretive and exclusive club was formed in 1923. Members bought land from the Southern Pacific Railroad and built a series of rock houses (22 in all) into the craggy hills to blend in with the desert landscape.

2,643 feet) and lifts visitors on a dizzying ride via suspended cable cars to traverse the length of rugged Chino Canyon, alighting in a crisp alpine climate at Mountain Station (elevation 8,516 feet) in **Mount San Jacinto State Park** (951/659-2607, www.parks.ca.gov). From Mountain Station, a network of trails (totaling 54 miles within the 14,000-acre wilderness) leads to pine forests, meadows, and striking views. Stop at the **Long Valley Ranger Station** (0.25 mile west of Mountain Station) for maps and info. All trails (except the Long Valley Discovery Trail and Desert View Trail) require that you check in and complete a **day-use permit.**

Because of the drastic change in elevation, the hiking season generally runs **April–November.** Keep in mind that temperatures may be very cold and trails may be impassable due to snow and ice. Expect a 30- to 40-degree temperature difference from the valley floor.

LONG VALLEY DISCOVERY TRAIL
Distance: 0.6 mile round-trip
Duration: 0.5 hour
Elevation gain: Negligible
Effort: Easy
Trailhead: Upper Terminal Mountain Station via the Palm Springs Aerial Tramway

This easy, level nature trail lies outside the back entrance of **Mountain Station,** after a thrilling lift from the **Palm Springs Aerial Tramway** to the top of Mount San Jacinto State Park. The signed trail starts at the bottom of the walkway and follows a 0.6-mile loop through pine forest and past a gorgeous meadow with interpretive signs providing an introduction to the park's plants and animals.

DESERT VIEW TRAIL
Distance: 1.6 miles round-trip
Duration: 1 hour
Elevation gain: 160 feet
Effort: Easy-moderate
Trailhead: Upper Terminal Mountain Station via the Palm Springs Aerial Tramway. Exit Mountain Station via the back entrance. The signed trail starts at the bottom of the walkway leading to trails, wilderness, and a ranger station.

Slightly longer than the Long Valley Discovery Trail, this trail offers another option from the **Mountain Station** after your **tram ride** to the top. Enjoy the striking contrasts between this fresh alpine haven and the austere desert below via an easy to moderate loop trail that clocks in at less than two miles. The trail, which can be hiked clockwise or counterclockwise, undulates through rich

Desert View Trail

pine forest, passing five rocky lookouts (notches) that give way to sweeping views of the Coachella Valley below. Each notch gives a different panoramic perspective and up close views of colorful rock outcroppings.

ROUND VALLEY LOOP TO WELLMAN DIVIDE

Distance: 4.5-6.5 miles round-trip
Duration: 3-4 hours
Elevation gain: 1,300 feet
Effort: Moderate
Trailhead: Long Valley Ranger Station
Directions: Take the Palm Springs Aerial Tramway to the Upper Terminal Mountain Station. From Mountain Station the Ranger Station is 0.25 mile to the west. Check in and complete a day-use pass before beginning your hike.

Hike the Round Valley Loop with lovely Round Valley and its luxuriant meadow as your destination (4.5 miles round-trip) or tack on a steep addendum (6.5 miles round-trip) to see the spectacular views from Wellman Divide.

From the Long Valley Ranger Station follow the well-marked trail (**Low Trail** on maps) southeast toward Round Valley. The trail climbs steadily through pine forests. In early summer you may be crossing or traveling alongside bubbling seasonal snowmelt streams. At 1.8 miles the trail splits. Continue right toward Round Valley and the meadow. You will reach **Round Valley** at 2.1 miles; it's a satisfying destination. Many people use it as an overnight spot, camping at the Round Valley **backcountry campground** or Tamarack Valley to the north.

Continuing from Round Valley the trail gets real, climbing 660 feet over 1 mile. The views from **Wellman Divide** make the short and steep trek worth it. They're spectacular, casting a visual net toward venerable Tahquitz Peak and deeper over the Santa Rosa Mountains. From here it's only 2.7 miles to San Jacinto Peak.

Assuming you've had enough for the day (continuing on to San Jacinto Peak will add an additional 5.4 miles round-trip), return 0.3 mile to a trail junction past Round Valley. Mix it up by taking the right loop (**High Trail** on maps). This will add a mere 0.3 mile to your hike but will vary your return scenery and give you unexpected views of Mountain Station as you descend the last mile to the ranger station.

SAN JACINTO PEAK

Distance: 12 miles round-trip
Duration: 6 hours
Elevation gain: 2,300 feet
Effort: Strenuous
Trailhead: Long Valley Ranger Station
Directions: Take the Palm Springs Aerial Tramway to the Upper Terminal Mountain Station. From Mountain Station the Ranger Station is 0.25 mile to the west. Check in and complete a day-use pass before beginning your hike.

Naturalist John Muir proclaimed the view from San Jacinto Peak to be one of the most sublime on earth. Topographically, it makes sense. San Jacinto Peak is the highest peak in the San Jacinto Mountains and one of the most prominent peaks in the contiguous United States, its north escarpment rising 10,000 feet in seven miles from the San Gorgonio Pass and its low desert wind farms. The peak towers over Palm Springs to the west and the mountain village of Idyllwild to the south. The vistas from the top are amazing, taking in the Coachella Valley, Salton Sea, and looking north to the impressive San Bernardino Mountains and lofty San Gorgonio Mountain.

There are several routes to San Jacinto Peak including from the town of Idyllwild. The most direct (and shortest) route begins from the top of the Palm Springs Aerial Tramway. From the Long Valley Ranger Station, follow the well-marked trail (**Low Trail** on maps) southeast toward Round Valley. The trail winds up steadily through pine forests. In early summer if there has been a good season of winter snowfall, you may come across lively seasonal streams. At 1.8 miles the trail splits. Continue right toward Round Valley, reaching **Round Valley** at 2.1 miles. From here the trail begins to climb more seriously toward

Wellman Divide, climbing 660 feet over the course of 1 mile. Take in the spectacular views from **Wellman Divide;** Tahquitz Peak and the Santa Rosa Mountains are in your sights. From here it's only 2.7 miles to San Jacinto Peak. Follow the trail north toward San Jacinto Peak as it switchbacks steeply and the views grow increasingly sweeping. Just below the peak (0.3 mile) the trail splits again. Follow the steep trail up to the giant granite massif that is **San Jacinto Peak**. Soak in the views from the steep (and sometimes windy) pinnacle.

Return the way you came. After Round Valley you will reach a split with the Low and High Trails. Both return to the Long Valley Ranger Station. The **High Trail** (right split) adds a small amount of mileage (0.3 mile), but it takes you over ground you haven't covered. The good news: either way you're close to some well-earned food, drinks, and continued views (from the comfort of a chair) at Mountain Station.

BIKING

Palm Springs is a great biking town: the area is flat, scenic, and there are established bike paths and routes that lead through historic neighborhoods and along the base of the rocky foothills. If you are cruising around downtown, the city also offers conveniently located bike locking racks throughout the area. Biking is best **October–May.** Summers can be way too hot. If you do bike in summer, start early and return no later than mid-morning.

A network of paved bike paths traverses Palm Springs, extending from Indian Canyon Drive northeast of the Palm Springs Visitors center south toward the Indian Canyons and Murray Canyon Drive and southeast to Golf Club Drive. There are several types of bike paths: Class One (road-separated trails with exclusive right-of-way for bicycles and pedestrians), Class Two (striped lanes for one-way bike travel on city streets), and Class Three (signed trails that share roads with motor vehicles and no on-street striping).

Bike Paths
CITYWIDE TOUR

For a great introduction to town, take the **Citywide Tour** (13 miles). This ride brings you on a wide loop around Palm Springs, from residential neighborhoods to golf courses and country clubs to civic buildings. Start on the north end of town at Palm Canyon Drive and Tachevah Drive. The trail begins by heading west toward the mountains to explore historic residential neighborhoods including Las Palmas. It then heads south, skirting the foothills of the San Jacinto Mountains and passing the Palm Springs Art Museum. The trail continues south to weave through the country clubs and golf course on the south end of town. On the return the loop makes an arc through the eastern side of town paralleling the Palm Springs International Airport and some of Palm Springs' civic buildings.

DOWNTOWN TOUR

Cruise around downtown Palm Springs on the **Downtown Tour** (3 miles), a quieter take on Palm Springs' bustling center. Begin at Palm Canyon Drive and Alejo. The first part of the loop runs along the foot of the mountains along Belardo Road. It parallels the main downtown thoroughfares of Palm Canyon Drive and Indian Canyon Drive and dips past the Palm Springs Art Museum. The route continues down to Ramon Road where it begins its northward return path at the north/south Calle El Segundo.

DEEPWELL TOUR

For an easy and scenic trip, try the **Deepwell Tour** (3.5 miles). This route begins at Mesquite Avenue and Sunrise Way to follow Calle Palo Fiera and Camino Real south (with a quick eastward jog on E Palm Canyon Dr.) to take you through the palm-lined residential streets of one of the city's older neighborhoods on the south end of town. The loop returns via LaVerne and Sunrise Way to connect again with Mesquite Avenue.

Bike Rentals

Many hotels offer complimentary cruiser bikes for tooling around town. If your hotel does not have bikes, they are available for rent at two locations.

BIKE Palm Springs Bike Rentals (194 S Indian Canyon, 760/832-8912, www.bikepsrentals.com, 9am-5pm daily) is in downtown Palm Springs next to the Hard Rock Hotel. They rent premium cruisers and road bikes ($25 for four hours, $33 per day), townies ($23 for up to four hours, $30 per day), tandems ($40 for four hours, $50 per day), electric bikes ($40 for four hours, $50 per day), as well as child bikes and bike carriers ($15 for four hours, $20 per day). The shop may close or hours may vary in the off-season (summer). Rentals include free maps with touring routes, locks, and helmets.

Big Wheel Tours (760/779-1837, www.bwbtours.com) features KHS brand bicycles for rent in the Palm Springs area. Cruisers, mountain bikes, hybrids, and road bikes are available for rent by the hour ($12-18), half day ($25-40), full day ($35-60), and week ($90-195). Big Wheel Tours is based in Palm Desert, 15 miles southeast of Palm Springs in the Coachella Valley, but their bikes are available for delivery ($25 per delivery; $35 west of Gene Autry in Palm Springs; call to reserve).

Big Wheel Tours also offers bike tours. Its **Earthquake Canyon Express Tour** (four hours, departs 8am and 1pm daily Oct.-May, 7am daily June-Sept., $105 pp) for beginner to intermediate riders travels the San Andreas fault zone along the Colorado and Mojave Desert transition with views of the Salton Sea. Customized Palm Springs mountain bike tours are also available (4-6 hours, $105-185 pp).

HORSEBACK RIDING

Beyond its reputation as a sleek resort town, Palm Springs has a Wild West side. The last of the traditional ranch-style inns offering city slickers an escape to simpler times is the historic **Smoke Tree Stables** (2500 S Toledo Ave., 760/327-1372, www.smoketreestables.com, Oct.-May, $120 pp). Established in 1927, they offer guided horseback trail rides that allow you to experience the striking Palm Springs desert. Trips follow more than 150 miles of riding trails along the mountain foothills surrounding Palm Springs and through the palm oasis-filled Indian Canyons.

Rides are offered hourly during the season. Reservations are not necessary, but you should call prior to your ride to confirm times, weather, and availability and plan to arrive 20 minutes prior to departure. **One-hour trail rides** (8am-3pm, $50 pp) follow a trail along the base of the Santa Rosa Mountains. **Murray Canyon Haul Rides** (9am, 11am, and 1pm daily, $120) follow the streams and palms of Andreas and Murray Canyons. Two-hour rides may also be available.

PARKS

Palm Springs is nestled near such spectacular wilderness parks as Joshua Tree National Park and Mount San Jacinto State Park, but within the city limits there are grassy places to relax and picnic, play tennis, swim, skateboard, or let the dog run free.

Centrally located close to downtown Palm Springs, **Ruth Hardy Park** (700 Tamarisk Way, until 10pm daily) is great for picnics and family celebrations. The 22 acres of tree-lined green lawns feature outdoor grills and picnic tables, a children's playground, eight lighted public tennis courts, three sand volleyball courts, a basketball court, and restroom facilities.

Spanning 61 acres, **DeMuth Park** (4365 Mesquite Ave., open until 10pm daily) is Palm Springs' largest park with ball fields, basketball and tennis courts, picnic tables, soccer fields, a children's playground, and restroom facilities. It is good for picnics as well as outdoor sports and activities.

The **Palm Springs Swim Center** (405 S Pavilion Way, 760/323-8278, www.palmspringsca.gov, 11am-5pm daily, $5) features an Olympic-size pool for recreational and lap swimming. Adjacent to the Swim Center, the

Palm Springs Skate Park (Sunrise Plaza, 401 S Pavilion Way, 760/656-0024, noon-10pm Mon.-Fri., 9am-10pm Sat.-Sun.) taps into Southern California's history of pool skating to offer bowls for smooth, fast skating with several feet of vertical walls, pool coping, and transitions. The skate park also features street skating elements like rails, pyramids, stairs, ramps, and quarter pipes. Actual skaters were consulted in the building of this park with a fun and genuine result for board and in-line skaters of all skill levels.

The leash-free, 1.5-acre Palm Springs Dog Park (N Civic Dr., 760/323-8117, www.palmspringsca.gov, 6am-10pm daily, closed noon-3pm Tues. and Fri.) is behind City Hall. Separate areas for large and small dogs offer your pets a place to run free. Park benches, shade canopies, and drinking fountains round out the amenities.

Food

NORTH PALM SPRINGS AND UPTOWN DESIGN DISTRICT
Breakfast and Coffee

Breakfast and lunch at ★ Cheeky's (622 N Palm Canyon Dr., 760/327-7595, www.cheekysps.com, 8am-2pm Thurs.-Mon. in summer, $7-13) is wildly popular for good reason. Enjoy fresh pressed juices, garden-fresh craft Bloody Marys, and specialty cinnamon rolls as well as California classics like the heirloom tomato BLT with jalapeño bacon and huevos rancheros on the patio or in the bright dining room. People rave about the bacon flight. While you wait for a table, the patio next door is open with cooling misters and coffee.

★ Ernest Coffee (1101 N Palm Canyon Dr., 760/318-4154, www.ernestcoffee.com, 6am-8pm daily) is a wonderful way to start the day. This chic space has polished concrete floors, plenty of natural light, warm wood tables, and splashes of bright color. They serve the Portland-originated Stumptown coffee and daily fresh-baked pastries. They also offer an excellent list of beer, wine, and a few small plates including cheese and charcuterie. It shares the space with the Bootlegger Tiki Bar next door. The coffee shop is named after Ernest Raymond Beaumont Gantt, better known as Don the Beachcomber, who opened the Palm Springs location of the famed tiki bar (Don the Beachcomber) in 1953.

Locals' favorite ★ Rick's Restaurant (1973 N Palm Canyon Dr., 760/416-0090, www.ricksrestaurant.biz, 6am-3pm daily) doesn't do anything on a small scale. Breakfast and lunch diner classics are served in heaping and well-executed quantities. Ignore the questionable 1980s decor at this American-style diner and dig into their giant pancakes (crispy on the edges), giant cinnamon rolls, or omelets for breakfast. Order a side of the excellent bacon to go with anything. Lunch transitions into salads, cold and hot sandwiches (including Cuban pressed sandwiches), and hot plates with American and Cuban specialties.

The original location of Koffi (515 N Palm Canyon Dr., 760/416-2244, www.kofficoffee.com, 5:30am-7:30pm daily) has been gracing Palm Springs with its strong brews since 2008. The fresh, small batch house blends are fragrantly ferried up from a roasting facility in the Coachella Valley. Food is an afterthought: standard coffee shop offerings including scones and muffins and such. Come here for the fresh high octane, convenient location, and friendly service.

California Cuisine

Maybe only in Palm Springs does an upscale, retro, tropical-themed restaurant with mood lighting and a neon color scheme not only make sense but also seem like a great idea. The ★ Tropicale Restaurant and Coral Seas Lounge (330 E Amado Rd., 760/866-1952, www.thetropicale.com, 4pm-10pm Sun.-Thurs., 4pm-11pm Fri.-Sat., brunch 11am-3pm Sat.-Sun., $13-32) serves a very eclectic menu with a focus on Pacific Rim plates. Pizzas and sandwiches are thrown in for good measure. Deep banquette booths, chandeliers, and a buzzing tropical patio and bar are a throwback to the dinner clubs and themed cocktail bars Palm Springs does so well.

Trio (707 N Palm Canyon Dr., 760/864-8746, www.triopalmsprings.com, 11am-10pm Mon.-Thurs., 11am-11pm Fri., 10am-11pm Sat., 10am-10pm Sun.) taps into Palm Spring's signature sleek party persona with its splashy lighting, historic mid-century setting, lively bar, and crowd-pleasing entrées (comfort food meets California contemporary) from seared ahi tuna to mushroom linguine. Specialty cocktails are fresh, fruity, and seasonal. Be sure to make a reservation, especially on weekends. This place is popular with both locals and tourists and can be packed with groups and bachelorette parties.

The chic farm to table ★ Workshop Kitchen and Bar (800 N Palm Canyon Dr., 760/459-3451, www.workshoppalmsprings.com, 5pm-10pm Sun.-Thurs., 5pm-11pm Fri.-Sat., 10am-2pm Sun., $24-37) shines most as a temple to outstanding architecture and design. The bones of the 1926 Spanish Colonial have been laid bare and recast with sleek concrete booths, a communal table, and long strands of custom lighting emphasizing the ceiling's height and the striking symmetry of the space. The soaring wood ceiling trusses have housed a bank, furniture store, and myriad other incarnations before its 2012 redesign—which snagged the prestigious 2015 James Beard Foundation Award for best restaurant design or renovation in North America. Consider it part of your touristic duty to, at least, have a carefully crafted cocktail at the altar-like bar. Soak in the space with drinks like the white rum and lime Hemingway Special or the vodka and pineapple Palm Springer. The restaurant is open for dinner serving richly nuanced small and large plates—from house-made pâté to seared scallops. Sunday brunch features plates like Jidori chicken & waffles and lobster breakfast burrito.

Part of the former Cary Grant estate, Copley's (621 N Palm Canyon Dr., 760/327-9555, www.copleyspalmsprings.com, 5:30pm-close daily Oct.-May, $32-39) offers new American fine dining in a romantic setting. The candlelit patio has the choicest seating

Ernest Coffee

and a stone fireplace. Entrées are geared toward the meat eater with perfectly executed steaks, duck, fish, and lamb. A fleeting happy hour at the tiny bar brings the restaurant pricing within reach for one hour on weekdays.

Make a reservation or prepare to wait for weekend meals at **Jake's** (664 N Palm Canyon Dr., 760/327-4400, www.jakespalmsprings.com, 11am-2:45pm and 5pm-8:45pm Tues.-Thurs., 5:30pm-9:45pm Fri.-Sat., brunch 10am-2:45pm Fri.-Sat., $20-32). It's a popular bistro with a fun patio scene. The extensive menu has every variation of new American, Southwest, Mediterranean-influenced dishes you can dream up in your wait for a table (sans reservation). The specialty cocktails have just as many twists (pun intended) from drinks like the Acai Basil Gimlet to the Rosemary Maple Bourbon Sour.

Italian and Pizza

Birba (622 N Palm Canyon Dr., 760/327-5678, www.birbaps.com, 5pm-11pm Wed.-Thurs. and Sun., 5pm-midnight Fri.-Sat., $10-29) offers a modern take on Italian classics serving up small plates and wood-fired pizzas topped with savory toppings from braised greens to meatballs. Their old-school cocktails are equally fresh and reimagined. Dinner is served on the bustling patio and in the sleek indoor space. The place books quickly; make reservations online in advance.

Mexican

It's Palm Springs. Chances are you've spent a hard day at the pool or enjoying some festive event. **El Mirasol** (266 E Via Altamira, 760/459-3136, 11am-10pm daily, $12-20), located in the Los Arboles Hotel, offers the type of Mexican comfort food that can easily hit the spot. The signature smoky, Doña Diabla sauce accompanies every meal in liter bottles. Strong margaritas and a charming patio make an easy choice for anyone staying in the hotel. The restaurant also serves poolside during the day. El Mirasol has a second location in **South Palm Springs** (140 E Palm Canyon Dr., 760/323-0721).

CENTRAL PALM SPRINGS AND DOWNTOWN
Breakfast and Coffee

★ **Pinocchio in the Desert** (134 E Tahquitz Canyon Way, 760/322-3776, www.pinocchiops.com, 7:30am-2pm daily) is a full-on party. By somewhere around noon, the eggs and hash browns are flying onto packed tables in the kitschy setting, and the cheap, bottomless mimosas are flowing. The patio gets cranked up to a fever pitch, fanned by the pink, fringed umbrellas, speedy service, and drink specials. It would be difficult to maintain such a pace, so they do everyone a favor and close at 2pm every day.

Once you manage to find the French-inspired **Farm** (6 La Plaza, La Plaza Shopping Center, 760/322-2724, Tues.-Sun. 9am-2pm, $11-30) tucked down a walkway and nestled past a wedding chapel, it oozes charm. Farmhouse-style wooden tables are scattered under a shady canopy. Brunch-goers enjoy a new American and Provencal-inspired menu with French press coffee, mimosas, chicken and mushroom crepes, banana French toast, and other brunch specialties. Farm prides itself on its menu. Translation: they do not allow substitutions, and the food can take a while. Be prepared to choose something and relax.

American

Two things: Dutch crunch bread and Bomb Sauce. **The Sandwich Spot** (240 N Palm Canyon Dr., 760/778-7900, www.sandwichspotpalmsprings.com, 11am-6pm daily, $8) serves up a smorgasbord of hefty sandwiches with provocative names like the MILF (cranberry, chicken, cheese, veggies) and the Dreamkiller (crunchy veggies and cheese). Choose a bread (did I mention the Dutch crunch?) and a sauce (Bomb or Secret) and dig into one of their gooey, crunchy, flavorful sandwiches.

From the front room **Woody's Burgers** (317 N Canyon Dr., 760/230-0188, http://woodysburgersps.com, 11am-midnight daily,

$8-10) looks like an innocent lunch counter serving up classic American burgers, fries, and milk shakes ($8-12). Every evening at 7pm, however, Woody's alter ego "Woody's After Dark" takes over. The back room serves up live jazz and blues along with beer, wine, and cocktails.

Tyler's Burgers (149 S Indian Canyon Dr., 760/325-2990, www.tylersburgers.com, 11am-4pm Mon.-Sat., $7-10 cash only) is Americana nostalgia made fresh. The small, casual café is set in an old 1936 Greyhound Bus depot, but the patio provides people watching for the very current Palm Springs. The menu features classic all-American fare—burgers (obviously), sandwich classics (egg and chicken salad, BLT, and others), soups, and chili. Veggie options include a veggie burger and grilled cheese. Come for the burgers, stay for the coleslaw—they're known for it. Beer and wine are also available.

Sherman's Deli and Bakery (401 E Tahquitz Canyon Way, 760/325-1199, 7am-9pm daily, $8-19), a beloved Palm Springs tradition, is a kosher-style deli serving up mile-high sandwiches and heaping plates. The staggering menu includes deli sandwiches, soups and salads, appetizers, chef specialties, breakfast, plates and platters, deluxe dinners, and a kids' menu. Oh, and save room for their arsenal of fluffy cream pies, cakes, and pastries for dessert.

Asian

The elegantly hip ★ **Rooster and the Pig** (356 S Indian Canyon Dr., 760/832-6691, www.roosterandthepig.com, 5pm-9pm Wed.-Mon., $9-19) is a small, progressive Vietnamese American restaurant. The menu features appetizers like pork belly and charred brussel sprouts, fresh, tangy salads, spring rolls, and larger-format dishes like crispy whole fish, a rice noodle bowl, and a banh mi burger. These are served family-style and recommended for sharing. The tasty menu is accompanied by a small but good selection of beer, wine, and cocktails. There can be lines to get in, but they generally move quickly.

Red emperor-style doors, neon-hued lighting, and Chinese screens and statues set the stage for the inventive fusion cuisine of **Wang's in the Desert** (424 S Indian Canyon Dr., www.wangsinthedesert.com, 5pm-close daily, $11-26) restaurant and bar. A Pan-Asian menu tackles everything from dim sum to pad thai. The bar serves a popular happy hour (3pm-7pm) and there is live entertainment on weekends.

California Cuisine

The bright and airy **Lulu's California Bistro** (200 S Palm Canyon Dr., 760/327-5858, www.lulupalmsprings.com, 8am-10pm Sun.-Thurs., 8am-midnight Fri.-Sat., $10-30) is a no-brainer with its central location on the downtown strip. The sprawling menu is solid, offering salads, panini, pastas, and entrées. The tiered dining areas, central bar, and efficient service make for a buzzing scene.

Eight4Nine Restaurant and Lounge (849 N Palm Canyon Dr., 760/325-8490, www.eight4nine.com, 11am-3pm and 5pm-10pm Mon.-Thurs., 11am-3pm and 5pm-11pm Fri., 9am-3pm and 5pm-11pm Sat., 9am-3pm and 5pm-10pm Sun., $16-22) offers a striking white decor for its restaurant and lounge. In 1954 the building housed the Palm Springs Post Office. Now, the contemporary, crisp white space is accented with colorful art and jewel tones. The restaurant offers fresh California nouveau classics with sea, land, and farm mains featuring salads, sandwiches, and entrées like sourdough-crusted Chilean sea bass as well as brunch items like lobster roll eggs Benedict. Dinner offers choices ranging from a poblano chili relleno to grass-fed New York strip steak. The lounge stays open all day offering a bar menu every day from 11am to close. An outdoor patio offers mountain views.

★ **Shanghai Red's Bar & Grill** (233 S Indian Canyon Dr., 760/322-9293, www.fishermans.com, 5pm-10pm Mon.-Thurs., 5pm-11:30pm Fri., 11am-3pm and 5pm-11:30pm Sat., 11am-3pm and 5pm-10pm Sun., $5-35) offers some of the finest fish tacos out there. Anthony Bourdain said so himself. Located inside the Fisherman's Market & Grill Restaurant Complex, this dark hole-in-the-wall consists of a long, wooden bar and a few tables. The small space allows the person cooking behind the counter to whip up your fluffy shrimp and fish tacos doused with pico de gallo, shredded cabbage, and white sauce and hand them straight over to you without further ado. The menu also includes a full array of steamed, grilled, and fried seafood, soups, salads, and pastas. There is live music on the patio on weekends.

Bring your parents, your mom, your partner, your mom's partner, your business friend, your oldest friend, or all of the above to ★ **Spencer's** (701 W Baristo Rd., 760/327-3446, www.spencersrestaurant. com, 8am-2:30pm and 5pm-10pm daily, brunch 8am-2:30pm Sat.-Sun., $10-40), a Palm Springs mainstay. Tucked away in the historic Palm Springs Tennis Club, Spencer's exemplifies Palm Springs upscale resort style for the clientele and decor. The restaurant serves new American and French Pacific Rim-influenced dishes. Brunch is the best meal for the value here and a fun place to see and be seen. Dinner is more romantic, while lunch is fit for the power set.

European

A sleek modern spot tucked into an unassuming corner location in downtown, **Johanne's** (196 S Indian Canyon Dr., 760/778-0017, www.johannesrestaurants. com, 5pm-10pm Tues.-Thurs. and Sun., 5pm-10:30pm Fri.-Sat., hours vary seasonally, $20-40) offers a fresh continental menu in an airy, upscale setting. The Austrian chef-run kitchen puts out sophisticated versions of Austrian and Pacific Rim specialties including schnitzel and seared scallops. The menu can be pricey, but they also offer a bar menu that includes several of their signature schnitzels served in a bright bar that offers a view into the street and good downtown people watching.

Le Vallauris (385 W Tahquitz Canyon Way, 760/325-5059, www.levallauris.com, 11:30am-2:30pm and 5pm-10:30pm daily, $20-48) delivers elegant French dishes from duck to lobster ravioli with a setting to match. The formal, old-world dining and romantic patio add up to a choice evening. Special prix fixe menus are offered from time to time and are worthwhile for the indulgent range and value.

Italian and Pizza

The family-owned **Johnny Costa's** (440 S Palm Canyon Dr., 760/325-4556, www. johnnycostaspalmsprings.com, 5pm-10:30pm Mon.-Sat., $20-30) has been serving classic Italian specialties since 1976. Sink into a deep booth and dinner lighting at this low-key spot with an old-school feel. They offer a large and satisfying menu with a wide range of dishes—steak, veal, chicken, seafood, and pastas. Try the Steak Sinatra (the restaurant founder cooked for Sinatra at his estate) or comforting choices like linguine with clams and baked eggplant parmigiana.

Mexican

★ **Rio Azul** (350 S Indian Canyon Dr., 760/992-5641, www.rioazulpalmsprings. com, 5pm-9pm Wed.-Thurs., 11am-10pm Fri.-Sat., 11am-9pm Sun., $12-22) goes a huge step beyond the status quo of the refried bean, rice, and bubbling cheese plate of formulaic Mexican restaurants. They do offer this standard fare (we practically demand it as vacationing Americans), but their menu gets way more complex and nuanced with house specialties like the traditional Yucatan Cochinita Pibil (slow-roasted pork in banana leaf), grilled quail, and seafood enchiladas. They kill it with their skinny margarita, organic tequila, fresh lime, agave, and a sweet, salty, chili rim. The space is vibrant with wood booths, good lighting, and a separate bar area.

SOUTH PALM SPRINGS
Breakfast and Coffee

With three locations, **Koffi** (1700 S Camino Real, 760/322-7776, www.kofficoffee.com,

5:30am-7:30pm daily) is positioned to give you your fix wherever you are. This second location (the first is in downtown Palm Springs, third in Palm Desert) offers a much-needed jolt to the guests staying at the cluster of party and relaxation hotels in South Palm Springs. Come for the coffee and leave with a better attitude. They offer basic breakfast survival food—muffins, scones, and the like.

The choice to go to **Elmer's Pancake House** (1030 E Palm Canyon Dr., 760/327-8419, www.eatatelmers.com, 6am-9pm daily) is as solid as its massive breakfast plates. Part of a Pacific Northwest diner chain dating from 1960, Elmer's makes its one California star appearance in Palm Springs. The service is good in this family-style retro diner with canted ceilings and plenty of windows. They serve all the breakfast favorites as well as their signature German pancakes. Lunch and dinner offer up sandwiches, soups, salads, and comfort food entrées straight out of Twin Peaks diner territory.

American

Located inside the Ace Hotel, ★ **King's Highway** (701 E Palm Canyon Dr., 760/969-5789 www.acehotel.com/palmsprings, 7am-11pm daily, $12-27) offers reimagined locally sourced nouveau American classics in an airy space with Naugahyde booths and original terrazzo floors. This roadside diner that was formerly a Denny's has a menu that features inventive breakfast dishes like the Moroccan scramble and sweet corn fritters with poached eggs, while lunch and dinner options include hearty fare like mahimahi tacos or buttermilk fried jidori chicken.

The upscale diner fare at ★ **Norma's** (4200 E Palm Canyon Dr., 760/770-5000, www.theparkerpalmsprings.com, 7am-3pm and 5pm-10pm daily, $18-26) is pricey but worth it. Within The Parker Palm Springs, the stylish comfy eatery offers perfectly executed breakfast and lunch with specialties like a fruit-stuffed waffle or lobster, fish, and chips. Dinner brings out indulgent comfort classics like lobster mac and cheese and spaghetti and

meatballs. Bonus: you can ogle the hotel's chic Jonathan Adler design and wander the manicured Alice in Wonderland garden grounds of The Parker.

The stylish **Smoke Tree BBQ Bar and Grill** (1775 E Palm Canyon Dr., 760/778-6521, www.smoketreebbq.com, 11am-9pm Mon.-Sat., $12-25) is one of the new guard of restaurants clustered in South Palm Springs. Its decor is refreshingly contemporary with marble and light wood furnishings. The rustic chic setting is small with communal tables, a small bar, patio, and private dining room. Craft beers, smoky barbecue (ribs, tri-tip, brisket, turkey chicken), and veggie options make it a satisfying stop.

The new owners of **Mr. Lyon's** (233 E Palm Canyon Dr., 760/327-1551, www.mrlyonsps.com, 5pm-11pm Tues.-Sat., 4pm-9pm Sun., $32-59) breathed new life into an old establishment, creating a sleekly designed upscale steak house with a modern twist. Dry, aged beef and prime rib are house specialties with seafood and veggie options available. The dark, friendly bar offers classic cocktails and a lounge menu with items like a burger and moules frites ($10-20).

California Cuisine

Kiyosaku (Plaza Del Sol Shopping Center, 1555 S Palm Canyon Dr., 760/327-6601, www.kiyosakusushi.menutoeat.com, 5:30pm-9pm Thurs.-Mon., $17-30) sushi is the real deal—traditional, family owned, and high quality. Instead of trendy rolls, the husband and wife team focus on excellent sushi and sashimi—he makes the sushi, she serves it in full kimono. (Yes, it's sushi in the desert, but they know what they're doing.) Beer, wine, and sake are served.

European

Central European meets Mediterranean cuisine in the cozy, well-appointed atmosphere of ★ **Miro's** (Plaza Del Sol Shopping Center, 1555 S Palm Canyon Dr., 760/323-5199, www.mirospalmsprings.com, 5pm-9:30pm daily, $26-39). The skilled kitchen staff takes basic ingredients like whole Mediterranean sea bass, cabbage, beef, mushrooms, and Yukon Gold potatoes and practices some magical cooking alchemy to turn every piping plate into a nuanced blend of satisfying goodness. Try dishes like beef Stroganoff, osso buco, scallops, and schnitzel paired with their (should-be-trade-secret) cabbage salad and a choice from the extensive wine list. The service is truly refined without being stuffy. Tip: Make a reservation! Even if you have to make it on your phone before you walk through the doors.

Italian and Pizza

Appetito Cal Italian Deli (1700 S Camino Real, #2, 760/327-1929, www.appetitodeli. com, 11am-10pm Sun.-Thurs., 11am-11pm Fri.-Sat., changes seasonally, $10-20) is another one of the bright (literally) new restaurants that's opened in South Palm Springs. A huge bank of windows frames views of the mountains; polished concrete floors reflect creative lighting and an industrial, exposed ceiling. The casual open space matches a friendly menu that features fresh pastas, pizzettes, sandwiches, salads, and snacks. Ingredients like arugula and local dates add California freshness to richer Italian fare. Despite the great choices, food can be hit-or-miss. Happy hour is a good bet with deals on snacks, craft beer, wines, and Italian cocktails.

The Chicago-inspired ★ **Guiseppe's Pizza and Pasta** (Smoke Tree Village Shopping Center, 1775 E Palm Canyon Dr., 760/537-1890, www.giuseppesps.com, 11am-9pm Sun.-Thurs., 11am-9:30pm Fri.-Sat., $15-20) is a fresher version of a comfortable

neighborhood joint dating back generations. The warm space has exposed brick walls, a relaxed dining room, and cozy bar. It's good for families, friends, or dates. Try the pan or thin-crust pizzas (their eggplant pizza is award-winning for good reason) as well as pastas (from mushroom ravioli to shrimp scampi linguine). Gluten-free options are also available.

Mexican

The casual **El Mirasol** (140 E Palm Canyon Dr., 760/323-0721, 11am-10pm daily, $12-20) is a great walkable option for the handful of hotels stretching along this section of South Palm Canyon Drive. They serve up plates of comfort food and strong margaritas to diners in their stripped-down dining room and patio. The signature smoky, Doña Diabla sauce accompanies every meal in liter bottles. El Mirasol has a second location in the **Los Arboles Hotel** (266 E Via Altamira).

Vegetarian

Palm Springs has the original location of the **Native Foods** (Smoke Tree Village Shopping Center, 1775 E Palm Canyon Dr., #420, 760/416-0070, www.nativefoods.com, 11am-9pm daily) vegan chain. They offer freshly made plant-based mock meat and other vegan fare in a fast-casual setting. Go guilty pleasure with the popular Chicken Run Ranch Burger (their most popular item) or chili cheese fries (it's okay—it's vegan!). They also serve a creative selection of burgers, sandwiches, bowls, and salads magically whipping whole foods like kale and quinoa into beloved creations like the Reuben and taco salad.

Accommodations

December-May is when lodging rates are at their highest and hotels can book weeks in advance. Rates especially skyrocket in April, when thousands of revelers flock to Palm Springs and the Coachella Valley for a number of large-scale events and festivals. In April, hotels can be booked *months* in advance—although with the sheer number of hotels in the area, last-minute reservations will likely be available at a few places. Fall (Oct.-Dec.) is still considered high season, although rates tend to be slightly lower than winter and spring. Summer is the low season, due to soaring desert temperatures. But if your main goal is to lounge in a pool, there are great hotel rates to be had June-September.

NORTH PALM SPRINGS AND UPTOWN DESIGN DISTRICT
$100-150

Within the historic Old Las Palmas neighborhood, the ★ Coral Sands Inn (210 W Stevens Rd., 760/325-4900, www.coralsandspalmsprings.com, $139-189) is cinematic with its bright pink facade, neon sign, and six themed rooms. Lounging by the kidney-shaped pool with the mountain backdrop, you'll feel like you're starring in the best road trip movie of the summer. Ruby Montana is a warm hostess, an avid collector with a cult following. She dreamed up and furnished the kitschy rooms including the western Yippy Ky Yo Ky Yay Rodeo Room and the Liberace Room. It's a fun place to lounge the weekend away, and the inn is also available to rent out for special events for you and your friends.

In addition to the Coral Sands Inn, Ruby Montana also has other properties nearby. Casa Redonda is a gorgeous 1937 Spanish-style hacienda. It was originally built for two sisters who each took a wing of the house. The space has two, two-bedroom mirror image standalone bungalows and a casita (side house)—enough to comfortably sleep 10. Spanish tile floors, period furnishings, rooftop cocktail decks, and unobstructed views of the mountains make this a stunning and relaxing getaway.

Situated in the center of the Uptown Design District, Alcazar (622 N Palm Canyon Dr., 760/318-9850, www.alcazarpalmsprings.com, $120-180 Mon.-Thurs., weekend rates up to $300) is a hip and relaxing 34-room boutique hotel with Spanish Colonial red-tile roofs and a sleek, modern sensibility. Mountain and poolside king rooms and poolside and courtyard queen rooms are available including some suites with whirlpool tubs and kitchenettes and some with patios. Rooms feature Italian linens and flat-screen TVs. A resort fee covers the amenities of a saltwater pool, Jacuzzi, and loaner townie bikes. Alcazar also boasts two of Palm Springs' favorite restaurants: Cheeky's (760/327-7595, www.cheekysps.com, 8am-2pm Thurs.-Mon. in summer) for a farm to table brunch and Birba (760/327-5678, www.birbaps.com, 5pm-11pm Wed.-Thurs. and Sun., 5pm-midnight Fri.-Sat.) for dinner and cocktails. The complimentary continental breakfast comes from Cheeky's.

$150-250

Once you go past the unassuming concrete facade of the Skylark Hotel (1466 N Palm Canyon Dr., 760/322-2267, www.skylarkps.com, $170-200), the inside is bursting with color. A rainbow of lounge chairs rings the inviting pool and hot tub and offer spectacular views of the San Jacinto Mountains. The hotel was originally constructed in 1955 and retains its mid-century exterior while offering newly furnished, updated, and contemporary poolside hotel rooms. Sundays can be a scene at the Skylark pool with mimosas and party tunes playing over the hotel's sound system. On an unrelated note, the hotel allows children, something of a rarity in Palm Springs. Continental breakfast is included. The blend of fun, easy style and value makes the Skylark a solid choice.

The historic, hacienda-style **Los Arboles Hotel** (784 N Indian Canyon Dr., 760/459-3605, www.losarboleshotel.com, $150-220) has 21 Spanish-tiled rooms, a pool garnished with lush greenery, and the on-site El Mirasol Mexican restaurant. There's clearly no reason to leave the grounds. All 21 spacious rooms are set in single-story stucco with red-tile roofs, just steps from the pool. It's a peaceful place to read, nap, or drink margaritas poolside.

The star of the cozy boutique **Avanti Hotel** (354 E Stevens Rd., 760/327-3866, www.avantihotelps.com, $180-250) is its small kidney-shaped pool, sunk into a central courtyard, ringed by potted flowers, greenery, and 10 hotel rooms. Quarters are intimate and peaceful with rooms opening directly poolside, offering mountain views, and most with private patios. The rooms tend to be comfortable as opposed to stylish, but you're likely to find everything you need including snacks, water, televisions, and kitchenettes. The hotel also offers complimentary continental breakfast, happy hour beer and wine, and cruiser bikes. There is a hot tub on site. The Avanti is adults only but dog-friendly.

Noted for its modernist architecture and movie star past, the mid-century **Movie Colony Hotel** (726 N Indian Canyon Dr., 760/320-6340, www.moviecolonyhotel.com, $170-290) dates to 1935, designed by architect Albert Frey. It exemplifies modernist style featuring sleek lines, original art, and period furniture. The hotel offers 17 themed rooms, some with terraces or private patios. Amenities include a continental breakfast, evening wine around the fire pit, a pool, a hot tub, and loaner bikes.

Posh Palm Springs Inn (530 E Mel Ave., 760/992-5410, www.poshpalmsprings.com, $150-319, 2-night minimum on weekends), dating from the 1930s, is a small, mid-century hotel offering a boutique bed-and-breakfast experience. The courtyard-style guest rooms feature king-size beds, plush robes, flat-screen TVs, and a kitchen or wet bar. Other amenities include a freshwater pool and hot tub, hot, homemade breakfast daily, and a Posh martini happy hour with snacks 4pm-5pm (no additional resort fees).

Over $250

The Irwin-Schuman-designed **Riviera Palm Springs** (1600 N Indian Canyon Dr., 760/327-8311, www.rivierapalmsprings.com, $200-300) opened in 1959 as the city's first resort hotel and played a key role in Palm Springs history as a glamour celebrity destination. The hotel was renovated in 2006 and continues as a deluxe resort with 398 rooms and 73 suites (although you're more likely to see bachelorette parties rather than celebrities basking around the pool). Hotel amenities include two resort pools (with pool bars), a spa and fitness center, two lounges, and an on-site restaurant.

Colony Palms Hotel (572 N Indian Canyon Dr., 760/969-1800, www.colonypalmshotel.com, $300-400) was opened in 1936 as the Colonial House by reputed mobster Al Wertheimer, member of the Detroit-based Purple Gang. The private hotel hosted a number of illicit activities including gambling, a speakeasy, and a brothel entered via a secret staircase. Since then, Colony Palms has classed things up. This 56-room luxury boutique hotel features Mediterranean-style decor with designer guest rooms (some with fireplaces and clawfoot tubs), courtyards for relaxing, a heated outdoor pool, hot tub, a Moroccan spa, gym, meeting space, and concierge. The Purple Palm Restaurant and Bar gives a nod to the old days.

Technically located in the prestigious Movie Colony neighborhood of Palm Springs, **Triada Palm Springs** (640 N Indian Canyon Dr., 760/844-7000, www.triadapalmsprings.com, $210-300) is a Spanish hacienda-style boutique hotel featuring 56 Mediterranean-style rooms. Some of the rooms have patios making them feel like private villas. Two pools and an on-site upscale restaurant and bar round out the luxury experience.

LGBT

Bearfoot Inn (888 N Indian Canyon Dr., 760/699-7641, www.bearfootinn.com, $139-179), a refurbished mid-century hotel located in the Movie Colony neighborhood, is a clothing-optional resort that caters to a gay male clientele. The hotel is a short distance to a number of gay bars and clubs. The 11 guest rooms feature platform beds, extra-firm bamboo memory foam mattresses, extra-large walk-in showers, refrigerators, in-room coffee, and flat-screen TVs. Property amenities include a heated saltwater pool and spa in the central courtyard and gym access.

Secluded, lush grounds make the **East Canyon Hotel & Spa** (288 E Camino Monte Vista, 760/320-1928, www.eastcanyonps.com, $199-299, three-night minimum) a retreat in the heart of Palm Springs. The luxury accommodations at this boutique gay resort hotel feature suites with king-size beds, Italian linens, separate living areas, oversize showers, rain showerheads, and plush towels. A private Jacuzzi is available in the grand suite. A courtyard pool and hot tub are surrounded by lush foliage and mountain views. On-site spa services are available. This resort hotel caters to a male clientele and is the only non-clothing-optional gay resort in Palm Springs.

CENTRAL PALM SPRINGS AND DOWNTOWN
$100-150

The spelling of the ★ **Orbit In** (562 W Arenas Rd., 760/323-3585, www.orbitin.com, $140-270) is intentional. Coming from your travels to land amid the atomic-style furnishings of this mid-century boutique hotel will truly feel as if you just orbited in. The Orbit In is actually two properties on the same block. Herb Burns, who introduced Palm Springs to the luxury, ultramodern motor court inn, built both the Orbit In and **The Hideaway** (370 W Arenas Rd., 760/323-3585, www.orbitin.com,

$140-270). They both feature large studio-style rooms with sitting areas and kitchenettes surrounding a saltwater pool. The Orbit In is funkier with nine poolside rooms, terrazzo bar, hot tub, and vintage orange sun umbrellas. The Hideaway is sleeker and more muted with 10 poolside studios and great mountain views. At "Orbitini Hour" (5pm) guests of both properties gather at the Orbit In to chat over fruity Orbitinis.

The classic mid-century ★ **Desert Hills** (601 W Arenas Rd., 760/325-2777, www.desert-hills.com, $120-155) was built in 1956. The apartment-style hotel rooms hearken back to a time when vacationers had their priorities straight and chose Palm Springs for extended vacations, often wintering here. The 14 casual, stylish rooms, some with kitchens and patios, stretch out around a central pool and hot tub. A three-night minimum encourages quiet relaxation with nothing to do but chat with other hotel guests or contemplate the mountains, another dip in the pool, some light reading, or what you'll be cooking up on the property grill for dinner. Guests also have access to the Palm Springs Tennis Club and loaner bicycles. Adults only. No pets.

Chase Hotel (200 W Arenas Rd., 760/320-8866, www.chasehotelpalmsprings.com, $90-170) is a small mid-century hotel built in the 1940s that offers a low-key desert retreat although it is just steps from the shops, restaurants, and bars of Palm Canyon Drive. Amenities include a heated saltwater pool in a garden setting, shuffleboard, barbecue area, Wi-Fi, and continental breakfast. Some rooms offer kitchenettes. The hotel is family-friendly, an unusual status in Palm Springs.

Founded in the 1920s, historic **Casa Cody** (175 S Cahuilla Rd., 760/320-9346, www.casacody.com, rooms/studios $80-170, 1-2 bedrooms $200-300) is the oldest operating hotel in Palm Springs. The romantic adobe inn has 29 Southwestern-inspired rooms with tile or hardwood floors, many with private patios and fireplaces. Amenities include two outdoor pools and daily breakfast.

$150-250

Hard Rock Hotel Palm Springs (150 S Indian Canyon Dr., 760/969-6665, www.hrhpalmsprings.com, $200-300) is part of the rock-and-roll-themed chain offering a resort experience. Rooms feature custom furniture and select artwork, balconies and patios, flat-screen TVs, minibar and mini-fridge, and Rock Spa bath products. On-site the resort amenities include a restaurant, lobby bar and lounge, spa, fitness center, outdoor pool with poolside bar, cabanas, and daybeds.

The stone and redwood ★ **Del Marcos Hotel** (225 W Baristo Rd., 760/325-6902, www.delmarcoshotel.com, $150-210) welcomes guests through its boldly angled entrance to a bright lobby with white terrazzo floors and floor-to-ceiling glass looking out to the saltwater pool. Designed in 1947 by William Cody, the hotel received a historic designation for its post-WWII modern resort design. The Del Marcos' 17 suites are impeccably styled with individual charm from the Eames Poolside Suite with terrazzo floors and Eames furnishings to the Desert Oasis Deluxe with a tiki bar and private patio. Beach cruisers are available for tooling around town. A daily complimentary happy hour is a nice touch.

The Amado (1821 E Amado Rd., 760/537-0053, www.theamado.com, $175) is a classic mid-century gem offering boutique accommodations. The five-unit complex features five king suites with private kitchens, bathrooms, dining rooms, and living rooms. A two-bedroom suite takes it up a notch with the addition of a vintage gas fireplace and full bath. Desert-chic styling, polished concrete floors, a central courtyard, barbeques, and plenty of lounging opportunities make this contemporary retreat a good bet. Book one room or the whole property ($1,350) for you and your friends.

The **Avalon Hotel** (415 S Belardo Rd., 760/320-4117, www.avalonpalmsprings.com, $180-350), formerly the Viceroy, is a Palm Springs luxury classic. The 68 guest rooms and bungalows wind through manicured property. Mediterranean exteriors give way to retro Regency-style interiors sporting a white, black, and yellow motif. The rooms are fun and over the top designwise—wingback chairs, flocked wallpaper, and chandeliers galore. There are three pools on the premises; two are adults only,

The Orbit In

while one is open to families. The hotel's on-site restaurant, Chi-Chi, offers breakfast, lunch, dinner, and poolside drink service. The lobby bar offers signature cocktails.

Over $250

The ★ **Korakia Pensione** (257 S Patencio Rd., 760/864-6411, www.korakia.com, $250-400) was built as a Moroccan-inspired artist retreat in 1924, and continues in this spirit as its incarnation as a stylish bed-and-breakfast resort. The 28 suites, studios, and bungalows are housed in two restored villas set on 1.5 acres of fountains. Many have private balconies or patios. Enter through the keyhole-shaped grand entrance flanked by ornately carved Moorish wooden doors. Moroccan fountains, a stone waterfall, and stone courtyard complete the outside vibe while the wood-beamed ceilings and antiques of the rooms ooze good taste.

The luxury boutique **San Giuliano Hotel** (375 W Arenas Rd., 760/325-7100, www.sangiulianohotel.com, $240-430) is perfect for a romantic getaway. Its eight hacienda-style suites surround the gleaming, secluded pool. They are lavishly appointed with private hot tubs, personal patios, HD TVs, DVD players, kitchenettes, and robes. The rustic Mediterranean hotel was built in the 1920s and is tucked away in the historic Tennis Club District at the foot of the striking San Jacinto Mountains, offering beautiful views.

★ **The Willows** (412 W Tahquitz Canyon Way, 760/320-0771, www.thewillowspalmsprings.com, $400-700) offers a romantic and elegant retreat in a former private mansion built in 1924. The historic Mediterranean-style eight-room inn is designed for seclusion and luxury: guests are pampered with a three-course breakfast, evening wine and hors d'oeuvres, and fresh fruit. The historic setting maintains a heated pool and Jacuzzi. Rooms are beautifully appointed with traditional antiques, but also include modern amenities like flat-screen TVs. A two-night minimum is required on weekends; there are no resort fees.

SOUTH PALM SPRINGS

$100-150

Caliente Tropics (411 E Palm Canyon Dr., 760/327-1391, www.calientetropics.com, $80-100) was once one of the hippest games in town with its A-frame entrance, tiki swank style, Congo Room Steak House, and Rat Pack clientele. Times have changed, but the bones of the place are still there. Manage your expectations and this Polynesian-styled budget hotel may pleasantly surprise you. It offers 91 basic budget rooms with king-size beds or double queens as well as suites. Service can be unpolished, but the large pool, manicured grounds dotted with tikis, and affordable rooms make it worth the stay. Afternoon weekends at the pool can be a zoo. Mornings and evenings are more mellow. Nighttime brings out the lit tiki torches. The crowds are a downside, but on the plus, the hotel is family-friendly and the pool is large.

$150-250

Sunny hospitality is what sets apart the ★ **Hotel California** (424 E Palm Canyon Dr., 760/322-8855, www. palmspringshotelcalifornia.com, $120-180). The historic Spanish Mission-style hotel was originally constructed in 1942. Recently updated rooms have a comfortable, rustic decor with Spanish tile floors, flat-screen TVs, and kitchenettes. King, queen, double queen, and suites are available. The communal space boasts a relaxing pool, lush greenery, hot tub, cruiser bikes, common kitchen, and grill. Bring your own supplies and relax for the weekend.

The 1950s-inspired decor of the **Desert Riviera** (610 E Palm Canyon Dr., 760/327-5314, www.desertrivierahotel.com, $190 with two-night minimum) maintains some of the mid-century charm of this 1951 hotel. A pool, Jacuzzi, fire pit, outdoor gas grills, communal kitchen, and loaner bikes make the Desert Riviera an oasis of fun times. The 11 rooms (double queen, king, suites, and studios) are warmly inviting.

The **Ace Hotel** (701 E Palm Canyon Dr.,

760/325-9900, www.acehotel.com/palm-springs, $160-350) has a pitch-perfect hipness with its mid-century, vintage-inspired style. This 176-room renovated hotel, spa, and resort (formerly a Westward Ho with a Denny's) offers two pools and a hot tub. The Ace Swim Club Pool has one of the major pool scenes in Palm Springs with regular deejays and events. The quieter Commune Pool has a more mellow and family-oriented vibe. The on-site Amigo Room bar serves poolside drinks and late-night atmosphere. The Kings Highway Diner offers a poolside menu and a day and evening menu in its roadside diner setting. Standard double, king, suites, and patio rooms feature clean, stylish design, flat-screen TVs and MP3 plug-ins. Some rooms offer vintage furniture, record players, or outdoor fireplaces. Children are allowed. There is an on-site gym and spa. Pets are also allowed for a fee.

Over $250

The ★ **Sparrows Lodge** (1330 E Palm Canyon Dr., 760/327-2300, http://sparrowslodge.com, $230-380) is an impeccably restored 1950s retreat. Originally constructed in 1952 as the Red Barn, a hangout for the Hollywood elite, the lodge was restored to its original charm in 2013.

Concrete and pebble-inlaid floors, exposed wood-beamed ceilings, open showers, and private patios grace the 20 poolside rooms and garden cottages. They're furnished with high-end rustic design classics like butterfly chairs and Swiss Army blankets. Imagine rustic mountain lodge meets mid-century ranch with a page from spare, traditional Japanese design. The vibe is understated and hip. It manages to exceed expectations and blend in with the landscape. A central pool and hot tub makes for a simple and relaxing scene. The barn-style communal area serves beer, wine, and specialty drinks including a refreshing house-made sangria. The continental breakfast of muffins, yogurt, granola, fruit, and French press coffee is as well thought out as everything else. Rooms are double occupancy and are restricted to guests over 21 only. Pets are allowed for a fee.

Jonathan Adler redesigned ★ **The Parker Palm Springs** (4200 E Palm Canyon Dr., 760/770-5000, www.theparkerpalmsprings.com, $260-400), which began life in 1959 as California's first Holiday Inn. It's hard to make that mental leap as you wander the sumptuous 13 garden acres with two pools, poolside bar, fire pit, tennis courts, croquet lawn, and luxury retro-hip suites. In the lobby,

Spanish Mission-style Hotel California

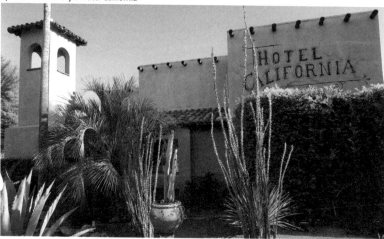

chandeliers merge with Moroccan-inspired antiques for a richly eccentric hippie chic. Patio, suite, and estate rooms are available. Hefty resort fees cover valet parking and bellman service at this upscale resort. Food and drink offerings include a lobby bar, **Norma's** (7am-3pm and 5pm-10pm daily), perfectly executed upscale diner fare, and **Mister Parker's** (6pm-close Wed.-Sun.), a posh French bistro.

Built in the 1930s, the **Smoke Tree Ranch** (1850 Smoke Tree Ln., 760/327-1221, www.smoketreeranch.com, $400-690) is the last of the traditional ranch-style inns that once fed Hollywood's love affair with the horse culture of the West. This exclusive resort offers 49 cottages (studios to multiroom) with a pool, horse stables, tennis courts, three-hole golf course, and spa services. Cottage rentals are traditionally sold with a meal plan for the property's Ranch House Dining Room (light dress code). Much of the property bordering the guest ranch, called "The Colony," has been privately owned through generations; owners share services with the ranch. (Walt Disney was among the early property owners.)

Designed in 1952 by renowned architect William F. Cody, **L'Horizon Hotel** (1050 E Palm Canyon Dr., 760/323-1858, www.lhorizonpalmsprings.com, from $485) has recaptured its glamour as a celebrity destination of the 1950s and 1960s. This low-slung hotel was newly redesigned by Steve Hermann around 25 well-appointed guest bungalows, angled wood beams, and long, low architecture that highlights the mountain panoramas. This exclusive luxury resort features an intimate landscaped setting, infinity pool, spa treatments, on-site dining, and bar.

LGBT

Less a hotel and more a well-appointed home, **Casa Ocotillo** (240 E Ocotillo Ave., 760/327-6110, www.casaocotillo.com, $179-299) is a historic property that brings together five uniquely designed bungalows and suites to create a luxury compound catering primarily to gay men. A heated pool and spa with outdoor fireplace form a central draw. Individual suites feature king-size beds with Ralph Lauren bed collections, private en-suite baths with rain head oversize showers, private porches and patios, and a guest kitchen stocked with breakfast.

Casitas Laquita (450 E Palm Canyon Dr., 760/416-9999, www.casitaslaquita.com, $165-305) is a Spanish-style resort catering exclusively to women, the only all-female resort in Palm Springs. The property offers 15 adobe casitas, most with full kitchens and some with fireplaces. The secluded pool is centrally situated amid palm trees and colorful gardens.

Set on a classic 1950s property, **Escape Resort** (641 E San Lorenzo Rd., 760/325-5269, www.escapepalmsprings.com, $139-199) is a laid-back, clothing-optional resort catering to gay singles and couples. A heated pool (cooled in summer) and 15-person hot tub are at the center of the tropical grounds. Join fellow guests and owners for weekend social hour. The 12 rooms, some with private patios, feature flat-screen TVs, luxury linens, spa bathrobes, and coffeemakers and some with full-size refrigerators and sitting areas.

La Dolce Vita (1491 S Via Soledad, 760/325-2686, www.ladolcevitaresort.com, $179-209) is a Spanish-style clothing-optional, gay resort offering a relaxing oasis. Its 20 guest rooms surround two swimming pools. Amenities include two whirlpools, a steam room, continental breakfast, Aveda bath products, and spa bathrobes. The rooms and suites feature hardwood floors, double French doors, and private patios.

The stylish **Santiago** (650 E San Lorenzo Rd., 760/322-1300, www.santiagoresort.com, $189-245) is a male-only, clothing-optional resort featuring chic, modern rooms, and landscaped grounds. The Spanish-style resort is fashionably styled: suites have Spanish tile floors, king beds, and woven rugs. Hammocks, a fire pit, and courtyard fountain complement the native landscaping. A pool and lounging area complete the tranquil atmosphere.

Transportation and Services

GETTING THERE

The two closest major cities to Palm Springs are Los Angeles to the west and San Diego to the southwest.

Air

Palm Springs also has its own airport. The tiny **Palm Springs Airport** (PSP, 3400 E Tahquitz Canyon Way, 760/318-3800, www.palmspringsca.gov) is a public airport that is served by 11 airlines. Connections are available from cities worldwide. The airport serves nonstop markets from 10 major airline hubs. If you are flying into the Palm Springs Airport, several hotels offer airport shuttle service including the Saguaro Palm Springs, the Smoke Tree Ranch, and corporate hotels like the Hyatt, Omni, Hilton, and Marriott. The major car rental carriers are located here, including Enterprise, Hertz, Dollar, and Alamo.

Los Angeles International Airport (LAX, 1 World Way, Los Angeles, 424/646-5252, www.lawa.org) has its advantages and disadvantages to fly into. Advantages: it's a major international airport with many carriers and flight options. All the major rental car companies are nearby with regular shuttles from the airport. Disadvantage: LAX can be very congested.

The **San Diego International Airport** (SAN, 3225 N Harbor Dr., San Diego, 619/400-2404, www.san.org) is a busy, single-runway airport located three miles northwest of downtown San Diego. Its major carriers include Southwest, American, United, Alaska, and Delta. A consolidated rental car center on the north side of the airport serves many major car rental car companies and makes it easy to rent a car from the airport.

If you're flying, your best option might be the **Ontario Airport** (ONT, Ontario, 909/937-2700, www.lawa.org), a medium-hub, full-service airport located 70 miles west of Palm Springs. Ontario Airport has all the major rental car companies on-site. It's big enough to have affordable flights with good time options and small enough to make it easy to navigate. From the Ontario airport, the drive to Palm Springs is slightly over an hour via I-10 east. You can avoid the congestion of the other major airports altogether and cut your drive time in half.

Car

Without heavy traffic, the drive from Los Angeles can take under two hours via I-10. Getting out of LA can be a slog, though, so you may need to factor in extra time if driving from LA. **From Los Angeles,** take I-10 east for approximately 100 miles. The 210 and 60 Freeways can sometimes provide good eastbound alternatives if the 10 is jammed. They eventually join up with I-10 before Palm Springs. After approximately 100 miles, exit on I-10 to take Highway 111 South toward Palm Springs. Highway 111B continues south to reach the Palm Springs city limit in just over 10 miles, turning into N Palm Canyon Drive, the main road through Palm Springs.

If traffic cooperates, the drive from San Diego takes just over two hours. **From San Diego,** take I-15 North (the same interstate that goes to Las Vegas) for about 50 miles. When I-15 splits off with I-215, follow the I-215N and signs for Riverside/San Bernardino. Follow I-215N for 30 miles until it intersects with CA-60. Take the exit for CA-60 heading east for 18 miles. Merge onto I-10 East and continue for another 18 miles until the CA-111 exit toward Palm Springs. Highway 111B continues south to reach the Palm Springs city limit in just over 10 miles, turning into N. Palm Canyon Drive, the main road through Palm Springs.

Public Transit

For public transportation to Palm Springs,

your best bet is to take Amtrak (800/872-7245, www.amtrak.com) via a combination train and bus from Los Angeles in a route that runs daily and takes 3-4 hours. The route begins from Union Station in downtown Los Angeles, taking the *Pacific Surfliner* train line. After a transfer, an Amtrak California Thruway Bus completes the journey at the Palm Springs Amtrak stop in North Palm Springs (N Indian Canyon Drive and Palm Springs Station Road, no amenities) 3.4 miles north of the Palm Springs Visitors center. Other stops on the Thruway route include Cabazon at the Morongo Casino Resort and Spa (49500 Seminole Dr., Cabazon) as well as two stops in the Coachella Valley: Palm Desert at the Palm Desert Westfield Mall (72-840 Highway 111, Palm Desert) and the La Quinta Town Center (Highway 111 and Adams, La Quinta).

There are no Greyhound stations directly in Palm Springs.

GETTING AROUND

Central Palm Springs is extremely easy to get around in. The main concentration of hotels and businesses span a 4.5-mile stretch. It's easy to plan much of your vacation to be walkable. In addition, many hotels provide free cruiser-style bicycles to guests, and Palm Springs has wide streets as well as bike lanes. Most hotels require bikes to be back before dark.

Bus

The city also offers a free shuttle called the Buzz Bus (www.buzzps.com, every 15 minutes 11am-1am Thurs.-Sun., free). The cheerfully painted shuttle is air-conditioned and wheelchair-friendly. It has its own stops along the two main streets (Palm Canyon and Indian Canyon). The bus runs from Via Escuela in the Uptown Design District to Smoke Tree in South Palm Springs. The bus is free, but it can be nice to tip drivers. Some drivers go out of their way when the bus isn't too crowded, and they'll drop you directly at your destination. For when you need a ride outside of the Buzz bus hours or want something even more convenient than the already convenient Buzz, the ride-sharing service Uber dominates the scene.

Taxis and Ride Shares

Palm Springs is swarming with Uber (www.uber.com) ride shares, but there are a few taxi services that serve Palm Springs and the Coachella Valley. American Cab (www.americancab.net) serves the entire Coachella Valley, including Palm Springs and Desert Hot Springs. Taxis are available to book 24 hours by phone, text, or an online app. Desert City Cab (760/325-8200, www.desertcitycab.com) offers 24-hour service to the entire Coachella Valley, including Palm Springs. Yellow Cab (760/340-8294, www.yellowcabofthedesert.com) is based in Palm Desert and serves Palm Springs, Cathedral City, Rancho Mirage, Palm Desert, La Quinta, Indio, and Indian Wells.

SERVICES

The first building you will pass on entering Palm Springs is the Palm Springs Visitors Center (2901 N Palm Canyon Dr., 760/778-8418, www.visitpalmsprings.com, 9am-5pm daily). The iconic building was designed in 1965 by renowned architect Albert Frey as a gas station for the Palm Springs Aerial Tramway. The fully staffed visitors center has a wealth of books and maps about the historic city. Other resources include the official Palm Springs tourism website (www.visitpalmsprings.com), which is helpful for planning. For a gay tourism perspective, check out www.visitgaypalmsprings.com or www.pspride.org for recommendations on lodging, dining, and activities.

The San Jacinto Mountains

Follow Highway 243 or Highway 74 up from the Coachella Valley desert floor and in under an hour you will find yourself in the much cooler San Jacinto Mountains. Originally the summer home of Cahuilla Indians migrating from the desert valleys below, the area began to be settled by homesteaders in the 1890s. Logging and tourism became the primary industry. Tourism won out, and now most of the land surrounding Idyllwild is protected through the Mount San Jacinto State Park, Santa Rosa and San Jacinto Mountains National Monument, and San Bernardino National Forest. In the 1960s and 1970s, an influx of hippies to the area changed the cultural fabric in Idyllwild. Browse the boutique shops in the town center now, and you'll find cowboy hats as well as healing crystals.

Planning Your Time

Summer is the high season with visitors taking advantage of cooler temperatures, campgrounds, and hiking trails. **Winter** brings snow tourism. Community events such as Jazz in the Pines (July) and the Art Walk and Wine Tasting (Oct.) give folks an excuse to visit year-round.

MOUNT SAN JACINTO STATE PARK AND WILDERNESS

Subalpine forests, granite peaks, and mountain meadows quilt the 14,000-acre **Mount San Jacinto State Park and Wilderness** (www.parks.ca.gov and www.fs.usda.gov) in the heart of the San Jacinto Mountains. Craggy San Jacinto Peak, the highest peak in the park and the second highest in the San Jacinto Range (after Mount San Gorgonio) reaches nearly 11,000 feet, snowcapped for much of the year. The steep mountain escarpments of the San Jacinto Range plunge 9,000 feet in less than four miles on the northeast side down to the desert floor.

Hiking trails offer sweeping views toward Palm Springs and over 100 miles to the southeast and the Salton Sea. It's a destination for day hikes, backpacking, snowshoeing, and camping. The famous Pacific Crest Trail (PCT), a continuous 2,650-mile trail system that runs from Mexico to Canada, passes through the San Jacinto Mountains, and Idyllwild is a destination for PCT hikers.

The two main jumping-off points for hiking and camping in the state park and wilderness are the town of Idyllwild and the Palm Springs Aerial Tramway.

A **Forest Adventure Pass** is required to park at trailheads and day-use areas. Adventure Passes are available at the Idyllwild Ranger Station or at **Nomad Ventures** (54415 N Circle Dr., 951/659-4853, www.nomadventures.com, 9am-5pm Thurs.-Mon.), as well as other ranger stations and retailers throughout the San Bernardino, Angeles, and Los Padres National Forests. Rules regarding where Adventure Passes are required are somewhat in flux (pay attention to signage; the default is that Adventure Passes are required).

Hiking

Hundreds of miles of hiking trails for all ability levels are accessible from the town of Idyllwild. Due to the short growing season and popularity of the area, there is a **wilderness permit** system in place. *Everyone must obtain a wilderness permit prior to day hiking or overnight camping.* Day-use permits are free and available at the **Idyllwild Ranger Station** (54270 Pine Crest Ave., 909/382-2921, 8am-4pm Fri.-Tues.). They are also available at the entrance station for **Idyllwild Campground** (25905 Hwy. 243) in San Jacinto State Park. Outside of business hours you can complete a form available on the porch of the campground's ranger station and drop it in the drop box. If you are hiking from the Palm Springs

Aerial Tramway, permits are available at the strategically located Long Valley Ranger Station once you arrive at the top.

★ TAHQUITZ PEAK (VIA SOUTH RIDGE TRAIL)

Distance: 7.6 miles round-trip
Duration: 4-5 hours
Elevation gain: 2,100 feet
Effort: Strenuous
Trailhead: South Ridge Trail
Directions: From the Idyllwild Ranger Station (Hwy. 243 and Pine Crest Ave.), head south on Highway 243 for 0.7 mile. Turn left onto Saunders Meadow Road just past the Mile High Café and before the Idyllwild School. Follow Saunders Meadow Road for 0.8 mile then turn left onto Pine Avenue. After 0.1 mile turn right onto Tahquitz View Road. The pavement ends 0.2 mile at Tahquitz View Drive, and the road forks. Take the right, signed fork for Forest Route 5S11 and continue one mile to the trailhead. (This last stretch is prone to washouts and may require high clearance.)

This striking, granite crag can be seen on the drive in from Highway 243. It stands sentinel over the town, and you'll catch glimpses of it from different vantage points. In addition to experiencing breathtaking views and a trip to a historic, furnished fire tower, if you kick off your time in Idyllwild with this spectacular hike, you'll get to feel a sense of smug accomplishment every time you look up.

The South Ridge Trail offers the most direct route and the most solitude on your trek to Tahquitz Peak. From the trailhead, the path climbs into the San Jacinto Wilderness region within a few yards. Manzanitas with their strange peeling rust-red bark, Jeffrey pine, live oak, and white fir line the trail.

Around one mile, views open up to the south toward Garner Valley and Lake Hemet. Impressive vistas continue for the rest of the hike. Over the next half mile you will pass along the **Desert Divide,** a spur ridge that runs through the southern section of the San Jacinto Mountain Range. Views from here are sweeping to the east.

Take a breather and a water break at **Window Rock** at 1.5 miles. This unique geologic feature frames rugged granite crags to the north. From here, the trail climbs gently, passing through lodgepole pine forest until about 2.2 miles.

The last mile and a half of switchbacks climbs steeply up to **Tahquitz Peak** and the **lookout tower.** Climb the steps up to the deck of the lookout tower to get an eyeful. The tower was used historically as a fire lookout, positioned because of its 360-degree views. It

views from South Ridge Trail to Tahquitz Peak

has been preserved with historic furnishings, and volunteers maintain the space and greet hikers at the top on some weekends in season (May-Nov.). It adds an extra layer of richness to the experience to be able to tap into some of the region's history and pick the volunteers' brains about trails and surrounding geography as well as enjoy the natural beauty. From the lookout tower deck, the Coachella Valley sprawls to the east, bounded by Joshua Tree National Park and the Little San Bernardino and Cottonwood Mountains. To the north, Marion Mountain looms, blocking views of San Jacinto Peak and the Palm Springs Aerial Tramway. To the southeast, the views extend as far as the Salton Sea.

ERNIE MAXWELL SCENIC TRAIL

Distance: 5.3 miles round-trip
Duration: 2-3 hours
Elevation gain: 550 feet
Effort: Easy
Trailhead: Tahquitz View Drive, at the end of a dirt road on the south end of Idyllwild
Directions: From the Idyllwild Ranger Station (Hwy. 243 and Pine Crest Ave. in Idyllwild), head south on Highway 243 for 0.7 mile. Turn left onto Saunders Meadow Road just past the Mile High Café and before the Idyllwild School. Follow Saunders Meadow Road for 0.8 mile then turn left onto signed Pine Avenue. After 0.1 mile turn right onto the signed Tahquitz View Road. The trailhead is in 0.6 mile. The pavement ends 0.2 mile into Tahquitz View Drive, and the road forks. Follow the left fork signed for the Ernie Maxwell Scenic Trail. The trailhead is signed on the right. Park along the dirt road.

First off, here's a pro tip: Hike the trail starting from the dirt road trailhead in Idyllwild. This way, you will gain elevation on the beginning stretch and have an easier return.

A gentle elevation gain through a mostly shaded, forested trail makes this a good choice for a leisurely but satisfying hike. (This is a good pre-brunch, Sunday morning hike.) Starting from the **Tahquitz View Drive** trailhead, the path climbs gently through a mix of Jeffrey, ponderosa, and Coulter pines all the way to the **Humber Park** trailhead.

The trail provides intermittent views toward Idyllwild and the southwest. The real highlight here is the immersive forest experience and the mellow grades. The trail is particularly nice in **September** and **October**. Once you reach the Humber Park trailhead, turn around and return the way you came.

DEVIL'S SLIDE

Distance: 5 miles
Duration: 2-3 hours
Elevation gain: 1,300 feet
Effort: Moderate
Trailhead: Humber Park
Directions: To get there from the Idyllwild Ranger Station, head northeast on Pine Crest Avenue for 0.6 mile. Turn left onto Fern Valley Road and continue for 1.8 miles until you reach Humber Park. The trail begins on the upper level of the parking area.

The Devil's Slide trail offers a scenic climb through idyllic forest. It's a nice day hike on its own merits, but it's also a key connector trail that leads to the PCT as well as routes to San Jacinto Peak and Tahquitz Peak. This busy trail can be congested; **hike in the morning** to beat some of the traffic as well as catch cooler temperatures. Much of the trail is exposed to direct sunlight after noon.

The trail begins in the upper parking level of **Humber Park.** A short climb quickly gives way to stunning views of Tahquitz Rock, a local landmark sometimes called "Lily Rock." As the trail continues to climb, you'll have views of Idyllwild and Strawberry Valley to the southwest. You'll climb steadily all the way to **Saddle Junction.** Although Saddle Junction isn't really a destination in and of itself, it's a good goal for a hike that really is about the journey. Return the way you came or continue on to Tahquitz Peak (7 miles round-trip), San Jacinto Peak (16 miles round-trip), or an array of other backpacking or day hiking destinations.

Winter Sports

While Mount San Jacinto State Park was never developed for skiing (a boon, as this allowed the wilderness to be preserved and the mountain town of Idyllwild to remain peaceful), cross-country skiing and snowshoeing are accessible from Mountain Station at the top of the Palm Springs Aerial Tramway. A **Winter Adventure Center** (10am-4pm Mon. and Thurs.-Fri., 9am-4pm Sat.-Sun, hours and season vary) is open whenever there is snow. The center offers cross-country ski packages (skis, poles, and boots, $21 per day) and snowshoe packages ($18 per day). Mount San Jacinto State Park is also a good destination for families who just want some fun snow frolicking. Snow camping is even available at the hike-in campgrounds along the state park and wilderness network of trails.

IDYLLWILD

Idyllwild is a charming mountain town, a forest island nestled one mile high in the San Jacinto Mountains, surrounded by the outlying desert. The artsy, rustic community sits nestled amid pines, cedars, manzanitas, and scenic rock outcroppings. Picturesque cabins with A-frame roofs hint at snow, an exciting proposition in contrast with the sleekly flat mid-century desert dwellings below. Seasonal streams and hiking trails crisscross the hills. Inns with chainsaw-carved

wildlife sculptures and fireplaces welcome visitors escaping the heat and traffic of the urban areas below.

The adjacent communities of Fern Valley, Pine Cove, and Idyllwild are generally grouped together and are all considered "Idyllwild."

Shopping

Many shops here can feel like they're caught in a time warp catering to the New Age hippie at heart, while other boutique shops cover a range of specialties including gifts, sweets, art, clothing, and outdoor gear. The majority of the shops in Idyllwild are clustered in a three-block radius on North Circle Drive where it intersects with Highway 243.

Nomad Ventures (54415 N Circle Dr., 951/659-4853, www.nomadventures.com, 9am-5pm Thurs.-Mon.) provides outdoor gear and equipment covering climbing, mountaineering, backpacking, hiking, trail running, and kayaking. There is a second location in Joshua Tree (61795 Twentynine Palms Hwy., 760/366-4684, 9am-7pm daily in summer).

Wooley's (54274 N Circle Dr., 951/659-0017, www.wooleys.com, 10:30am-5pm daily) offers sheepskin products including

Devil's Slide trail

Idyllwild

sheepskin slippers, boots, and seat covers. They also stock clothing, cowboy hats, and winter hats—great if you're caught in the cooler temperatures of Idyllwild and need to make an emergency fashion purchase. Home furnishings include high-quality cowhide rugs, lambskin throws, and pillows.

Everitt's Minerals (54300 N Circle Dr., 951/659-7075, www.everittsminerals.com, 11am-5pm daily, but hours can vary) sells handmade jewelry and designs, exotic mineral specimens, rare fossils, and antique Japanese woodblock prints.

Recreation

Bicycles are available for rent at **The Hub Cyclery** (54425 N Circle Dr., 951/659-4070, www.hubcyclery.com, 10am-5pm Mon. and Wed.-Thurs., 9am-6pm Fri.-Sat., 10am-2pm Sun.). The shop rents mountain bikes and town bikes for day use only ($35-95).

In winter, there are sledding opportunities

at **Idyllwild County Park** (54000 Riverside County Playground Rd., 951/659-2656, www. rivcoparks.org, open sunrise-sunset).

Accommodations

The aesthetic here is rustic, and accommodations range from boutique mountain lodges with elaborate amenities to frayed cabins with charming exteriors and interiors that have seen better days. Make reservations in advance, as Idyllwild can book up completely on popular event weekends.

MOTELS

For a budget motel, the **Bluebird Cottage Inn** (26620 Saddle Dr., 951/659-2696, www. bluebirdcottageinn.com, $75-165) has character. The cabin-style motel dates to 1957. Its 17 units include studio lodge rooms, duplexes, triplexes, and one two-bedroom cabin. Amenities range from basic rooms to kitchens, fireplaces, and Jacuzzi tubs. The inn is located on the south end of town about a 20-minute walk or less than 5-minute drive to the town center.

LODGES AND CABINS

Silver Pines Lodge (25955 Cedar St., 951/659-4335, $85-119) is a classic mountain inn built in 1923, and it has been the Silver Pines Lodge since 1952. The main lodge has a pitch-perfect exterior and is stuffed full of leather couches, antlers, and other lodge-like furnishings. Silver Pines offers 13 rooms—five connected to the lodge and eight stand-alone cabins, duplexes, or triplexes. The lodges and cabins are a little worse for the wear but clean with decent amenities. Most rooms have fireplaces, and about half have kitchens. Private porches or decks offer peaceful reflection over seasonal Strawberry Creek unless the Town Hall next door is hosting a community event (including daily Jazzercise). The good news is that you're in the center of town with easy walking to restaurants and shops. The lodge also offers six new units at the **Silver Pines Village** 100 yards away.

The family-owned ★ **Idyllwild Inn** (54300 Village Center Dr., 888/659-2552, www.idyllwildinn.com, $99-185) dates from 1904 and is a favorite of PCT hikers and repeat visitors. Set on five wooded acres in the center of town, it features cabins, suites, and theme rooms. Its 12 one- and two-bedroom rustic cabins are original with knotty pine paneling, fireplaces, and private decks. Cabin #9 is carved with historic graffiti dating to the 1950s. Eight new rustic cabins are family-friendly with queen beds and sleeper sofas. New rustic suites offer Jacuzzi tubs, queen beds, and sleeper sofas. Eight themed rooms are a relatively recent addition.

Make sure you know what your spirit animal (or tree) is before you make reservations at **The Fireside Inn** (54540 N Circle Dr., 951/659-2966, www. thefiresideinn.com, $100-210). They offer seven lightly themed duplex cottages and a separate 1930s lodge, all with fireplaces and most with kitchens. The inn is set in a residential neighborhood in the center of town within easy walking distance to shops and restaurants.

From 1930 to 1950, Idyllwild became known for its knotty pine furniture. **Knotty Pines Cabins** (54340 Pine Crest Ave., 951/659-2933, www.knottypinecabinsidyllwild.com, $74-189), dating to the 1930s and 1940s, strongly upholds this tradition with knotty pine everything (furniture, paneling, and cabinets). Eight cabins and duplex cabins provide lodging for 2-8 people ranging from a studio cabin with a queen bed to a three-bedroom lodge. Amenities include kitchenettes, fireplaces, and decks or porches. They're conveniently near the Idyllwild Ranger Station and the town center.

The red and white cottage-style ★ **Fern Valley Inn** (25240 Fern Valley Rd., 951/659-8100, www.fernvalleyinn.com, $85-125) dates to 1950 and offers charming cottages and a seasonal pool. Of the 10 cottages, six are duplexes and four are private cottages. Each has a queen-size bed, wood-burning stove or fireplace, refrigerator, cable TV, and Wi-Fi.

Some have full kitchens. Some units have an additional sofa sleeper for a maximum occupancy of four persons. The inn is situated in the upper part of Idyllwild in the quieter Fern Valley neighborhood and close to Humber Park hiking trails. The town center is a five-minute drive or 20-minute walk.

B&BS

Too much rustic got you down? See no difference between staying in a mountain cabin and camping? **The Grand Idyllwild Lodge** (54820 Pinecrest Rd., 951/659-2383, www.grandidyllwildlodge.com, $285-325) might be the place for you. The Craftsman-style boutique lodge is situated at the top of the town in Fern Valley close to Aroma and Idyology restaurants and Humber Park hiking trails. They offer four suites and one guest room with private entrances, decks, gourmet breakfast, fireplaces, flat-screen smart TVs, gym, Swedish-style sauna, and spa services.

The Craftsman-style **Rainbow Inn** (54420 S Circle Dr., 951/659-0111, www.rainbow-inn.com, $120-165) offers five well-appointed rooms with rustic elegant design. They feature Wi-Fi, cable TV, DVD players, mini-fridges and coffeemakers, and some also offer Jacuzzi tubs and fireplaces; all have private baths. The inn is in the center of town.

Nine rustic, individually decorated rooms make up the **Strawberry Creek Inn** (26370 Hwy. 243, 951/659-3202, www.strawberrycreekinn.com, $119-249). The cozy rooms have Wi-Fi, private bathrooms, and TVs. Some also offer private decks, fireplaces, or canopy beds. A full, homemade breakfast is included. A two-story cottage on the property features a private entrance, full kitchen, and whirlpool tub. The inn is located in the center of town.

On the south side of Idyllwild a 20-minute walk to the town center, **Quiet Creek Inn** (26345 Delano Dr., 951/468-4208, www.quietcreekinn.com, $128-160) encompasses seven secluded acres along seasonal Strawberry Creek. Studios and one-bedroom suite cabins with queen and king beds all feature fireplaces and private decks plus Wi-Fi, refrigerators, and microwaves. One-bedroom suites offer kitchenettes.

Camping

There are many great camping options in and around Idyllwild from developed camping close to town to remoter sites. Note: Fire restrictions may be in effect during fire

Idyllwild Inn

season (summer months), and campfires may not be allowed at local campgrounds. Campgrounds may be closed intermittently due to drought and fire conditions. Check for current conditions.

Mount San Jacinto State Park's **Idyllwild Campground** (25905 Hwy. 243, 951/659-2607, www.reserveamerica.com, year-round, $25) has 33 sites under a canopy of pine and dotted with manzanitas for tent camping, RVs, and trailers. Showers, flush toilets, water, picnic tables, and fire rings are on-site. Since the site is walking distance to Idyllwild shops and restaurants, campers can spend time enjoying the stars instead of washing dishes.

Idyllwild County Campground (54000 Riverside County Playground Rd., 951/659-2656, www.rivcoparks.org, $33) is less than a mile south of the state park campground. Its 88 sites are situated under shaded pine forest and available year-round for tent, RV, and trailer camping. Amenities include picnic tables, fire rings, flush toilets, and showers. Designated accessible sites are 1, 23, and 39. These sites also have a grill. Reservations are accepted April through October; November to March, the park has sites 1-6 available for first-come, first-served camping. The park also offers a nature center and interpretive trails, and is walking distance to shops and restaurants.

Stone Creek Campground (Hwy. 243, www.reserveamerica.com, year-round, $20) is off Highway 243, about six miles north of Idyllwild. The campground offers 50 sites for tent camping, as well as trailer and RV sites (no hookups or dump stations). Amenities include fire rings, picnic tables, water, and vault toilets. Reservations at Stone Creek are managed by Mount San Jacinto State Park.

Other seasonal campgrounds are open in summer only; these are in the vicinity of the Stone Creek Campground and are operated by the **San Bernardino National Forest** (909/382-2921, www.fs.usda.gov).

At **Fern Basin** (reserve at www.recreation.gov, May-Sept., $10), about 6.5 miles north of Idyllwild, 22 sites are set amid manzanitas,

oaks, and conifers at 6,400 feet. Amenities include vault toilets, fire rings, and picnic tables, but there is no drinking water.

Up the road from Fern Basin, **Marion Mountain Campground** (reserve at www.recreation.gov, June-Nov., $10) has 24 campsites set in two loops amid a cedar and Ponderosa pine forest. Amenities include vault toilets, fire rings, drinking water, and picnic tables. Marion Mountain is located about seven miles north of Idyllwild.

Dark Canyon Campground (first-come, first-served, May-Sept., $12) has 12 shaded, tent-only campsites set next to a seasonal creek at 5,900 feet elevation. Amenities include vault toilets, fire rings, drinking water, and picnic tables. Dark Canyon is located about eight miles north of Idyllwild.

Food
BREAKFAST AND COFFEE
The family-run **Idyllwild Bake Shop and Brew** (54200 N Circle Dr., 951/659-4145, 6:30am-6pm Mon.-Thurs., 6:30am-8pm Fri., 7am-8pm Sat., 7am-6pm Sun.) bakes breakfast pastries and savory items on-site with fresh coffee and fresh-squeezed juice to wash them down. For a little later in the day they switch gears to grilled sandwiches, craft beers, and wine.

If you want the classic, cozy coffee shop vibe where you can hang out and take advantage of Wi-Fi, **Higher Grounds Coffee** (54245 N Circle Dr., 951/659-1379, www.highergroundscoffee.com, 7am-7pm Sun.-Thurs., 7am-9pm Fri.-Sat.) is the place to go. Food is standard fare including bagels and muffins.

The **Town Baker** (54385 N Circle Dr., 951/659-8606, 6:30am-3:30pm Thurs.-Mon.) serves up fresh coffee, breakfast, and baked goods to take out or enjoy in the cheerful cottage setting. Pro tip: they also offer prepackaged sandwiches and sides to grab and go on your mountain adventures.

The ★ **Red Kettle** (54220 N Circle Dr., 951/659-4063, www.redkettleinc.com, 6am-2pm daily, $8-11) is a great place to fuel up before a hike or to savor a casual weekend. They serve up classic American breakfasts like country ham and eggs and lunch specials like chili, burgers, soups, and salads in a quaint cottage setting. Coffee served at 6am and hot food served from 7am on.

AMERICAN

Chandeliers, upholstered parlor furniture, and sepia lighting make **Idyology** (54905 N Circle Dr., 951/659-5962, www.idyology. org, 4pm-11pm Tues.-Fri., 11am-11pm Sat.-Sun., $8-15) a perfect place to cozy up with a craft beer, glass of wine, or specialty cocktail. They offer a full food menu with upscale comfort food like buttermilk-fried chicken and Cherry Coke pulled pork, but the food is wildly hit-or-miss. The bar stays open later than the restaurant and is a popular hangout for tourists and locals.

The burgers are perfectly executed, the fries are hot, and the beers are cold at this stripped down watering hole and café. ★ **The Lumber Mill** (25985 Hwy. 243, 951/659-0315, www.idymill.com, 11am-midnight Sun.-Thurs., 11am-1am Fri.-Sat., $11-16) offers burgers, sandwiches, chili, and bar appetizers. The on-site bar (open until 10pm Mon.-Wed.,

11pm Sun. and Thurs., 1am Fri.-Sat.) serves tasty drinks.

EUROPEAN

Take a 1970s ski lodge and spruce it up with design tips from The Hobbit, and you've got ★ **Gastrognome** (54381 Ridge View Dr., 951/659-5055, www.gastrognome.com, 10am-close daily, $10-34), the picturesque favorite of locals and visitors. A lengthy dinner menu features fish, chicken, lamb, steaks, and pasta dishes. The lunch menu is equally daunting with sandwiches, fish, seafood, pastas, vegetarian options, and steaks. The charm of the restaurant might be its biggest selling point, but the food is generally well executed. Reservations are recommended for dinner on weekends.

ITALIAN

Café Aroma (54750 N Circle Dr., 951/659-5212, www.cafearoma.org, 11am-9pm Mon. and Wed.-Thurs., 7am-10pm Fri.-Sat., 7am-9pm Sun., $14-33) is an artsy bistro featuring local art and live music on a woodsy patio. The menu is Italian-driven accompanied by local wines, beers, and a full bar. Breakfast is served daily. Lunch consists of soups, salads,

Idyllwild's Gastrognome has plenty of mountain charm.

and sandwiches, while dinner options offer steaks, seafood, and pasta.

The former chef of Café Aroma opened the beautifully designed **Ferro Restaurant** (25840 Cedar St., 951/659-0700, www.ferro-restaurant.com, 11am-4pm and 5pm-10pm Sun.-Thurs., 11am-4pm and 5pm-11pm Fri.-Sat., $10-34) in the summer of 2015. Edison lights and a pine canopy make for a lovely al fresco dining experience on the back patio with live music some nights. Despite the great atmosphere and sophisticated menu, food can be hit-or-miss. The wood-oven pizza is a good choice; the dough is excellent. The outdoor pizza oven with bar seating gives you front row seats. The menu also features pasta, pizza, and panini for lunch and pasta, risotto, polenta, seafood, chicken, steaks, and small plates for dinner. Reservations are recommended for dinner.

MEXICAN

In the Fern Valley neighborhood, ★ **La Casita Mexican Restaurant** (54650 N Circle Dr., 951/659-6038, www.idyllwildlacasita.com, 11am-9pm daily summer, 11am-8pm daily winter, $10-20) anchors the other end of town with satisfying plates of Mexican food and margaritas served in a pleasant setting with a large patio. Located near the entrance to the hiking trails in Humber Park, the small restaurant can get packed.

Located near the Idyllwild State Park campground, the stripped-down **Arriba Mexican Restaurant** (25980 Hwy. 243, 951/659-4960, 9am-9pm Mon.-Sat., 8am-8pm Sun., $10-20)

serves up heaping plates of Mexican specialties as well as margaritas and beers on its front deck or back patio. The restaurant's decor is low-key, but the service is attentive.

Transportation

There is no public transportation available in Idyllwild—no buses, taxis, or ride-sharing services. Idyllwild is a small town of less than three miles end to end, and it is easy to get around by driving or walking. The town center has sidewalks and lighting, and if you are staying directly in town, it is no problem to do everything on foot.

Outside the town center the sidewalks and lighting disappear. Both Highways 243 and 74 have steady traffic, and it can be a little nerve-wracking to be a pedestrian walking along the narrow shoulders of these dark roads at night. Carry a flashlight so that you are visible to drivers.

CAR

The town of Idyllwild is located in the San Jacinto Mountains above Palm Springs. To get here from Palm Springs, take N Palm Canyon Drive (Hwy. 111) north to I-10. Take I-10 west for three miles to the town of Banning. At Banning, take Highway 243 and drive 25 twisting mountain miles south to the town center. Note that Highway 243 may close due to snow or other inclement weather.

From the Coachella Valley, take Highway 74 west (from its intersection with Hwy. 111) and continue onto Highway 243 north to reach Idyllwild in 41 miles.

The Coachella Valley

The Coachella Valley sprawls southeast from Palm Springs. This suburban desert is flanked by the San Jacinto Mountains on its southwest border, and Joshua Tree National Park and the San Bernardino Mountains bound the northwest edge. It's primarily residential, a checkerboard of gated communities and golf courses. It trends northwest to southeast all the way to the Salton Sea, and while not a destination, there are a few stops worth making. In the middle of it all is the surprising Coachella Valley Preserve, a literal oasis with shining palms and shaded pools set against a heat-baked landscape.

PLANNING YOUR TIME

The sights in the Coachella Valley are **day trip** options or short drives from Palm Springs for sightseeing, recreation, dining, and casino accommodations. Towns and cities include **Desert Hot Springs** (a small mid-century resort community with hotel and spa opportunities), **Thousand Palms, Palm Desert,** and **Indio,** most of which can be accessed from I-10.

SIGHTS
★ Cabot's Pueblo Museum

Cabot Yerxa is the man responsible for the fascinating Hopi-inspired 35-room pueblo, an artistic masterpiece he built entirely out of found materials between 1941 and 1950. **Cabot's Pueblo Museum** (67616 E Desert View Ave., Desert Hot Springs, 760/329-7610, www.cabotsmuseum.org, 9am-4pm Tues.-Sun. Oct.-May, 9am-1pm Wed.-Sat. June-Sept., tours $11) offers guided tours of the home's interior, but you don't have to take the tour to visit the trading post and grounds, which include beautifully weathered outbuildings, a meditation garden, a well house, and "Waokiya," a 43-foot-tall Native American sculpture carved from a fallen cedar.

Living Desert Zoo and Gardens

The **Living Desert Zoo and Gardens** (47900 Portola Ave., Palm Desert, 760/346-5694, www.livingdesert.org, 9am-5pm daily Oct.-May, 8am-1pm daily June-Sept., $20 adults, $18 seniors, $10 children 3-12) is a

Cabot's Pueblo Museum

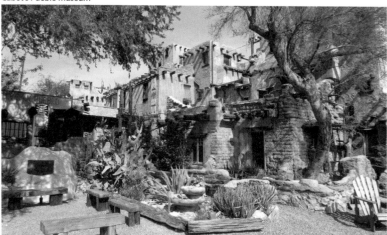

desert botanical garden and zoo with an amusement park feel. Paved paths wind through exhibits representing major desert regions. The place is a huge draw for families and can be very crowded on weekends and holidays.

Shields Date Garden

In the 1920s, Highway 111 was lined with date farms all vying for motoring tourists' patronage. Shields Date Garden (80-225 Hwy. 111, Indio, 760/347-0996, www.shieldsdategarden.com, 9am-5pm daily, $5) is the last one standing. This family-friendly roadside attraction features a gift shop with free date samples, packaged dates, date milk shakes, and other gifts. A film, *The Romance and Sex Life of the Date,* chronicles the history of the date farm and, well, how these delicious dates come to be. Visitors can wander through the date gardens and oasis, which has strangely been reenvisioned as a biblical sculpture garden complete with famous biblical scenes. There is also the on-site Café at Shields (760/775-0902, lunch 7am-2:30pm daily and dinner 5pm-9pm Tues.-Sat., $15-45) if you need a bite.

ENTERTAINMENT AND EVENTS

Casinos

Tucked at the foot of the San Jacinto Mountains 18 miles west of Palm Springs, Morongo Casino Resort and Spa (49500 Seminole Dr., Cabazon, 951/849-3080, www.morongocasinoresort.com) offers 150,000 square feet of Las Vegas-style gaming in a high-rise luxury resort hotel. The Tukwet Canyon Golf Club, a professional bowling center, and a range of dining options are also on-site.

The sleek Agua Caliente Casino Resort Spa (32-250 Bob Hope Dr., Rancho Mirage, 760/321-2000, www.hotwatercasino.com) is 10 miles southeast of Palm Springs just off I-10. This upscale resort features a concert theater and lounge for entertainment with a second lounge offering specialty cocktails.

The casino houses a selection of casino table games, slots, a live poker room, and a high-limit room. Dining options include a high-end steakhouse, two cafés, a deli, and a buffet.

The luxury high-rise Fantasy Springs Resort Casino (84-245 Indio Springs Pkwy., Indio, 800/827-2946 or 760/342-5000, www.fantasyspringsresort.com) is 25 miles southeast of Palm Springs. It's good for a weekend getaway, featuring Vegas-style gaming options, poolside lounging, a fitness center, an 18-hole golf course, bowling lanes, and fine and casual dining options.

Spotlight 29 (46-200 Harrison Pl., Coachella, 760/775-5566, www.spotlight29.com, 24 hours) is a large casino offering 1,600 slot machines and table games, a dance club, a lounge, and a sports bar. The 2,200-seat Spotlight Showroom hosts live music events. Dining options include a steak house and a casual café with a buffet. The casino is just south of I-10, just south of Fantasy Springs.

Festivals and Events
★ COACHELLA VALLEY MUSIC AND ARTS FESTIVAL

The Coachella Valley Music and Arts Festival (www.coachella.com, Apr.), known simply as Coachella (as in "Dude, are you going to Coachella this year? The lineup looks rad!") is an annual music festival held every April on the Empire Polo Club fields in the Coachella Valley. From folk rock to power pop to hip-hop to electronic music, the festival draws big names and huge numbers of fans. Past headliners have included cultural icons like The Beastie Boys, Radiohead, Bjork, The Black Keys, Red Hot Chili Peppers, Outkast, and Jack White. People come from far and wide to attend. The festival is so popular that it offers the same lineup two weekends back to back in April. Tickets are highly competitive to get and sell out within hours of going on sale in January. The crowd skews youngish, but it can be a fun time for anyone due to their predictably excellent band lineup. They don't shy away from the "art" aspect of the festival either, featuring a few choice Burning

Man-level technology and sculpture installations. On-site camping is available including stylish tepees all set up for you. Outside the festival, local hotels as far as Palm Springs 25 miles away book quickly. For transportation to and from the festival (if you're not camping on the grounds), prepaid and reserved shuttles are available at pickup points throughout the Coachella Valley and Palm Springs.

STAGECOACH FESTIVAL

The **Stagecoach Festival** (www.stagecoachfestival.com, end of Apr.) takes the Coachella Festival's place on those same polo fields to throw a massive outdoor country music festival at the end of April. Acts range from mainstream to outlaw country, old-timers to new blood, with some big names gracing the festival's three stages. Since its beginning in 2007, the festival has been on the rise. Past Stagecoach lineups have featured Merle Haggard, Emmylou Harris, Dwight Yoakam, and Hank Williams Jr. The three-day lineup (Fri.-Sun.) is all-ages and draws thousands of festivalgoers. Accommodations are tight and should be booked well in advance. There is limited on-site RV camping that fills up months ahead of time. Beyond this, visitors rely on campgrounds and hotels in the area outside the festival grounds. Shuttles (with prepaid weekend shuttle passes) transport festivalgoers from designated hotel shuttle stops in the Coachella Valley and Palm Springs.

SHOPPING
Cabazon Outlets

Coming from the west to Palm Springs, you'll pass the **Desert Hills Premium Outlets** (48400 Seminole Dr., Cabazon, 951/849-5018, 10am-9pm daily) along I-10 approximately eight miles west of the exit for Palm Springs. Despite being situated directly across from the striking San Jacinto Mountains and San Gorgonio wind farms, this block of high-end outlet shopping manages to hold its own as a draw, luring thousands of visitors off the highway and into the discounted maze of tempting stores like Le Creuset, Calvin Klein, Guess, Columbia, and Ralph Lauren. The slightly more discount **Cabazon Outlets** (48750 Seminole Dr. #100, Cabazon, www.cabazonoutlets.com, 10am-9pm daily) are next door with retail outlets including Adidas, Oakley, and Columbia Sportswear.

Cathedral City

The hotbed of mid-century home furnishing shopping may be in Palm Springs, but Cathedral City's shops on Perez Road have a few offerings. Set in an unassuming strip mall north of Highway 111, a short series of vintage design stores make for a destination in the otherwise uninspired suburban sprawl. **Hedge** (68-929 Perez Rd., Ste. F, Cathedral City, 760/770-0090, www.hedgepalmsprings.com, noon-5pm Thurs.-Sun.) displays a curated collection of pristine mid-century furniture and housewares including chairs, patio furniture, lamps, ashtrays, art, sculpture, and pottery. The collection at **Hom** (68929 Perez Rd., Ste. G, H, I, 760/770-4447, www.at-homps.com, 10am-5pm Mon.-Sat., 11am-5pm Sun.) spans three suites chock-full of vintage furniture, lamps, and art from mid-century to the 1960s and 1970s. An upstairs loft is stocked with vintage records favoring lounge and feel-good rock. **Spaces** (68-929 Perez Rd., 760/770-5333, paula@modern-spaces.net, call for hours) feels like a cluttered estate sale, stuffed with glassware, furniture, and housewares. You're sure to find a treasure. The limited number of items at **JP Denmark** (68-929 Perez Rd., Ste. N, 760/408-9147, call for hours) gives good clues as to the quality and price range of this shop featuring vintage Danish modern furniture and accents.

Palm Desert

The **Shops on El Paseo** (73-061 El Paseo, Palm Desert, 760/341-4058, www.theshopsonelpaseo.com, shops open daily) are the Rodeo Drive, Beverly Hills of Palm Desert and a destination for luxury shopping. The elite two blocks feature high-end designer brands such as Gucci, St. John, James Perse, and Burberry. They are located on El Paseo Drive between

Highway 74 and Sage Lane. Complimentary valet parking is provided. The shopping and dining district continues another four blocks to the east with anchors such as Louis Vuitton, Saks Fifth Avenue, and Tiffany & Co.

RECREATION

The Coachella Valley's **Bagdouma Park** (51-723 Douma St., Coachella, www.coachella.org) is a 46-acre park with four tennis courts, a swimming pool, other sports facilities, and restrooms.

South Jackson Park (Jackson St. and Date Ave., Indio, www.indio.org) offers two free tennis courts as well as barbecue areas, playground equipment, restrooms, and other sports facilities.

★ Coachella Valley Preserve

The 20,114-acre **Coachella Valley Preserve** (29200 Thousand Palms Canyon Rd., Thousand Palms, 760/343-1234, www.coachellavalleypreserve.org, 7am-6pm daily May-Sept. 7am-5pm daily Oct.-Apr.) is hidden unexpectedly in the middle of the suburban Coachella Valley, protecting a fragile and diversely beautiful desert habitat in an area otherwise overrun by suburban sprawl. Shaped by the San Andreas fault zone, the landscape features both rocky, barren ridges and lush oases. Across the preserve clusters of native California fan palms flash in the glaring sun, protecting hidden pools. A **visitors center** (760/343-2733, hours vary, closed June-Aug.) offers maps and information in the Palm House, a picturesque rustic cabin.

HIKING

The preserve is a peaceful and striking destination, good for a picnic or a hike on more than 25 miles of trails (closed to dogs and bikes). The most popular hike is the **McCallum Trail** (two miles round-trip), an easy, level trail cross-desert to a spectacular series of oasis pools. To extend the hike, continue onto the Moon Country Loop and wind through Colorado River Desert, by contrast barren and desolate (four miles round-trip in combination with the McCallum Trail and oasis).

GETTING THERE

The preserve is located east of Palm Springs and north of I-10. From Palm Springs, follow Ramon Road east to Thousand Palms Canyon Road. Turn left (north) and continue along Thousand Palms Canyon Road to Preserve

Coachella Valley Preserve

turn-off, a short dirt road which leads to the visitors center parking lot. Note that services here are limited.

Whitewater Preserve

The scenic riparian corridor at the Whitewater Preserve (9160 Whitewater Canyon Rd., Whitewater, 760/325-7222, www.wildlandsconservancy.org, 8am-5pm daily) features 2,851 acres surrounded by the San Gorgonio Wilderness. In spring of 2016, it was added to the newly established Sand to Snow National Monument (www. fs.fed.us), now spanning 154,000 acres. The national monument knits together several preserves and previously unprotected land, connecting it with Joshua Tree National Park to the east and the Santa Rosa and San Jacinto Mountains National Monument to the south.

Whitewater Preserve sits tucked behind the unlikely looking arid hills north of I-10. The preserve is named for the Whitewater River, a wild, year-round river winding through scenic Whitewater Canyon. Once used for cattle grazing, the river's crystal clear waters have since been restored.

A combined visitors center and ranger station is located in the Whitewater Trout Farm's historic building, graced by a picturesque trout pond and wading pool. If you plan to hike, pick up a trail map at the ranger station or online. All day hikers are required to register at the ranger station or sign in at the trailhead. Other facilities include individual and group picnic areas and seasonal activities (free, but registration required).

HIKING

A series of hikes ranging in length and difficulty start from the visitors center. They offer great views of the surrounding mountains and canyon, passage along the Whitewater River basin, and access to the famous Pacific Crest Trail, the continuous trail system that runs 2,650 miles from Mexico to Canada. The moderate Canyon View Loop Trail (3.5 miles round-trip) is a rewarding trail that gives you great canyon and mountain views as well as passage along the river. It leaves the Whitewater Ranger Station to follow a section of the PCT heading south across the riverbed. A small wooden footbridge leads across the river.

The hike to the colorful red rock outcropping known as Red Dome (four miles round-trip) begins near the ranger station to cross the canyon's river basin. The trail continues on the west bank of the canyon, connecting with the PCT to reach the destination to the left of the trail—a large colorful rock outcropping.

GETTING THERE

Whitewater Preserve is north of Palm Springs off I-10. From I-10, take Exit 114 and follow Tipton Road to Whitewater Canyon Road. Drive five miles north on Whitewater Canyon Road to the preserve entrance. The preserve gates are open for hiking 7am-6pm daily September 1-November 1; 7am-5pm November 2-March 9; 7am-6pm March 10-May 31. Visitors must park and then walk in outside of visitors center hours. June through August the gates are closed.

Santa Rosa and San Jacinto Mountains National Monument

The Santa Rosa and San Jacinto Mountains National Monument (www. blm.gov and www.fs.usda.gov) encompasses the mountain ranges to the west of the Coachella Valley towering above the desert floor. With its highest elevation reaching 10,834 feet, it provides a spectacular, sometimes snowcapped, backdrop to the desert communities. An array of destinations and hikes—from lush palm oases to rugged peaks, wilderness areas, and a scenic section of the Pacific Crest Trail—makes the national monument an outstanding destination.

The monument spans more than 280,000 acres, extending from the Coachella Valley to the alpine hamlet of Idyllwild near Mount San Jacinto State Park. The vast sprawl encompasses two federal wilderness areas

(Santa Rosa and San Jacinto), the San Jacinto Ranger District, and public BLM lands within the California Desert Conservation Area. The monument's extensive network of trails and backcountry can be accessed from Idyllwild and the Coachella Valley.

The ranger-staffed **visitors center** (51-500 Hwy. 74, Palm Desert, 760/862-9984, 9am-4pm Thurs.-Mon. in winter, 8am-3pm Thurs.-Mon. in summer) is your best resource for exploring this region, with maps and books for hikes and recreation. The visitors center is located in the Coachella Valley, four miles south of Highway 111 in the town of Palm Desert.

Golf

The Coachella Valley is a golfing mecca. Moderate year-round temperatures and spectacular mountain views have given rise to a wealth of golf courses and clubs throughout the valley. Golfing is a lifestyle as well as a destination in the Coachella Valley, and there are a number of courses open to the public including municipal courses, semiprivate clubs, and resort facilities. Courses vary widely for a range of skill levels and price points from basic courses for knocking around to luxury resort settings to PGA Classic Courses. Many courses enforce dress codes.

Most golf courses maintain online booking for tee times on their website. Pricing for many courses is dynamic, reflecting real-time conditions including weather, demand, and other market factors. Other booking resources include Stand-By Golf and Golf Now. **Stand-By Golf** (760/321-2665, www. standbygolf.com, 7am-7pm daily) is a comprehensive booking site that is able to search for tee times in all Coachella Valley communities including Palm Springs, Cathedral City, Rancho Mirage, Palm Desert, Indian Wells, La Quinta, and Indio. You can search by desired tee time, price range, and course. Book directly through this website 365 days a year. **Golf Now** (800/752-9020, www. golfnow.com, 5am-5pm daily) offers an online

tee time retail service for Palm Springs and other international golfing destinations.

DESERT HOT SPRINGS

The semiprivate **Mission Lakes Country Club** (8484 Clubhouse Dr., 760/329-8061, ext. 198, www.missionlakescountryclub.com, $54-69) features an 18-hole golf course open to the public. Other amenities include warm-up cages, pitching/putting practice area, a fully stocked pro shop, and full-service restaurant and bar as well as a café and lounge. Summer rates are lower ($29).

CATHEDRAL CITY

Cathedral Canyon Golf Club (68311 Paseo Real, 760/328-6571, www.jcgolf.com/cathedral-canyon, $32-69) offers an 18-hole championship course with 16 lakes and undulating greens. Amenities include a practice green and bunker, complete golf shop, golf instruction and clinics, and a grill-style restaurant. Golf club rentals are available.

Cimarron Golf Resort (67603 30th Ave., 800/701-1656, www.cimarrongolf.com) has a more desert feel than the green-grass layouts common to Palm Springs and a links style of play with British-Isles-type bunkers. It offers 36 holes across two championship layouts: the Boulder course, 6,858 yards, par 71 ($44-84) and the Pebble course ($29-35).

RANCHO MIRAGE

The **Westin Mission Hills Golf Resort & Spa** (760/328-3198, www.playmissionhills. com, $60-109) is a resort facility with two golf courses available for public guests as well as resort guests. The **Gary Player Signature Course** (70705 Ramon Rd., Rancho Mirage) is straightforward with wide fairways while the **Pete Dye Course** (71501 Dinah Shore Dr., Rancho Mirage) is more difficult with challenging greens. Amenities include shared golf carts and a pro shop. The resort also offers a golf academy, daily clinics, private lessons, and golf schools.

Omni Rancho Las Palmas Resort & Spa (42-000 Bob Hope Dr., 760/568-2727, www.

omnihotels.com, $59-99) has three distinct layouts across a 27-hole championship course characterized by a gently rolling terrain with palm trees and six lakes.

PALM DESERT

Desert Willow Golf Resort (38995 Desert Willow Dr., 760/346-0015, www.desertwillow. com) offers two 18-hole regulation courses featuring desert landscaping, large lakes, and bunkers. Amenities include a golf academy, complete practice facility ($30 pp), PGA instruction, a restaurant with patio dining, and a full-service pro shop. Golf club rentals are available. Sunrise and prime tee times run $75 (includes two sleeves of golf balls), and twilight and sunset tee times $45 (no golf balls).

Mountain Vista Golf Club (38180 Del Webb Blvd., 760/200-2200, www.mountainvistagolfclub.com, $53-88) offers two 18-hole championship courses on a landscape that features waterfalls, lakes, and palm trees. Amenities include a clubhouse with small pro shop, café, and bar. Golf club rentals are available. **Marriott's Shadow Ridge Golf Club** (9002 Shadow Ridge Rd., 760/674-2700, www. marriott.com, $127-189) is open to the public with a clubhouse, pro shop, and practice facility. Club rentals are available. Reserve tee times by calling or book online.

The 18-hole course at **Woodhaven Country Club** (41555 Woodhaven Dr. East, 760/345-7636, www.woodhavencc.com, $49-65) has a reputation as a golfer-friendly course with typical rounds averaging less than four hours. Amenities include golf and pull cart rentals, a driving range, a putting green, chipping area, practice bunker, a school, and food and bar service. Rental clubs are available.

The semiprivate, high-end **Classic Club** (75200 Classic Club Blvd., 760/601-3600, www.classicclubgolf.com, $99-169) is a daily-fee golf facility. This 18-hole course features a rolling terrain across 30 acres with pine, California pepper, and olive trees, lake and water features, and stone bridges. Facilities include a driving range, practice

greens, power carts, food and beverages, a clubhouse, and forecaddies. Golf club rentals are available.

JW Marriott Desert Springs Resort & Spa (74855 Country Club Dr., 760/341-1756, ext. 1, www.marriott.com, $99-160) is a luxury golf resort that encompasses 36 holes across two championship layouts—the Palms Course (par 72) and Valley Course (par 54). Resort amenities include a clubhouse and golf shop, rentals and lessons, driving range and putting green, golf program available for juniors, and a Kids Golf-4-Free program.

The **Oasis Country Club** (42300 Casbah Way, 760/345-2715, www. theoasiscountryclub.com, Nov.-Dec. $30-50, Jan.-Apr. $35-59) is a privately owned club open to the public and featuring a par 60 executive golf course with 22 lakes. Other amenities include an 18-hole putting course, putting green, practice driving range, three tennis courts, and clubhouse with dining room and lounge. Public reservations are available 3-4 days ahead of time; to make a reservation, call the Oasis Pro Shop. Golf cart rentals are $10 per person.

INDIAN WELLS

The **Indian Wells Golf Resort** (44500 Indian Wells Ln., www.indianwellsgolfresort.com, $49-109) offers two 18-hole courses: the Celebrity course and the Players course. The Celebrity course features undulating fairways, split-level lakes, waterfalls, brooks, and floral details. The Players course features wide playing corridors and sculpted bunkers. Resort amenities include a driving range, practice greens, power carts, locker rooms and showers, a golf performance center, a golf academy, bar and grill, and clubhouse. Accommodations, golf packages, and rental clubs and shoes are available.

LA QUINTA

A former home course of the PGA, **SilverRock Resort** (79179 Ahmanson Ln., 888/600-7272 or 760/777-8884, www.silverrock.org, call for rates) features an 18-hole regulation golf course that sprawls over 200 acres with water features and native bunkers. The Clubhouse is a historic, renovated ranch hacienda situated amid rocky outcroppings. Amenities include a grill-style restaurant.

La Quinta Resort (50200 Ave. Vista Bonita, 760/564-4111, www.laquintaresort.com, $49-109) offers two 18-hole regulation golf courses—the Dunes Course with traditional Scottish design and the Mountain Course known for its dramatic mountain backdrop and challenging course. Both courses are open to resort and public guests. Golf amenities include the Mountain Dunes clubhouse with a grill-style restaurant and golf shop (6am-6pm daily). Fees include shared cart and unlimited day-of-play use of practice facilities. The resort also offers resort accommodations and golf packages. Golf club rentals are available.

Three 18-hole regulation PGA West golf courses are also part of the luxurious La Quinta Resort ($89-179). **PGA West Greg Norman** features 60 acres of fairways and nine ponds spanning 18 acres. The world-famous **PGA West TPC Stadium Course** is considered to be one of the greatest 100 courses in the world and has been viewed on TV by millions. The **PGA West Jack Nicklaus** is a more manageable version of the PGA West TPC. Both courses are open to resort and public guests. Tee time reservations are available online. Fees include shared cart and unlimited day-of-play use of practice facilities. Other amenities include two clubhouses with restaurants and golf shops.

The **Golf Club at La Quinta** (60151 Trilogy Pkwy., 760/771-0707, www.thegolfclubatlaquinta.com, $55-139) offers an 18-hole championship course set at the base of the Santa Rosa Mountains. Amenities include a fully stocked pro shop (6am-5pm daily) and a bistro with outdoor dining.

INDIO

The 18-hole **Eagle Falls Golf Course** (84245 Indio Springs Pkwy., 760/238-5633, www.eaglefallsgolf.com, $35-65 weekdays, $55-95 weekends) features elevations and water features. Amenities include pro shop, snack bar, golf carts with up-to-date GPS, driving range, putting greens, and forecaddies. Golf club rentals are available.

The Golf Club at Terra Lago (84000 Terra Lago Pkwy., www.golfclub-terralago.com) features 36 challenging holes on the North Course ($50-115) and South Course ($45-100), with green fairways interwoven into native vegetation. On-site amenities include a pro shop, practice driving range, putting greens, and a practice hole open to the public ($7 for a medium bucket, $10 for a large bucket). Clubhouse dining and golf club rentals are available; a dress code is enforced.

Heritage Palms Golf Club (44291 S Heritage Palms Dr., 760/772-7334, www.heritagepalmsindio.com, $25-115) is an 18-hole championship course with wide, rolling fairways, four large lakes, and greenside bunkers. Regular, twilight (starting at 1pm), and super-twilight (starting at 2pm) tee times are offered. On-site amenities include a driving range (6am-dusk daily), pro shop (6am-6pm daily), and a bar and grill.

The 27-hole championship golf course at the **Indian Palms Country Club & Resort** (48630 Monroe St., 800/778-5288, www.indianpalms.com/golf-course, $35-90) features three nine-hole courses. The resort also offers a practice facility with a driving range, two putting greens, and a complete short game area. Other amenities feature a pro shop, café, and on-site accommodations. Golf club rentals are available.

The 18-hole championship golf course at the **Indian Springs Country Club** (79940 Westward Ho Dr., 760/200-8988, www.indianspringsgc.com, $60-89) is considered to be a great course for the value, with eight lakes, streams, waterfalls, and immaculate tournament speed greens. The course features Precedent golf cars, a practice range, two putting greens, and a food and beverage cart. Golf club rentals are available.

Shadow Hills Golf Club (80875 Ave. 40, 760/200-3375, www.shadowhillsgolfclub.

com, $71-91) features two distinct golf courses open to the public. The South Course offers a traditional 18-hole championship course. The North Course is a par 3 course with an undulating fairway and water features. On-site amenities include a practice area, clubhouse, pro shop, restaurant, and snack bar.

Tennis

Like golf, tennis is a big draw to Palm Springs and the Coachella Valley. The lovely weather and year-round sun put Palm Springs on the map even before golf became a favorite pastime. There are a number of public, semiprivate, and resort facilities open to the public.

Indian Wells Tennis Garden (78200 Miles Ave., Indian Wells, 760/200-8200, www.iwtg.net, 8am-8pm Mon.-Fri., 8am-5pm Sat.-Sun. Oct. 1-May 31; 7am-noon and 5pm-9pm Mon.-Fri., 7am-noon Sat.-Sun. June 1-Sept. 30) is the second-largest tennis stadium in the world. The full-service tennis club features 29 concrete courts, 23 lighted courts, locker rooms, a fitness area, and a pro shop. A regular calendar of private lessons, group lessons, clinics, and camps are available for both adults and juniors. Additional services include ball-machine rental ($30), racquet stringing and repairs, and game arrangements.

The **Oasis Country Club** (42300 Casbah Way, Palm Desert, 760/345-2715, www.theoasiscountryclub.com, $10) is a privately owned club open to the public and featuring a par 60 executive golf course with 22 lakes and three tennis courts. Other amenities include a clubhouse with dining room and lounge and pro shop.

Spas

Situated along the San Andreas fault line, Desert Hot Springs' claim to fame is the abundance of hot natural mineral springs that propelled the development of the town's spas and resorts. The 1950s were a heyday, and some of the operating boutique hotels sport the clean lines and neon signs of desert resort mid-century architecture. Desert Hot Springs has never achieved the popularity of nearby Palm Springs. The town has seen growth in recent years but much of it in the form of newer residences. Desert Hot Springs' spas are mixed in amidst the more recent housing. The town attracts snowbirds and other visitors looking for a more low-key and affordable experience than Palm Springs. Its spas range from retro-hip to sleekly luxurious.

Desert Hot Springs Spa Hotel (11740 Mesquite Ave., Desert Hot Springs, 760/673-8689, www.dhsspa.com, 8am-10pm daily, $7 day pass) takes a quantity-over-quality approach. A day pass gets you access to the 1940s resort hotel's eight mineral pools in a large, palm-studded courtyard. The hotel also has an on-site café and sports bar. The hotel is well known as a party spot and has live music on weekends.

The charming Moroccan-themed **El Morocco Inn** (66810 4th St., Desert Hot Springs, 760/288-2527, www.elmoroccoinn.com, 9am-4pm daily, $50 pp or free with one-hour spa treatment) offers a huge, covered hot spa, outdoor mineral pool, sauna, and spa services.

A range of spa services including massage therapy and facial and body treatments is available at the impeccably maintained mid-century **Lido Palms** (12801 Tamar Dr., Desert Hot Springs, 760/329-6033, www.lidopalms.com, 9am-8pm daily, $40 for four hours without spa service). Spa services include four hours of mineral pool day use. No alcohol may be brought on premises for day-use guests.

The **Miracle Springs Resort & Spa** (10625 Palm Dr., Desert Hot Springs, 760/251-6000, www.miraclesprings.com, 9am-6pm daily, age 21 and over only, $14) offers eight pools and spas for day use. They also have an on-site salon (manicures and pedicures) and a full-service spa with a range of services. The on-site Capri restaurant serves breakfast, lunch, and dinner, and has a full bar and poolside lunch service.

At **The Spring Resort & Spa** (12699

Reposo Way, Desert Hot Springs, 760/251-6700, www.the-spring.com, call for reservations 7:45am-8:45pm, $120-350) guests receive two hours' use of mineral pools with day spa services. They offer several different packages combining massages, scrubs, and wraps from 1.5 to 3 hours.

The quiet **Tuscan Springs Hotel & Spa** (68187 Club Cir., Desert Hot Springs, 760/251-0189, www.tuscansprings.com, $45 for four hours) offers mineral pool day use (free when purchasing any treatment from the on-site La Bella Spa).

The setting at family-friendly **Sam's Family Spa Hot Water Resort** (70875 Dillon Rd., Desert Hot Springs, 760/329-6457, www.samsfamilyspa.com, $14 Mon.-Fri., $20 Sat.-Sun. and holidays) includes a spring-fed swimming pool and a series of hot mineral pools tucked amidst palm trees in a park-like setting.

ACCOMMODATIONS

When it comes to accommodation options in the Coachella Valley, you're limited to resort hotels from the chains or casino hotels. Desert Hot Springs offers the best range of lodging choices, many of which include access to the area's renowned hot springs.

Desert Hot Springs

Many hotels in Desert Hot Springs offer day-use services for non-hotel guests. For a fee that varies by hotel, visitors can enjoy the cold mineral pools, hot spas, or spa treatments and massages at a range of hotels in Palm Springs from tranquil retreats to party spots.

The Casablanca-inspired digs at ★ **El Morocco Inn** (66810 4th St., 760/288-2527, www.elmorroccoinn.com, $149-169) walk the line between luxurious, kitschy, and chic. The hotel is strewn with extravagant Moroccan lamps that the owner brings back from his travels. Rooms in this hideaway feature canopy beds, while the hotel spoils guests with complimentary mint tea, snacks, breakfast, and a nightly Morocco-tini hour. There's also a desert garden with hammocks, a bocce ball

court, a relaxation tent, and a movie and game library. The pool and gigantic covered spa are open 24 hours daily.

The impeccably maintained **Lido Palms** (12801 Tamar Dr., 760/329-6033, www.lidopalms.com, $160) offers a chance to relax and rejuvenate. The nine-room mid-century retreat opens onto a neatly landscaped courtyard with ocotillos, yuccas, agave, barrel cactus, and palms. Inside, rooms feature tile floors, full kitchens, and fluffy robes. Amenities include a pool, hot tub, and a spa that are open 24/7, plus a grill for guest use on-site. Children and pets are not permitted.

The upscale, modernist **Sagewater Spa** (12689 Eliseo Rd., 760/220-1554, www.sagewaterspa.com, $195-285) offers a restful and serene experience. The seven guest rooms have views and full kitchens.

Spare mid-century style and desert chic meet over polished concrete floors at **Hope Springs Resort** (68075 Club Circle Dr., 760/329-4003, www.hopespringsresort.com, $185-200), which offers 10 rooms with king-size beds (four rooms include kitchens) that open onto a communal pool and spa. Guests take advantage of the continental breakfast, communal kitchen, and grill, which means you never have to leave. Children and pets are not permitted.

The contemporary **Spring Resort & Day Spa** (12699 Reposo Way, 760/251-6700, www.the-spring.com, $169-189) offers 12 understated guest rooms in view of the San Jacinto Mountains. Most rooms surround the courtyard pool, and include rainfall showerheads and Egyptian cotton linens. Guests can look forward to a complimentary breakfast, a fire pit, and three mineral pools.

Set on 77 lush acres, **Two Bunch Palms Resort & Spa** (67425 Two Bunch Palms Trail, 760/329-8791, www.twobunchpalms.com, $220-290) offers charm dating back to 1930. Choose from the original "Grotto" rooms with king beds, or "Soulstice" rooms, which come in a range of layouts with either a king bed or two double beds; some rooms have patios or

Desert Hot Springs

© AVALON TRAVEL

courtyards. Amenities include two mineral springs pools, a shaded "grotto" for soaking, and tennis courts, as well as the on-site farm to table restaurant **Essense.**

Iconic architectural home turned desert oasis, the **Hotel Lautner** (67710 San Antonio St., 760/832-5288, www.hotellautner. com, $200) was designed by John Lautner in 1947 and features concrete, redwood, lots of glass, and skylights. Four private units with private patios share a communal space with

a saltwater plunge pool, a fire pit lounge, and a grilling area.

Resort Hotels

Most Coachella Valley resort hotels come with accompanying golf courses and cater to the needs of leisure travelers who rarely need to leave the premises. Resort fees will add to the cost of your stay.

The historic Spanish revival-style **La Quinta Resort** (50200 Ave. Vista Bonita, La

Quinta, 760/564-4111, www.laquintaresort.com, from $180) is a restored desert hideaway dating to 1926. Set on 45 acres, this resort features six golf courses, tennis courts, six restaurants, a swimming pool, gym, and a spa. Cozy casitas offer mini-fridges and LCD flat-screen TVs; some rooms have fireplaces. Upgrades and suites can add hot tubs, private patios, and sitting areas. Villas are also available.

JW Marriott Desert Springs Resort & Spa (74855 Country Club Dr., Palm Desert, 760/341-1756, www.marriott.com, $250-500) is a luxury hotel and golf resort featuring an extensive spa and fitness facility. Contemporary guest rooms offer luxurious bedding and bathrooms, plus LCD flat-screen TVs and mini-fridges; some rooms have private balconies. The resort features two championship golf courses, tennis courts, five swimming pools, and six restaurants.

The **Indian Palms Country Club & Resort** (48630 Monroe St., Indio, 800/778-5288, www.indianpalms.com, $120) offers a 59-room boutique hotel with modern accommodations, a championship 27-hole golf course, an on-site restaurant, a swimming pool, and a Jacuzzi offering stunning views of the San Jacinto Mountains.

Westin Mission Hills Golf Resort & Spa (71333 Dinah Shore Dr., Rancho Mirage, 760/328-5955, www.playmissionhills.com, $260-530) features deluxe rooms with luxury bedding, an in-room cooler or mini-fridge, and private balconies or patios; suites add a living or dining space. Resort amenities include two golf courses, five swimming pools, a restaurant, lounge, and poolside dining on landscaped grounds.

Omni Rancho Las Palmas Resort & Spa (42-000 Bob Hope Dr., Rancho Mirage, 760/568-2727, www.omnihotels.com, $330-400) boasts 444 guest rooms, a 27-hole golf course, two-acre water park, tennis courts, and full-service spa set on 240 acres. Elegantly appointed contemporary guestrooms offer views and private balconies or patios. Suites add dining and entertaining spaces.

Casino Hotels

Morongo Casino Resort and Spa (49500 Seminole Dr., Cabazon, 951/849-3080, www.morongocasinoresort.com) is a high-rise luxury resort hotel with 272 contemporary guest rooms, 36 suites, and 6 luxury casitas. Some rooms have views of the mountains. Perks included in your resort fee: Wi-Fi, flat-screen TVs, stocked minibars, the Oasis pool (with a lazy river, sandy beach, and hot tubs), shuttle to nearby outlets, access to Tukwet Canyon Golf Club, fitness center, professional bowling center, and 150,000 square feet of gaming. The resort also has a range of casual and fine dining options.

The **Agua Caliente Casino Resort Spa** (32-250 Bob Hope Dr., Rancho Mirage, 760/321-2000, www.hotwatercasino.com) is an upscale resort. Deluxe rooms offer 42-inch flat-screen TVs, Wi-Fi, robes, and oversize sunken tubs, while suites will garner you parlors, a wet bar, and jetted whirlpool tubs. Resort amenities include two outdoor pools, a hot tub, cabana rentals, an outdoor bar and grill, a fitness center, and spa and salon services. Dining options include a high-end steak house, two cafés, a deli, and a buffet.

The luxury high-rise **Fantasy Springs Resort Casino** (84-245 Indio Springs Pkwy., Indio, 800/827-2946 or 760/342-5000, www.fantasyspringsresort.com) is a 250-room hotel with numerous amenities and casual dining options.

CAMPING

Campgrounds in the Coachella Valley tend toward developed RV resorts. For tent camping, your best bet is to head to Joshua Tree National Park (and pray for a spot).

The 91 sites at **Lake Cahuilla Recreation Area** (58-075 Jefferson St., La Quinta, 760/564-4712, www.rivcoparks.org, $40-70) are set around the 135-acre lake and offer picnic tables, barbecues, restrooms, showers, and a primitive tent camping area. Though the lake is closed to swimming, a pool (hours vary) offers a chance to cool off. Reservations are accepted up to six months in advance.

RVers can choose from **Emerald Desert RV Resort** (76-000 Frank Sinatra Dr., Palm Desert, 877/624-4140, www.emeralddesert.com, from $85), with 255 spaces, and **Indian Waters RV Resort** (47202 Jackson St., Indio, 760/342-8100, www.indianwatersrvresort.com, from $45), with 274 spaces, and **Shadow Hills RV Resort** (40655 Jefferson St., Indio, 760/360-4040, www.shadowhillsrvresort.com, from $50), with 100 sites.

FOOD
Desert Hot Springs

Dining options in Desert Hot Springs are very limited; some people drive to Palm Springs 12 miles south or take advantage of the kitchens and barbecues provided in some of the resorts. Serving up Mexican specialties and smoky salsa in a vibrant setting, ★ **Casa Blanca** (66370 Pierson Blvd., 760/251-5922, www.casablancamenu.com, 8am-10pm daily, $6-18) is a popular choice for locals and visitors. Try the signature spinach enchiladas. There is a second location in **Cathedral City** (35850 Date Palm Dr., 760/328-2150).

You can also enjoy the traditional Mexican plates and deep booths at **South of the Border** (11719 Palm Dr., 760/251-4000, 11am-9:30pm Sun.-Thurs., 11am-10pm Fri.-Sat., $9-12).

Located off the wide-open lobby of the Miracle Springs Resort & Spa, **Capri Restaurant** (10625 Palm Dr., 760/329-6833, www.miraclesprings.com, 4:30pm-close daily, $11-24) offers Italian dinner specialties, as well as breakfast (7am-11:30am daily, $5-9) and a daytime poolside menu (11:30am-4pm daily, $6-9).

Locals swear by the food at **Thai Palms** (12070 Palm Dr., 760/288-3934, 11am-3pm and 5pm-9pm daily, $16) where spicy curries, seafood, chef specials, Siam noodles, and fried rice are all washed down with beer, wine, and sake.

Essense (67425 Two Bunch Palms Trail, 760/329-8791, www.twobunchpalms.com, 7:30am-9pm Sun.-Thurs., 7:30am-10pm Fri.-Sat., $18-39) is the farm to table restaurant in the Two Bunch Palms Resort, offering traditional breakfast options like house-made granola and omelets ($7-14), lunch plates ranging from papaya chicken salad to garden gyro ($7-15), and dinner specialties such as vegan orecchiette and seared duck. Specialty cocktails, wines, local and organic beers, and snacks are served in the lounge.

Rancho Mirage

Lord Fletcher's (70385 Hwy. 111, Rancho Mirage, 760/328-1161, www.lordfletcher.com, from 5:30pm, last seating at 8:30pm, $25-38) specializes in upscale classic English fare from prime rib to chicken and dumplings set amid an impressive collection of English bric-a-brac and antiques. They also offer a pub menu served bar-side (from 5pm, $7-13). Reservations are recommended.

Chef-driven **Catalan** (70026 Hwy. 111, Rancho Mirage, 760/770-9508, www.catalanrestaurant.com, 5pm-9pm Tues.-Sun., $12-49) serves small, farm-to-table plates and large-format dishes inspired by Italy, Spain, and California.

Palm Desert

An old-school American diner, **Keedy's Fountain Grill** (Palms to Pines Shopping Center, 73633 Hwy. 111, Palm Desert, 760/346-6492, 5:30am-3pm daily, $7-13) has been getting folks fed since 1957. They're slinging omelets, burgers, and other American diner fare at the coffee counter and stripped-down dining room.

European-style deli **Bouchee** (72785 Hwy. 111 #1, Palm Desert, 444/666-3296, www.boucheecafeanddeli.com, 9am-5pm Mon.-Fri., 9am-4pm Sat., 9am-3pm Sun., $8-11) serves gourmet fare, including salads and signature sandwiches.

The Mediterranean-influenced eatery **Clementine Gourmet Marketplace & Café** (72990 El Paseo #3, Palm Desert, 760/834-8814, www.clementineshop.com, 8am-3pm daily) features a patisserie with coffee, deli, and take-out, plus a weekday menu, weekend brunch, and bar and happy hour menu in a quaint space.

Pacifica Seafood Restaurant (73505 El Paseo, Palm Desert, 760/674-8666, 11:30am-9:30pm Mon.-Thurs., 11:30am-10:30pm Fri.-Sat., $12-36) serves a variety of fresh seafood and steaks, as well as a vodka menu and wine list.

Indian Wells

An Indian Wells staple since 1965, **The Nest** (75188 CA-111, Indian Wells, 760/346-2314, www.gotothenest.com, 4pm-midnight Sun.-Thurs., 4pm-1:30am Fri.-Sat., $23-57) offers a full-service restaurant and lively venue with live music, drinks, and dancing nightly. Their restaurant features American specialties like steaks, pastas, and seafood as well as traditional family recipes including cabbage rolls and moussaka.

Indio

On the edge of the Coachella polo fields where the Coachella Music Festival is held, ★ **Tack Room Tavern** (81800 Avenue 51, Indio, 760/347-9985, www.empirepoloevents.com, 3pm-12:30am Mon., 11am-12:30am Tues.-Sat., 9am-12:30am Sun., $11-15) is open to the public. This fun, local watering hole with a patio and saddle bar seats serves excellent sandwiches, burgers, and salads, drawing everyone from ladies sipping manhattans to dudes chanting over the big game.

Ciro's (81963 Hwy. 111, Indio, 760/347-6503, www.cirosofindio.com, $7-18) serves subs, salads, pizzas, and classic Italian dishes in a casual setting. Head to **Jackalope Ranch** (80400 Hwy. 111, Indio, 760/342-1999, www.thejackaloperanch.com, 11:30am-10pm Sun.-Wed., 11:30am-midnight Thurs.-Sat., $11-39) for BBQ, steaks, and seafood served in a stone lodge with a saloon, outdoor bar, and live music.

TRANSPORTATION AND SERVICES

The Coachella Valley sprawls southeast of Palm Springs encompassing the towns of Desert Hot Springs, Cathedral City, Rancho Mirage, Thousand Palms, Palm Desert, Indian Wells, La Quinta, Indio, and Coachella, all of which are accessed from I-10. A car is the only way to navigate this region surrounding Palm Springs.

Car

Desert Hot Springs is located north of Palm Springs and I-10. To get here, follow North Indian Canyon Drive north from Palm Springs or take Highway 62 north from I-10 and turn east on Pierson Boulevard.

Cathedral City abuts Palm Springs to the east and is accessible via I-10 by following Vista Chino or Ramon Road east from Palm Springs. Continuing east, Rancho Mirage is the next in line, accessible from I-10 via Bob Hope Drive or along Highway 111 from Palm Springs.

Thousand Palms and **Palm Desert** sandwich I-10 north and south (respectively). Monterey Avenue (Exit 131) from I-10 links the two.

Tiny **Indian Wells** sits off Highway 111 between Palm Desert and La Quinta. To get here from Palm Springs, follow Highway 111 east. To get here from I-10, exit at Cook Street (Exit 134) or Washington Street (Exit 137) and drive south to Highway 111.

As Highway 111 continues its journey east, it passes through **La Quinta, Indio,** and **Coachella** to connect with Business I-10 in Indio. Note that Business I-10 continues south, merging with Highway 111 and Highway 86 north of Mecca and toward the Salton Sea. To continue on I-10 east and the South Entrance to Joshua Tree, turn northeast on Dillon Road to I-10.

THE SALTON SEA

On clear days, standing on a high peak in Joshua Tree National Park or a rugged ridge near Idyllwild, you'll see an enormous body of blue water shimmering to the south. This is the Salton Sea, deep in the arid Colorado Desert, directly on the San Andreas fault, and covering a massive area 35 miles long

Pleasures and Plagues

Famed architect Albert Frey designed the North Shore Beach and Yacht Club on the Salton Sea.

The Salton Sea occupies the ancient Salton Sink, which acted as a flood basin for the Colorado River over thousands of years. The river would overflow its banks, running along dry flood channels, fill the sink with a temporary lake, and then disappear. Native American oral history tells of a lake around 1600-1700. Between 1824 and 1904 the river flooded the basin no less than eight times. All this flooding and evaporating created a nutrient-rich soil, and in the early 1900s, the California Development Company tried to cash in by developing an industry of year-round, irrigated agriculture. By the end of 1904, 10,000 settlers were farming the newly irrigated land. The success was short-lived. By 1905, the irrigation channels had silted up, and engineers made an infamous cut into the bank of the Colorado River to try to increase flow. You could say they succeeded. However, the water that flowed out crashed through the engineered canal creating a raging torrent that swamped the Salton Basin in successive floods for two years before the deluge was stopped. Witnesses described huge waterfalls 20, 40, and 80 feet high. The Salton Sea was born.

Recreation became the fledgling industry. In fact, one of the original settlers, Captain Charles E. Davis, set the region on its course. He had fortuitously built his early camp in 1898 on top of an extinct volcano near what would become the shores of the Salton Sea. After the flooding, the site of his camp became Mullet Island. Hell's Kitchen was the name of the café, dance hall, and boat landing he built in 1908. By the late 1920s the Salton Sea was well on its way to becoming a wildly popular recreation destination. Tourists flocked to the shores of the "Salton Rivera" for fishing, boating, waterskiing, swimming, golf, and partying. Albert Frey, an architect who pioneered the desert modernist aesthetic, was responsible for the distinct lines of the **Salton Bay Yacht Club** and the nautical-themed **North Shore Beach and Yacht Club** in 1958.

In the late 1970s the sea's popularity began to sink with the rise of the sea and flooding due to agricultural runoff and above-average rainfall. By the early 1980s most of the planned vacation communities around the Salton Sea were abandoned. With no natural outlet, the saline levels of the Salton Sea have continued to rise, causing problems with the sealife and birds who depend on the lake.

and 15 miles wide. In this desert valley, where summer temperatures often top 115°F and the average rainfall is less than three inches, the story of the Salton Sea is a saga of boom and bust, a disaster turned happy accident turned disaster again as a combination of ancient geography and contemporary folly created the perfect storm—or in this case, flood.

Today the Salton Sea is a strangely beautiful place, surrounded by the stark Chocolate Mountains and the semi-ghost towns of once-vibrant resort communities. Photographers come here to capture the abandonment and decay, while road-trippers marvel at the juxtaposition of natural beauty and desolation. The communities still exist, though they are mostly abandoned. Some are home to those who were stuck when the Salton Sea crashed, while others became a refuge for eccentrics, artists, and those looking to live off-the-grid in an out-of-the-way place.

For the best documentary about the Salton Sea, watch *Pleasures & Plagues on the Salton Sea,* narrated by John Waters.

Mecca, Bombay Beach, and Slab City

There are still some functioning businesses from the old days. One enterprising family opened **The International Banana Museum** (98775 Hwy. 111, Mecca, 619/840-1429, www.internationalbananamuseum.com, 11:30am-7:30pm Fri.-Mon., but call to confirm) on the site of the bar and tackle shop they had owned since 1958 during the Salton Sea's heyday.

In the town of Bombay Beach, the **Ski Inn** (9596 Avenue A, Niland, 760/354-1285, 8am-midnight daily, cash only) is operated by owners Jane and Wendell, and has achieved cult status among dive bars. On any given day old-timers, locals, OHV riders, and the occasional

curious visitor sip cold beers in the dim coolness of the bar.

In the 1930s military operations moved in, but were all decommissioned by the mid-1990s. The remains of one World War II Marine base near the town of Niland has since been taken over as a recreational vehicle squat called **Slab City.** Today it attracts artists, snowbirds, and wanderers who live off the grid. Just outside the boundary of Slab City, **Salvation Mountain** is an adobe and straw painted visionary sculpture created by outsider artist Leonard Knight from 1980 to his death in 2011. The bright colors and spiritual text convey his universal message that "God is Love." Within Slab City, the artist community of **East Jesus** (http://eastjesus.org) has received attention for its impressive sculpture installations.

Salton City

On the opposite side of the sea near the intersection of Highway 86 and the Borrego-Salton Sea Way is **Capt'n Jims** (2108 Salton Arena St., Salton City, 760/394-1155, noon-8pm Mon.-Thurs., noon-1am Fri., 11am-2am Sat., 10am-8pm Sun.), a welcoming watering hole for locals, bikers, and travelers.

Getting There

When it comes to accommodations, food, and services around the Salton Sea, lower your expectations now. This is a remote desert region—distances are far and services are very, very few. Fill up the gas tank in Palm Springs or Indio before heading out here, and bring water and food.

From Palm Springs, take I-10 south for 24 miles to the split with Highway 86. To reach Salton City on the west side, follow Highway 86 south for 37 miles. To reach Bombay Beach on the east side, take Highway 111 south for 40 miles. Plan at least one hour for either drive.

Joshua Tree and the Yucca Valley

The stunning, alien landscape of Joshua Tree both startles and charms.

Powerful geologic forces have whipped the rocks here into twisted shapes and scrambled boulder piles. Among the eroded chaos spiky Joshua trees reach out in unpredictable angles, forming jagged, moody backdrops against dusty desert roads. This is the Mojave, the high desert: gorgeous in spring and fall, brutal in summer, and dusted by snow in winter.

Farther south the landscape changes yet again, straddling the boundary between the Mojave and Colorado Deserts. The lower Colorado sits austere and arid, with wide alluvial fans to guard its mountain canyons. Instead of Joshua trees, creosote bushes and spindly ocotillos dot the pristine desert wilderness.

Joshua Tree's surreal appeal draws casual day-trippers, spring wildflower hounds, serious hikers, and hard-core rock climbers in droves, all wanting to experience its beauty and strangeness. The park's location near major urban centers like Palm Springs and Los Angeles contributes to its popularity, as does its easy access for locals living in the gateway towns of Joshua Tree and Twentynine

Palms. The tiny towns surrounding the park are filled with outsider art, alien-inspired feats of aeronautical engineering, and some of the best live music around.

PLANNING YOUR TIME

Joshua Tree is doable as a **day trip** from Palm Springs; it's a drive of about one hour to the Joshua Tree Visitors Center at the West Entrance. (From Los Angeles, plan 3-4 hours for the drive and definitely spend the night.) Some visitors only spend one day in the park, and most of that in the car driving the Park Boulevard loop into, and then out of, each entrance station. Such limited time affords equally limited exposure to how much the park has to offer—and that involves getting out of the car and onto the trail. Do yourself a favor and plan to spend at least an overnight; **3-5 days** are even better.

Plan your visit during the cooler months of **October-April** (although these are also the most crowded). If you're **camping,** try to arrive by Thursday afternoon for weekend stays in order to snag a coveted site in the park. Visitors seeking accommodations

---

Previous: stunning views from the Mastodon Mine; Noah Purifoy Outdoor Desert Art Museum. **Above:** orange Mojave mound cactus flowers.

Look for ★ to find recommended sights, activities, dining, and lodging.

Highlights

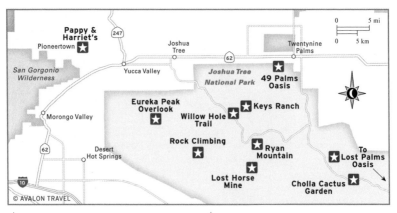

★ **Eureka Peak Overlook:** While everyone crowds the popular Key's View overlook, this lightly visited peak offers equally spectacular views (page 104).

★ **Keys Ranch:** Take a ranger-guided tour of the ranch house, buildings, and grounds owned by one of Joshua Tree's most colorful characters (page 105).

★ **Cholla Cactus Garden:** A brigade of fuzzy, multihued cacti stretch out to form this surreal desert garden (page 108).

★ **Ryan Mountain:** A vigorous hike leads to panoramic views of the Pinto Basin, Hidden Valley, and the Wonderland of Rocks (page 115).

★ **Lost Horse Mine:** Follow an old mining road to this well-preserved stamp mill with rock house ruins and stunning views toward the Queen Valley (page 115).

★ **Willow Hole Trail:** This easy trek delves into the heart of the wildly eroded Wonderland of Rocks (page 117).

★ **49 Palms Oasis:** Hike to this mirage-like fan palm oasis (page 121).

★ **Lost Palms Oasis:** From lush Cottonwood Spring, this trail crosses desert ridges to a secluded oasis of fan palms with detours to mine ruins and panoramic views (page 124).

★ **Rock Climbing:** The park's boulder-strewn oasis makes it a world-class destination for rock climbers (page 125).

★ **Pappy & Harriet's:** Built as part of a Wild West film set, this historic restaurant and saloon serves up excellent barbecue and live music (page 136).

Joshua Tree and the Yucca Valley

© AVALON TRAVEL

SEE "YUCCA VALLEY" MAP

SEE "HIDDEN VALLEY" MAP

Twentynine Palms Marine Corps Base

Rimrock

Pioneertown

PAPPY & HARRIET'S

Yucca Valley

Morongo Valley

Desert Hot Springs

Palm Springs

Cathedral City

Rancho Mirage

PALM SPRINGS INTERNATIONAL AIRPORT

Palm Desert

Indian Wells

La Quinta

Coachella

Indio

Coachella Valley Preserve

Sky Valley

Joshua Tree

BLACK ROCK NATURE CENTER

EUREKA PEAK OVERLOOK

WEST ENTRANCE STATION

WILLOW HOLE TRAIL

JOSHUA TREE VISITOR CENTER

PARK BLVD

KEYS VIEW

Hidden Valley

INDIAN COVE

KEYS RANCH

RYAN MOUNTAIN

NORTH ENTRANCE STATION

DESERT QUEEN MINE

29 PALMS OASIS

Twentynine Palms

Cleghorn Lakes Wilderness

LOST HORSE MINE

GEOLOGY TOUR RD

Little San Bernardino Mountains

CHOLLA CACTUS GARDEN

Cottonwood Canyon

COTTONWOOD VISITOR CENTER

Cottonwood Spring

SOUTH ENTRANCE STATION

LOST PALMS OASIS

PINTO BASIN RD

OLD DALE RD

BLACK EAGLE MINE RD

Eagle Mountains

Joshua Tree National Park

Mecca Hills Wilderness

Desert Center

Sheephole Valley Wilderness

0   10 km
0   10 mi

Joshua Tree in One Day

Even with limited time, it's still possible to soak in many of the parks' sights and wonders. Start in the **Indian Cove** area with an invigorating and scenic hike to the **49 Palms Oasis** (3 miles) for your first taste of the hidden wonders Joshua Tree National Park has in store. The two-hour hike winds up a rocky canyon with views of the town of Twentynine Palms before emerging above a natural palms oasis tucked into the craggy hills.

After the hike, drive east on Highway 62, making your way to the park's less-crowded **North Entrance.** Stop by the **Oasis Visitors Center** for a great selection of books, maps, and information, then head southeast on Park Boulevard to make a loop through the park from east to west. From here on out, it's all about the journey as you marvel at the passing landscape.

On Park Boulevard, drive 10 miles west (20 minutes) to the **Queen Valley,** an excellent destination thanks to its boulder-strewn and Joshua tree-filled landscape and history. A series of networked hiking trails lead to ranching sites, mining remains, and the site of Native American settlements. The trail to the **Wall Street Mill** (3 miles round-trip, 1.5 hours) leads to a well-preserved ore-processing mill dating from the 1930s, while the remains of the **Desert Queen Mine** (1-3 miles, 0.5 hour) clings to the steep side of Desert Queen Wash. The **Lucky Boy Vista** loop (3.6 miles, 2 hours) traverses an ancient Native American village with views of Hidden Valley. **Barker Dam** (1.3 miles, 0.5 hour) is a popular nature trail leading to the edge of the Wonderland of Rocks and a ranch-era dam created on the site of a Native American settlement. Bring your lunch and picnic at nearby Split Rock or Live Oak picnic areas.

Cap off your time wandering the canyons with a perspective-building drive to popular **Keys View.** This scenic overlook gives sweeping panoramas of the park's southwest, taking in the Santa Rosa Mountains, San Andreas fault, Palm Springs, San Jacinto Peak, and San Gorgonio Peak. The paved observation point is wheelchair-accessible.

For a last hurrah, meander your way northwest along **Park Boulevard** toward the **West Entrance,** passing through the impressive rock formations of the **Hidden Valley** on your way; plan one hour for the drive.

with luxuries such as running water should book a room at one of the multiple lodging options in the towns surrounding the park entrances—**Yucca Valley, Joshua Tree,** and **Twentynine Palms.**

You'll need a **car,** a full tank of gas, and plenty of patience driving the long distances both on the park roads and between the desert towns. Bring all the **water** you'll need to drink, clean with, or bathe in (at least two gallons per day of drinking water), as there are no services inside the park.

Joshua Tree National Park

Joshua Tree National Park (www.nps.gov/jotr, open daily year-round, $20 per vehicle, $10 per motorcycle, bike, or on foot) is famous for its large stands of Joshua trees, scenic desert landscape. Wildly eroded rocks make the park a world-class rock climbing destination. Most visitors spend their time on the west side of the park where the only paved road access (Park Boulevard) exists.

From the West Entrance near the town of Joshua Tree, Park Boulevard delves deep into the Hidden Valley (the most popular section of the park filled with trailheads and campgrounds) to emerge in the town of Twentynine Palms. While the Black Rock Canyon area and Indian Cove offer developed (and reservable) campgrounds, their access does not extend farther into the park. At the South

Entrance, Cottonwood Spring offers a less-visited glimpse of the park's Colorado Desert geography.

VISITORS CENTERS

Joshua Tree Visitors Center

The **Joshua Tree Visitors Center** (6554 Park Blvd., Joshua Tree, 760/366-1855, 8am-5pm daily) is in the town of Joshua Tree on Park Boulevard before the western park entrance. This fully staffed visitors center offers a well-stocked bookstore with travel guides, nature guides, maps, and gifts. There are restrooms and a café. The **Park Rock Café** (760/366-8200, 8am-5pm daily) is right next door and serves sandwiches, soups, salads, espresso, beer, wine, smoothies, and boxed lunches for dining in or as takeout.

Black Rock Nature Center

The **Black Rock Nature Center** (9800 Black Rock Canyon Rd., Yucca Valley, 760/367-3001, 8am-4pm Sat.-Thurs., 8am-8pm Fri. Oct.-May) is a small visitors center used primarily as a check-in for campers heading to the Black Rock Canyon Campground and other visitors to the Black Rock Canyon area. Several trails lead from here including ones to Warren Peak

and the Panorama Loop through the Little San Bernardino Mountains. The ranger-staffed center has maps, books, and nature guides for purchase. Park entrance fees may also be paid here.

Oasis Visitors Center

Oasis Visitors Center (74485 National Park Dr., Twentynine Palms, 760/367-5500, 8:30am-5pm daily) is en route to the park's North Entrance in the gateway town of Twentynine Palms. The fully staffed visitors center offers a well-stocked bookstore with travel guides, nature guides, maps, and gifts. Water, restrooms with flush toilets, and picnic tables are also available. A short 0.5-mile interpretive trail from the visitors center leads to the Oasis of Mara, a historic fan palm oasis with a large standing pool originally settled by the Serrano Indians.

Cottonwood Visitors Center

Located at the remote south entrance to the park, the **Cottonwood Visitors Center** (Cottonwood Spring Rd., 8:30am-4pm daily) provides check-in for visitors entering through the more sparsely traveled south entrance. The fully staffed visitors center offers a bookstore with travel guides, nature guides,

The Oasis Visitors Center welcomes visitors in the town of Twentynine Palms.

maps, and gifts. Water, restrooms with flush toilets, and picnic tables are also available. A short botanical garden interpretive loop leaves from the visitors center. The visitors center is convenient to the Cottonwood Campground as well as Cottonwood Spring and the Hidden Palms Oasis hiking trail.

Twentynine Palms Visitors Center

Located en route to the North Entrance, the **Twentynine Palms Visitors Center and Gallery** (6847 Adobe Rd., Twentynine Palms, 760/361-1805, 10am-4pm daily fall-spring, 9am-3pm Mon.-Fri., 9am-2pm Sat.-Sun. in summer) welcomes you to the gateway town of Twentynine Palms and Joshua Tree National Park. The visitors center and gallery features maps, brochures, local books, Wi-Fi, a gift shop, electric car charging station, a community art gallery, and the Twentynine Palms Chamber of Commerce.

ENTRANCE STATIONS

There are three main entrances into the park:

The **West Entrance** (5 miles south of Hwy. 62 and Park Blvd.) is accessed from the gateway town of Joshua Tree and sees the heaviest volume of visitors. Lines can be long on busy weekends. Visitors to the park go through a ranger-staffed entrance kiosk to pay entrance fees ($20, $30 annual pass), while season pass-holders are often offered a shorter line. Restrooms are available.

The **North Entrance** (3 miles south of Hwy. 62 and Utah Trail) is located in the gateway town of Twentynine Palms and sees slightly less traffic and shorter lines. Visitors pass through a ranger-staffed kiosk to pay entrance fees. Restrooms are available.

The **South Entrance** (off I-10, 25 miles east of Indio in the Coachella Valley) accesses Cottonwood Spring and sees the fewest visitors. There is no entrance kiosk; instead, visitors entering from the south should stop at the ranger station to pay fees and gather information. Restrooms and maps are available.

DRIVING TOURS

If you want to get off the pavement, Joshua Tree has several rugged backcountry roads that are best for four-wheel drive vehicles. There are also graded dirt roads that still offer scenery and some seclusion, but that can be navigated with most passenger cars. Note that the speed limit on park roads is 45 mph or lower.

Black Rock Canyon
COVINGTON FLATS
10.9 MILES

The series of dirt roads in **Covington Flats** gives access to the sweeping views from Eureka Peak, several hiking trails (including the Upper Covington Flats section of the California Riding and Hiking Trail), and some of the largest stands of Joshua trees, junipers, and piñon pines in the park. Covington Flats is situated between Black Rock Canyon and the town of Joshua Tree in the northwestern section of the park. Compared to other sections of the park, this area is lightly traveled and makes for some pleasant scenery-watching.

To access Covington Flats, take La Contenta Road south from Highway 62 in Yucca Valley. A 10.9-mile drive leads to Eureka Peak and spectacular views of Palm Springs, the Morongo Basin, and the San Jacinto Mountains. The Covington Flats area has signed intersections that make it easy to navigate; while there is occasional sand, the dirt roads are navigable by most cars despite some elevation gain near Eureka Peak. To reach **Eureka Peak** follow La Contenta Road south; the road quickly turns to dirt. After driving 7.8 miles, look for a signed intersection that directs you right toward Eureka Peak. As the road begins to climb, continue straight to a picnic area and the trailhead access in 0.9 mile. At 9.6 miles, another right turn takes you to a small parking area within a few hundred yards of the peak. A left turn here leads south to Upper Covington Flats and access to the **California Riding and Hiking Trail.**

Hidden Valley
QUEEN VALLEY
13.4 MILES

In **Queen Valley,** a series of short dirt roads totaling 13.4 miles connects **Barker Dam** with the **Pine City** backcountry area. Steeped in ranching lore and Native American history, the Queen Valley area also gives rise to thick stands of Joshua trees. The one-lane dirt roads (**Queen Valley Road, Bighorn Pass Road, and O'Dell Road**) are accessible to most vehicles, though the narrow roads might make it a tight squeeze for passing.

GEOLOGY TOUR ROAD
18 MILES

Geology Tour Road (passenger cars okay for the first 5 miles, then 4WD beyond) is a pleasant 18-mile backcountry drive that descends south into the broad Pleasant Valley and an ancient dry lake. Along the way it gives long views of the dramatic erosion and uplift that have formed Joshua Tree's unique geologic phenomena. Pick up a free interpretive pamphlet from the Joshua Tree Visitors Center, which details the route with 16 numbered points of interest. (They're also available from a small metal box at the start of the drive.)

Begin from a signed intersection on Park Boulevard about two miles west of **Jumbo Rocks Campground.** The dirt road knifes south into Pleasant Valley, situated between the Hexie Mountains and Little San Bernardino Mountains. Sights along the way include stark **Malapai Hill,** distinct for its black basalt formation, and Pleasant Valley, with its heavily oxidized rocks (called desert varnish) and the Blue Cut earthquake fault.

As stark as the landscape may seem, the drive will take you past places that saw human—not just geologic—action. **Squaw Tank** (Stop 9) was dammed with concrete by ranchers who were really just bolstering a watering source used by Native Americans in the area for centuries. **Pleasant Valley** (Stop 10) was once home to a periodic lake and cattle ranching operation when the area was wetter and full of grasses, again on the site of land historically used by indigenous groups. The steep Hexie Mountains are riddled with **mining shafts** (Stop 12) that date to the late 1800s and early 1900s.

The first five miles of graded dirt road to Squaw Tank are passable by most cars (no RVs) during dry weather. (During wet weather, don't go beyond Squaw Tank in any vehicle, as the road can become flooded or

views of Malapai Hill and Pleasant Valley from Geology Tour Road impassable.) Beyond Squaw Tank, the road is labeled **four-wheel drive only** by the park service due to deep ruts, sand, and steep grades. There are some rough spots, but you may be able to handle the drive in a compact SUV, depending upon your backroad driving experience and the current road conditions. Past Squaw Tank the road completes a one-way loop clockwise along the Hexie Mountain foothills and through Pleasant Valley. From this point you're committed to the drive, a leisurely round-trip that can take up to **two hours**.

BERDOO CANYON ROAD (4WD) 15.4 MILES

Stemming from the southern tip of the Geology Tour Road, **Berdoo Canyon Road** continues 15.4 miles south to end beyond the park boundary at **Dillon Road** in the Coachella Valley. The unmaintained road heads through Pleasant Canyon and then navigates rugged Berdoo Canyon to the southern park boundary. Outside the park boundary, the final 3.9 miles of the road passes the remains of **Berdoo Camp,** established for builders of the California Aqueduct in the 1930s. Berdoo Canyon Road requires **high-clearance 4WD.**

Cottonwood Spring
OLD DALE ROAD (4WD) 23 MILES

The **Old Dale Road** begins at a signed intersection on Pinto Basin Road, 6.5 miles north of Cottonwood Visitors Center. This rugged, 23-mile unmaintained Jeep trail crosses the Pinto Basin for 11 miles, then crawls beyond the park boundary into the eastern hills of the Pinto Mountains and a nest of old mines that make up the **Old Dale Mining District.** (A number of side roads split off to these sites.) The Old Dale Mining District drew prospectors looking for gold from as early as 1881. At peak production in 1898, there were as many as 3,000 miners in the region. Production limped along on a small scale until 1939 and the outbreak

of World War II. Today the historic mining district is located on BLM land. The main road eventually spills north out onto Highway 62, 15 miles east of the town of Twentynine Palms.

BLACK EAGLE MINE ROAD (4WD) 9 MILES

The **Black Eagle Mine Road** shares its start with the Old Dale Road, off Pinto Basin Road 6.5 miles north of the Cottonwood Visitors Center. The road strikes east across the Pinto Basin and into the northwest Eagle Mountains where it ends at a barricade at the park boundary at just over nine miles. The road continues beyond the barricade on BLM land near several old mining sites.

SIGHTS
Black Rock Canyon

The Black Rock Canyon region is in the northwest corner of Joshua Tree with a campground and several great hikes as well as easy access to the shops and restaurants of the Yucca Valley. The Black Rock area is characterized by craggy rolling peaks and piñons, juniper, and oak trees, giving it a different feel from the more popular Hidden Valley section of Joshua Tree. Though the Black Rock Canyon area is located near the West Entrance, there is no direct access into the center of the park.

★ EUREKA PEAK OVERLOOK

At 5,521 feet **Eureka Peak Overlook** offers panoramic views of Joshua Tree and surrounding valleys. Not only are the views spectacular, Eureka Peak is way less crowded than the very popular Keys View, a paved, drive-up viewpoint in the middle of the heavily visited central section of the park. From the summit, the Coachella Valley, Desert Hot Springs, and the San Jacinto Mountains (including the often snowcapped San Jacinto Peak) lie to the southwest, while views to the north take in the Morongo Valley. Look east into the park and you'll glimpse into the Wonderland of Rocks.

Hidden Valley

Of course, there's a catch: Eureka Peak is not accessed via the park's main entrances. Instead, entry is via a graded dirt road from Yucca Valley (near the Black Rock Canyon Campground) that leads into Covington Flats, ending within a few hundred yards of the peak. It's also possible to hike to Eureka Peak via the trail from Covington Flats (8 miles round-trip) or the Black Rock Canyon Campground (10 miles round-trip).

From Highway 62 (29 Palms Highway) in the town of Yucca Valley, take La Contenta Road south. The road quickly becomes dirt and has some sandy places. In normal weather conditions, it should be passable for most two-wheel drive cars. At 7.8 miles, turn right toward Eureka Peak. At 9.6 miles, turn right again toward Eureka Peak (signed). At 10.9

miles, you will reach a small parking area a few hundred yards below the peak.

Hidden Valley

From the park's West Entrance in Joshua Tree, Park Boulevard travels 35 miles southeast making a loop with the North Entrance in Twentynine Palms. This paved stretch is the most popular region of the park, with access to Queen Valley, Hidden Valley, Quail Springs, the Wonderland of Rocks, as well as the majority of campgrounds and trailheads.

★ KEYS RANCH

Colorful homesteader, rancher, and miner Bill Keys was an industrious and resourceful pack rat who fashioned a homestead and a life in the isolated desert. From 1917 to 1969,

Wonderland of Rocks

he and his family carved out a desert domain that included a ranch house, a schoolhouse, a store, and a workshop. Today, visitors can tour the well-preserved ruins of the Desert Queen Ranch, now listed on the National Register of Historic Places.

From October through May, park rangers lead guided, 90-minute tours of **Keys Ranch** (by reservation only: call 760/367-5522 9am-4:30pm daily, $10 over age 12, $5 children age 6-11, children under 6 free) This popular tour guides you to a preserved historic homestead near the Hidden Valley Campground. The schedule varies, but tours are usually held once daily Friday-Sunday and offer your only peek at these historic remains. Tickets are also available at the Joshua Tree and Oasis Visitors Centers prior to the day of the tour.

WONDERLAND OF ROCKS

Dubbed the **Wonderland of Rocks**, for reasons which quickly become apparent, this region is characterized by a wildly eroded maze of striking granite rock formations studded with secret basins, gorgeous views, and history. The Wonderland of Rocks covers the area southeast of Indian Cove Campground and northeast of Hidden Valley Campground. Its compelling rock formations are visible to the east and north driving along Park Boulevard, the main park road. Indian Cove Campground and the parking area for the Barker Dam Nature Trail are the closest driving points into the belly of the beast. The area lures rock climbers and hikers. Four trails (Barker Dam Loop, Boy Scout Trail, Willow Hole, and Wonderland Wash) knife short distances into the Wonderland of Rocks. Rock climbing use trails are signed and established.

RYAN RANCH

Ryan Ranch was named after the Ryan brothers, Thomas and J. D. "Jep," who bought interest in the nearby Lost Horse Mine and set up camp at the Lost Horse Well at the base of Ryan Mountain. The homestead ruins date to 1896, but the region had been used by Native Americans prior to the mining era thanks to the availability of water in the area. A short 0.5-mile stroll leads to remains of the ranch and its adobe bunkhouse, windmill, and outbuildings. A deeper search of the area reveals a pioneer cemetery and evidence of Native American habitation, including grinding stones. This interpretive site is accessed from a pull-out on Park Boulevard, between the Ryan Mountain trailhead and the turnoff for Ryan Campground.

KEYS VIEW

Impressive views spill from the lip of windswept **Keys View,** an observation point in the Little San Bernardino Mountains. Take in a panorama that stretches to the Salton Sea, Santa Rosa Mountains, San Andreas fault, Palm Springs, San Jacinto Peak, and San Gorgonio Peak. The paved observation point is also wheelchair-accessible. Find it seven miles south of the Hidden Valley Campground, a 20-minute detour from Park Boulevard along Keys View Road.

QUEEN VALLEY

The **Queen Valley** is like a cross section of Joshua Tree's greatest hits with Joshua tree stands, mining ruins, Native American village sites, scenic hikes, and views! A series of short dirt roads crisscrosses the Queen Valley, chugging through one of the largest pockets of Joshua trees in the park. Mining ruins range from large gold operations, like the Desert Queen Mine, to way humbler affairs marked by the rusty remains of tent encampments. Evidence of Native American settlements dot the boulder-strewn landscape. Established hiking trails follow a series of old mining roads to the **Desert Queen Mine, Lucky Boy Vista,** and the **Wall Street Mine.** To reach the Queen Valley area, follow the unpaved Queen Valley Road or Desert Queen Mine Road east to their terminus at Pine City.

Cottonwood Spring

Located near the South Entrance to the park (off Pinto Basin Road, north of I-10), the Cottonwood region encompasses a visitors center, campground, and several hikes. **Cottonwood Spring** itself is a fan palm oasis named for a surprising crop of native cottonwood trees that are mixed into

JOSHUA TREE
JOSHUA TREE NATIONAL PARK

Eroded granite creates a dramatic landscape in the Wonderland of Rocks.

the luxuriant vegetation surrounding the spring. Cottonwood Spring has served as a vital water source for centuries with Native American settlement signs around to prove it. One example of how few and far between such water sources are in the desert: One ill-fated Matt Riley started off with a friend from the Dale Mining District intending to refill their small, shared canteen at the spring 25 miles away. Beaten down by the heat, the friend turned back and survived. Riley pressed on and died on July 4, 1905, within 200 yards of the spring. Your access is a lot easier today. Cottonwood Spring is located on a paved road past the Cottonwood Campground in the vicinity of the Cottonwood Visitors Center.

★ CHOLLA CACTUS GARDEN

Driving south through the endless landscape of the Pinto Basin, the **Cholla Cactus Garden** appears like an army of prickly planted teddy bears—their sheer numbers impress in this already surreal landscape. Though these cacti may look fuzzy, their multicolored arms are effective against predators. Urban legend-style photos show hapless visitors covered in cholla (aka jumping cactus), with segments that have attached themselves to those who got too close. You'll be fine if you keep your hands to yourself and use common sense. A small parking area allows visitors to stop and wander the 0.3-mile interpretive trail through a surreal crop of this strange flora. The trailhead for this nature walk is located 20 miles north of the Cottonwood Visitors Center on Pinto Basin Road.

HIKING

Joshua Tree offers fantastic hiking in an otherworldly landscape. The park has a range of hikes from easy nature trails to difficult cross-country adventures. Some of the longer trails lend themselves to backpacking (all backpackers overnighting in the backcountry must self-register for a free permit at any backcountry board).

Regardless of trail length, dehydration is the biggest factor while hiking in Joshua Tree. Always carry at least **two gallons of water per day per person,** especially during strenuous activities, and plan your hike to coincide with cooler times of the day, such as early morning or late afternoon.

Black Rock Canyon
HI-VIEW NATURE TRAIL
Distance: 1.3 miles round-trip

cholla cactus along Pinto Basin Road

Duration: 0.5 hour
Elevation gain: 320 feet
Effort: Easy
Trailhead: near Black Rock Campground
Directions: Immediately before the entrance to Black Rock Campground, turn right onto a dirt road and drive 0.8 mile to a parking area.

For such a short trail, you'll be rewarded with panoramic views and desert knowledge. To hike the trail, follow the gentle grade clockwise. Take in the sweeping views of the Yucca Valley to the northeast, **Black Rock Canyon** and campground to the south, and the San Bernardino Mountains to the west. See if you can spot the highest peak in the San Bernardino Mountains, snowcapped San Gorgonio Mountain at 11,503 feet.

The trailhead can also be reached from a spur trail connecting from the **Black Rock Ranger Station**, where interpretive brochures are available.

PANORAMA LOOP

Distance: 7.4 miles round-trip (8.6 miles round-trip to Warren Peak)
Duration: 4-5 hours
Elevation gain: 1,120 feet
Effort: Strenuous
Trailhead: Black Rock Canyon Backcountry Board or the southern end of the campground near site #30
Directions: Follow Black Rock Canyon Road 0.3 mile south of San Marino Road. Just before a split in the road, look for a small dirt parking area and the Black Rock Canyon Backcountry Board on the left, just past the campground entrance.

Hike this crown of peaks—five in all—and you'll be rewarded with sweeping views extending from the Salton Sea to Mount San Jacinto and the Yucca Valley. Starting from the well-marked trailhead, travel south along a sandy trail that can feel like walking on a desert beach. The trail splits at 0.3 mile; head right to follow a sign pointing toward **Black Rock Canyon.** For the next 0.5 mile, you'll hike Black Rock Wash through open desert and a Joshua tree forest framed by a serrated landscape of ridges and peaks. The trail is easy to follow, but splits into smaller washes and use trails at times. Pay attention to official trail markers (**PL** for Panorama Loop; **WP** for Warren Peak), as well as stone boundaries that mark the trail.

At just under two miles, you'll reach the base of the foothills and **Black Rock Spring.** The spring usually does not have standing pools, but the ground may be damp. Oaks and other vegetation are abundant here (a good sign of water) and the area can be swarmed

Enjoy continuous views from the Panorama Loop.

Black Rock Canyon

© AVALON TRAVEL

WARREN VIEW

Warren Peak
5109 feet

Warren Peak Tr.

Panorama Loop Tr.

Black Rock Canyon

Black Rock Canyon Tr.

Black Rock Spring

Panorama Loop Tr.

Burnt Hill Tr.

Black Rock Wash

BLACK ROCK CANYON

BLACK ROCK CANYON BACKCOUNTRY BOARD

California Riding and Hiking Tr.

Eureka Peak Tr.

Covington Road

Eureka Peak
5518 feet

EUREKA PEAK OVERLOOK

California Riding and Hiking Tr.

with flies, another giveaway. From Black Rock Spring, the trail narrows and cuts through the region's signature black rock formations.

At two miles the trail splits at a **signed intersection.** A straight left continues into the first loop entrance to hike the Panorama Loop clockwise, but we are going to follow the loop counterclockwise. (The trail can be hiked in either direction, but hiking it counterclockwise gives you a slightly gentler grade going uphill and a steeper hike downhill.) Stay right to reach the second loop entrance in 0.4 mile. From the **second intersection,** continuing straight (right) takes you to Warren Peak in 0.6 mile. (If you're up for it, I highly recommend this 1.2-mile round-trip detour to get the full eyeful and bragging rights. Six peaks in a day? Sure!) If you're only following the Panorama Loop, this will be a **left turn** at the intersection.

The three-mile Panorama Loop begins by climbing a steady grade through the foothills, following the remains of an old road. The grade tops out at a sharp ridge with spectacular views to the southeast across the Coachella Valley—you can see all the way to the Salton Sea on a clear day. Across the valley to the southwest are the impressive San Jacinto Mountains and Mount San Jacinto. At 5,154 feet, this ridge marks the highest point in the hike (including Warren Peak).

From here the trail continues to be one big reward as you wind your way along four more peaks on an open ridge that gives you an eyeful far across the Yucca Valley. Once you've made your way back down to the canyon floor (6.6 miles), turn right to follow the Black Rock Canyon wash the final two miles to the trailhead.

WARREN PEAK

Distance: 6 miles round-trip
Duration: 3-4 hours
Elevation gain: 1,070 feet
Effort: Strenuous
Trailhead: Black Rock Canyon Backcountry Board or from the southern end of the campground near site #30

Directions: Take Black Rock Canyon Road 0.3 mile south of San Marino Road. Just before a split in the road, look for a small dirt parking area and the Black Rock Canyon Backcountry Board on the left just past the campground entrance.

At 5,103 feet, Warren Peak is the 10th-highest peak in the park. Considering that the highest peak, Quail Mountain, clocks in only 713 feet higher at 5,814 feet, Warren Peak's ranking is more impressive than it might sound at first. The trail to Warren Peak manages to be a moderate hike with a huge view payoff.

Starting from the well-marked trailhead, follow the trail for the **Panorama Loop** (PL; see previous hike) to the second intersection where it junctions with the trail to Warren Peak (WP). Stay right to continue to **Warren Peak.** At the next intersection at 2.4 miles, stay straight (right). You're only 0.6 mile from Warren Peak, and it comes into clear view. The trail climbs steeply up to the knobby peak where you're rewarded with panoramic views—the San Jacinto Mountains, Coachella Valley, Yucca Valley, and toward Hidden Valley and the Wonderland of Rocks in the heart of Joshua Tree. When you're done basking in the views, return the way you came. A use trail exiting the peak dead-ends at a ridge; pay attention to where you entered the peak.

EUREKA PEAK

Distance: 10 miles round-trip
Duration: 4-5 hours
Elevation gain: 1,535 feet
Effort: Strenuous
Trailhead: Black Rock Canyon Campground
Directions: Take Black Rock Canyon Road 0.3 mile south of San Marino Road. Just before a split in the road, look for a small dirt parking area and the Black Rock Canyon Backcountry Board on the left just past the campground entrance.

You definitely need to be in an "it's all about the journey" mind-set to hike Eureka Peak. The journey is a pleasant one, leaving Black Rock Canyon to navigate a series of mountain canyons, finally arriving at Eureka Peak and its spectacular views of the San

Jacinto Mountains and the Coachella Valley extending to the Salton Sea. However, after you've huffed and puffed your way to the top, you may be disappointed to find that a perfectly good dirt road, navigable by most vehicles, stops less than 0.2 mile from the peak. The idea may dawn on you that you could have had those same spectacular views in a much easier way. The road is lightly traveled, and your chances of solitude on the peak are good no matter how you get there.

For hiking purposes, a network of trails spiderwebs out from Black Rock Canyon, giving you various routes for reaching Eureka Peak. Beginning from the Black Rock Canyon Backcountry Board, follow the **California Riding and Hiking Trail** (CA R&H) for the first two miles. It quickly leaves the wash to climb into the foothills. Ignore a trail split at 1.5 miles to stay left on the CA R&H, climbing to an upper valley. At 1.9 miles, a signed junction indicates the **Eureka Peak Trail** (EP). Turn right to head up the wash. Continue to follow the main wash as it narrows and climbs, ignoring another junction at 2.3 miles. Intermittent signposts for the next two miles indicate that you're on the right path. At 4.3 miles, the trail twists up to the peak, arriving at a ridge just below the

summit at 4.9 miles. Turn left for the 5,518-foot peak.

Retrace your steps when you're done basking in the views. It is also possible to turn the hike into a loop by taking **Covington Road** (the dirt road just south of the peak) to its intersection with the California Riding and Hiking Trail. You can follow the CA R&H trail the whole way back to the Black Rock Canyon Backcountry Board.

Hidden Valley

This is the most popular area of the park, as it includes access to Queen Valley, Hidden Valley, Quail Springs, and the Wonderland of Rocks. Expect filled parking lots and plenty of company on the trails.

BARKER DAM

Distance: 1.3 miles round-trip
Duration: 0.5 hour
Elevation gain: Negligible
Effort: Easy
Trailhead: Paved parking area and signed trailhead off of Hidden Valley Road

Located on the southern edge of the Wonderland of Rocks, the popular 1.3-mile loop trail winds through closely lined boulders to a small pond that can be dry at

Warren Peak is steeper than it looks.

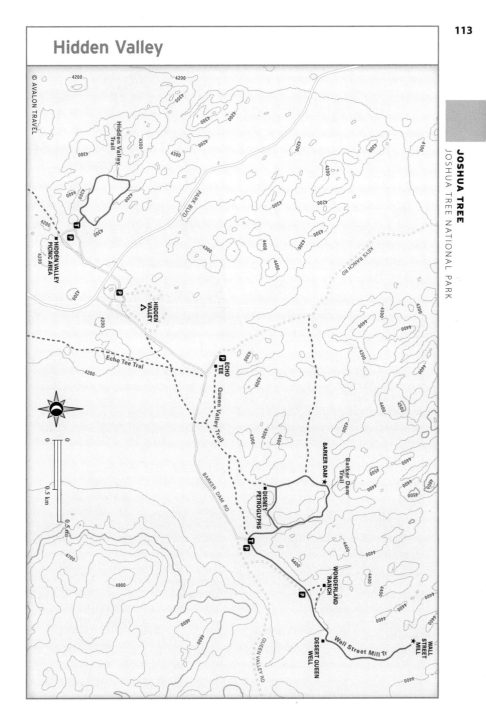

Hidden Valley

certain times of year. Ranchers dammed the natural pond for cattle, taking advantage of a site used by Native Americans for centuries. The trail is well-marked and easy to follow.

The watering hole is now a stop for migrating birds, bighorn sheep, and other wildlife. This area is also home to the **Disney petroglyphs.** During shooting for a film in the 1960s, a film crew painted over existing Native American petroglyphs to make them more dramatic for the shoot, possibly adding some of their own—a cultural travesty.

CAP ROCK

Distance: 0.4 mile round-trip
Duration: 0.5 hour
Elevation gain: Negligible
Effort: Easy
Trailhead: Parking area at intersection of Park Boulevard and Keys View Road

At first glance the Cap Rock nature trail seems like just another gorgeous destination—a flat, easy trail leads through whimsically eroded boulder formations, most notably a flat, cap-like rock balanced on top of a spectacular formation. But there are a few things that set this spot apart. First, it's **wheelchair-accessible.** The trail is wide, flat, and made of hard-packed sandy dirt. Second, although it may be hard to imagine with the paved parking area and interpretive signs, Cap Rock played backdrop to a rock-and-roll drama. In 1973, country rocker **Gram Parsons** died of a drug overdose at a motel in nearby Joshua Tree. His friends, trying to fulfill his wishes, brought his body out to Cap Rock and set it on fire so that he could be cremated in his beloved Joshua Tree. The site still attracts fans of the cult-famed rocker.

SKULL ROCK

Distance: 1.7 miles round-trip
Duration: 0.5-1 hour
Elevation gain: 157 feet
Effort: Easy
Trailhead: Parking for Skull Rock and the nature trail is located on Park Boulevard near the Jumbo Rocks Campground entrance. The trail begins to the right of

Anthropomorphic Skull Rock is a park landmark.

the landmark Skull Rock.

Skull Rock, anthropomorphically named for its gaunt eye socket-like depressions, is a popular rock formation along Park Boulevard. The concave hollows, called *tafoni*, originally began as small pits. Over time they cyclically filled with rainwater and eroded. After your photo op at the skull, follow the 1.7-mile nature trail as it winds through the scenic boulder and plant-strewn landscape. From the right side of the skull, the trail hooks over to **Jumbo Rocks Campground** passing interpretive signs on desert ecology along the way. Turn right when you reach the campground. The trail follows the campground road until it intersects with Park Boulevard. It crosses the road to wind back through more boulders with views of the surrounding desert before it completes the loop at Skull Rock.

ARCH ROCK NATURE TRAIL

Distance: 0.5 mile round-trip
Duration: 0.5 hour

Elevation gain: 30 feet

Effort: Easy

Trailhead: White Tank Campground across from site 9

The highlight of this trail is a delicately eroded arch, tucked into a boulder pile formation in the first third of the loop. The rest of the trail winds through **carved rock formations** to return to the starting point at **White Tank Campground.** Though the trail is short, several social trails split off from the official trail and can make it hard to follow. Pay attention to where you're going.

HIDDEN VALLEY

Distance: 1 mile round-trip

Duration: 0.5 hour

Elevation gain: 20 feet

Effort: Easy

Trailhead: Hidden Valley Campground and picnic area

This one-mile loop passes through granite boulders to emerge in scenic **Hidden Valley,** once wetter, grassier, and used for cattle grazing during the ranching halcyon of the early-mid 1900s. The well-signed trail circles the small, enclosed valley, delving into the monzogranite **boulder piles** with tempting bouldering opportunities.

★ RYAN MOUNTAIN

Distance: 3 miles round-trip

Duration: 1.5 hours

Elevation gain: 1,070 feet

Effort: Moderate

Trailhead: Signed parking area on Park Boulevard east of Ryan Campground

Although only three miles round-trip, this trail climbs a little more than 1,000 feet in elevation over its 1.5-mile ascent to the summit. Hikers are rewarded with panoramic views from the 5,457-foot wind-scoured vantage point where a **giant cairn** marks the peak. Soak in views of Pinto Basin, Hidden Valley, Wonderland of Rocks, and a bird's-eye view of Ryan Ranch and the Lost Horse Well. This is one of the **most popular hikes in the park.** While it's short on solitude, it's long on vistas.

★ LOST HORSE MINE

Distance: 4-7.4 miles round-trip

Duration: 2-4 hours

Elevation gain: 450-570 feet

Effort: Moderate to strenuous (very steep, rocky grades climbing Lost Horse Mountain)

Trailhead: Far end of the dirt parking area at the end of Lost Horse Mine Road

Directions: From Park Boulevard take Keys View Road south for 2.4 miles. Turn left onto the signed Lost Horse Mine Road and follow it for 0.9 mile to the parking area.

One of the **best preserved mining sites** in Joshua Tree National Park, the beautifully weathered stamp mill at the Lost Horse Mine was in operation from 1894 to 1931. The mill's breadth and sturdy construction are a testament to the mine's success as one of the highest producing in Joshua Tree history. The first person to file a claim was Johnny Lang of local lore who, in Wild West campfire tale fashion,

Lost Horse Mine

had recently had his horses stolen by a gang of local cattle rustlers. The mill and surrounding ruins (look for rock house foundations, equipment, and mining tunnels) are the highlight of the out-and-back hike, but the loop offers more surprises and history.

The signed loop trail is located in the middle of the parking lot and directs hikers counterclockwise. The trail climbs (gradually then steeper at 2.5 miles) around the flank of stark **Lost Horse Mountain** through a mix of Joshua trees, yucca, and juniper, following an old mining road. On the way it crosses paths with the **Optimist Mine;** only a picturesque stone chimney and scattered artifacts remain. Beyond these ruins the trail climbs precipitously, giving way to sweeping views toward the northeast, Wonderland of Rocks and Queen Valley. At 4.7 miles the rocky trail hits the ridge below the Lost Horse Mountain Summit, and the **Lost Horse Mine** comes into view below. Take time to check

out the area. Although the mill and tunnels are fenced off, remains of rock houses and artifacts make this an interesting place to explore. You've done the hard work—the way back is mostly downhill with pleasant views looking toward the Lost Horse Valley. Keep an eye out for additional rock structure remains and mining artifacts.

QUAIL SPRINGS TRAIL

Distance: 6 miles round-trip
Duration: 3 hours
Elevation gain: 243 feet
Effort: Moderate
Trailhead: Quail Springs Basin Picnic area; look for an unmarked, eroded trail on the west side of the paved parking area.

Quail Springs Historic Trail, as it is named on some topo maps, strikes out through peaceful open desert, intersecting with historic routes like the Johnny Lang Canyon (original claim-holder for the Lost Horse Mine) and connecting with a network of trails that extend to the west park entrance. It is also used to access **Quail Mountain,** the highest peak in Joshua Tree National Park at 5,814 feet.

The first three miles of the trail to the base of Quail Mountain are peaceful and open, crossing what looks like a grassy plain that doesn't necessarily fit into our ideas of boulder-strewn Joshua Tree. The silvery husks of downed Joshua trees, burned in a fire, further add to the prehistoric savanna feel. The silence is punctuated by the occasional sound of a bird or a car along Park Boulevard, the main road within distant sight for most of the hike and making this place feel that much more secret.

From the picnic area the trail is clearly defined. One mile in, the route splits with **Quail Springs wash,** and footprints are visible in both forks. Although the wash (right) will take you in generally the same direction as the trail (due west), the going is easier on the trail. Take the left fork to continue. At 2 miles, the trail crosses the access route to **Johnny Lang Canyon** veering off to the south (left). Continue straight.

At 2.9 miles you will reach signs indicating that the area used to be **private property.**

An out-of-place weathered parking curb as well as sun-silvered timber and metal odds and ends are strewn about. A pile of boulders a few hundred yards to the north marks the site of the 1920s **homestead of John Samuelson,** a Swedish immigrant who was ultimately denied his homestead claim in 1928 by the U.S. land office because of his Swedish heritage. His house burned down in the 1930s.

This is a good turnaround point or you can continue to Quail Mountain or to eventually intersect with Park Boulevard near the West Entrance. (Note: To continue along the Quail Springs Trail requires maps, planning, and possibly a car shuttle at the other end.)

★ WILLOW HOLE TRAIL

Distance: 7 miles round-trip
Duration: 3-4 hours
Elevation gain: Negligible
Effort: Moderate
Trailhead: Parking area for Boy Scout Trail

The Willow Hole Trail strikes into the heart of the Wonderland of Rocks. The flat, sandy track and lack of elevation gain mean that your main job is to admire the spectacular scenery. At 1.2 miles the trail splits at a signed intersection. The left fork continues as the **Boy Scout Trail,** ending at the **Indian Cove**

The Willow Hole Trail cuts into the Wonderland of Rocks.

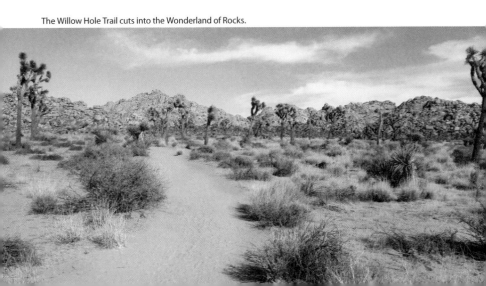

Campground in another 6.4 miles. Most people hike the Boy Scout Trail as a shuttle hike with a car at either end. To continue on the **Willow Hole Trail,** stay to the right. The trail officially ends unceremoniously in 3.5 miles, in a sandy, boulder-filled wash at so-named **Willow Hole.** As you may have guessed, Willow Hole itself is marked by a stand of willow trees. Depending on seasonal rains, the area can be filled with ephemeral pools of water.

PINE CITY SITE

Distance: 3 miles round-trip to Pine City; 4 miles round-trip to overlook of Pine Canyon
Duration: 2 hours
Elevation gain: 150 feet
Effort: Moderate
Trailhead: Parking area for Desert Queen Mine

The word "site" not "city" is the operative word here. Pine City is long gone, marked by piñons and a few scattered mining tunnels. The highlights of this hike are the easy, open trail winding through classic Mojave Desert flora, picturesque boulders, and its location off the beaten path of Park Boulevard.

The trail starts at the end of the graded, dirt Queen Valley Road, and although the trailhead is less than a mile from Park Boulevard, it offers more **solitude** than some of the more popular nearby hikes. The trail gains slight elevation as it heads toward the **Pine City site** (1.5 miles) or the **Pine Canyon overlook** (2 miles). The slight elevation makes this an easy desert trek but also gives rise to shifts in desert vegetation along the way. Hearty desert creosote gives way to yuccas and Joshua trees and eventually junipers and piñons. Cholla and barrel cactus also spike the landscape. At 1.3 miles you'll see your first pine trees interspersed in a picturesque bay of stacked monzonite boulders. The "city" itself is also marked by these pines at 1.5 miles. Here the trail splits slightly with the left (main) fork continuing another 0.5 mile to an overlook on the edge of Pine Canyon. The trail down into the canyon is unmaintained beyond the overlook. The right fork continues the extra few hundred yards to Pine City proper.

WALL STREET MILL

Distance: 3 miles round-trip
Duration: 1.5 hours
Elevation gain: 23 feet
Effort: Easy
Trailhead: Barker Dam parking area; the trailhead for the Wall Street Mill is clearly signed.

When local rancher **Bill Keys** wanted to build a mill for processing ores from local mines, he scrounged an existing one and relocated it, tapping into the time-honored desert tradition of moving defunct mining cabins and structures to new, profitable locations. The mill was originally located at Pinyon Well and had been in operation since 1891. Keys rebuilt the mill and used it from 1932 to 1942 to mill ore for different miners in the area. The mill was used briefly in 1949 and again as late as 1966. When Keys died, the National Park Service took over the mill site and has done an excellent job of preserving it. In addition to the mill, you'll find **abandoned cars** and other equipment and **artifacts.** The site also used to house a bunkhouse, now gone.

To get to the mill, begin at the marked trailhead for the Wall Street Mill in the Barker Dam parking area. The trail veers east, clearly marked with stone trail boundaries and occasional arrows. In 0.3 mile the trail hits a second, smaller parking lot then picks up again on the left. At 0.5 mile an unexpected psychedelic pink marks the remains of the **Wonderland Ranch,** tempting exploration. A short side trip will lead you to the foundations, crumbling walls, and scattered artifacts of the ranch.

Another historic bonus awaits in the form of the **Desert Queen Well** ruins one mile into the hike. A tall windmill, once used to pump water, still stands over piles of weathered timbers and an old tank.

The **Wall Street Mill** is definitely the highlight. Leave time to admire the well and poke around the area.

LUCKY BOY VISTA

Distance: 3.6 miles round-trip
Duration: 2 hours
Elevation gain: 150 feet
Effort: Moderate
Trailhead: Pine City/Desert Queen Mine parking area. Trailhead is unsigned at the south end of the parking area (on the right just past parking entrance).

What makes the Lucky Boy Vista such a nice hike is its combination of views, Native American history, mining history, solitude, and the pleasant walk through boulder-strewn desert piñon and yucca gardens. Heads up: there are a number of use trails, old mining roads, and washes crossing this area near the Desert Queen Mine, so it is easy to veer off your route if you're not paying attention; carry a map and compass and know how to use them.

Start from the Pine City/Desert Queen Mine parking area. The sandy trail is clearly defined but unmarked. It starts by heading south then curves through a series of washes lined with striking stacked rock formations. Look for signs of the Native American village that once inhabited this site in the form of a pair of *morteros* along this stretch. At 0.8 mile, the trail forks. The left (north) trail heads toward the Desert Queen Mine and Wash. Rock scrambling is required. To reach the Lucky Boy Vista, turn right (south) and follow the trail. Follow the trail to continue to head south/southeast over the next mile. You will pass through a **gate**, a holdover from the era of mines and private property. Beyond the gate, the trail forks and begins to climb slightly. Take the left fork to follow the old mining road. The **Elton Mine site** is easily identifiable from its shuttered mining tunnels at about 1.5 miles. The trail continues past the mine site to pause on a lofty plateau with views of Split Rock—the **Lucky Boy Vista.** Follow the return trail.

At 2.6 miles the trail forks at an easy-to-miss **No Camping post.** Stay straight (west) to complete the loop. Turning right will take you back to where you started the trail. At 3.1 miles you will reach the **Desert Queen Mine**

Road. Turn right for the last half of a mile to complete the loop.

DESERT QUEEN MINE AND WASH

Distance: 1-7 miles round-trip
Duration: 1-5 hours
Elevation gain: 160-660 feet
Effort: Easy to strenuous
Trailhead: Pine City/Desert Queen Mine parking area

This steep, rugged wash in the Queen Valley saw a lot of mining action from the 1890s until the 1960s. A short trek to the Desert Queen Mine reveals the rust-varnished equipment, mining tunnels, and massive tailings of a successful California gold mine. Continuing down the wash turns up more scattered mining debris and, eventually, scant remains of other, meaner mining camps, never as rich as the Desert Queen, hinting at a harsh life for miners scraping out a living.

To reach the Desert Queen Mine, take the **unsigned trail** from the Pine City parking area. At 0.3 mile you will see the picturesque remains of a **miner's stone cabin** on your right. Continuing straight, you will soon reach an overlook. This is a great stop or a destination. From the overlook you can see across the wash to the mines on the hillside and the old road snaking along the rocky embankment. Tailings, the huge piles of silvery rock excavated from the mining tunnels, are mounded, monuments to mining, on the wash floor.

To get a closer look at the **Desert Queen Mine's** equipment and tunnels, backtrack to the stone house and follow the road down into the wash, then back up to the mining site.

If this didn't satisfy your itch for exploration, a rugged hike through the wash brings you to a much smaller mining site. From the top of the Desert Queen Mine, return to the wash and turn right (north) to continue exploring the wash. After a few hundred yards, the canyon jogs and the hike trends generally east. The sandy-floored canyon is wild and scenic with steep walls, clusters of boulders, and scattered mining

Desert Queen Mine

debris, testament to the power of desert floods. **Two boulder jams** block your way, but they are passable by use trails. After the second boulder jam, the wash widens and you'll see tailings from the **Gold Hill Mine.** The miners' small tent community of John's Camp was located on a long, low shelf on the right side three miles from your starting point in the wash below the Desert Queen Mine. Return the way you came.

BOY SCOUT TRAIL

Distance: 8 miles one-way (arrange a car shuttle at one end)

Duration: 4-5 hours

Elevation gain: 1,265 feet (mostly downhill)

Effort: Moderate

South Trailhead: South Keys West Backcountry Board 0.7 mile east of the Quail Springs picnic area

North Trailhead: Indian Cove Backcountry Board, near the Indian Cove Ranger Station

This scenic eight-mile trail skirts the western edge of the Wonderland of Rocks before it winds through sharp mountains and rocky canyons to end in open desert at the Indian Cove backcountry board. With the shifting landscape and elevation along the Boy Scout Trail, the plant zones transition so that you have the chance to move through classic Joshua tree forest and mesquite, piñon, and oak at the higher elevations, yucca and boulder gardens, and creosote and cholla at the lower altitudes. This hike is the **most popular overnight backpacking hike** in the park. The Wonderland of Rocks to the east is a day-use area only: campsites must be west of the Boy Scout Trail. Sections of the trail are indistinguishable or unmarked, especially through washes. Carry a topo map.

From here the trail begins as a pleasant stroll through Joshua tree forest along a well-defined sandy track leading along the western edge of the Wonderland of Rocks. At 1.3 miles the trail splits with the **Willow Hole Trail.** Follow the signed junction to the left.

From here the trail climbs slightly before leveling on a high plateau, and the vegetation transforms with piñon, juniper, oak, and cholla cactus. At 3.8 miles the trail continues into an open wash marked by a **signpost.** For the next half a mile the trail can be hard to follow through a series of washes. You'll pass a split with the **Big Pine Trail** on your left at 4 miles. Beyond the split, look out for an old cement cattle trough as a landmark.

The trail exits the wash on the left at 4.4 miles and winds to the head of a deep canyon with austere desert views. From here the trail descends steeply to the canyon floor then heads right into the wash. Follow the rugged canyon for a mile, heading northeast. Yucca and barrel cactus line your way.

Exit the canyon at 6.2 miles, bearing right at a signpost. The trail spills into an open *bajada*. The final leg of the trail crosses open desert to end at the **Indian Cove** backcountry board.

Indian Cove
★ 49 PALMS OASIS
Distance: 3 miles round-trip
Duration: 2-3 hours
Elevation gain: 360 feet
Effort: Moderate
Trailhead: The trailhead is accessed from a parking area at the end of Canyon Road, about 1.7 miles east of Indian Cove Road, off of Hwy. 62.

Directions: From Hwy. 62, turn right onto Canyon Road, signed for 49 Palms Oasis. (Note: It is only signed heading east.) A small animal hospital on Hwy. 62 is a good landmark. Follow Canyon Road (signed for 49 Palms Oasis) for 1.7 miles to the trailhead.

This natural oasis surrounded by **native fan palms** secluded in a rocky canyon is a striking destination. From the trailhead, the trail climbs up over a ridge and then winds down through arid hills. The trail is easy to follow, passing through a flinty landscape that gives no indication of its secret oasis until you are close. You'll see the oasis from a distance, nestled against the jagged hills, before you reach it. There are only 158 fan palm oases in North America, and five in Joshua Tree; this is clearly a special place, used historically by Cahuilla Indians and offering precious habitat for bighorn sheep, quail, and coyotes. Tread lightly in this fragile ecosystem.

CALIFORNIA RIDING AND HIKING TRAIL

The California Riding and Hiking Trail is a continuous **36-mile trail system** cutting across piñon and juniper forests, Joshua tree stands, and creosote-strewn lowlands in the main western section of the park. Long on views and solitude, this trail can be hiked as

the remains of the Desert Queen Mine

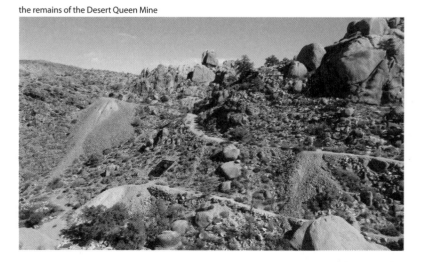

a **three-day backpacking trip** or broken into smaller day or overnight hikes. For backpacking, you will want to cache water. You must register at designated backcountry boards if you plan to stay out overnight.

There are **six main trailheads** anchoring **five trail sections.** For thru-hiking, the trail is best hiked west to east.

- Section 1: **Black Rock Canyon Trailhead to Upper Covington Flats.** Starting from the Black Rock Canyon Campground, this 7.5-mile section of the trail hooks through creosote lowlands before it climbs 1,000 feet, gaining the steepest elevation of the entire hike, to 5,130 feet. From here, the trail rolls downhill to Upper Covington Flats.

- Section 2: **Upper Covington Flats to Keys View.** This is the remotest section of the trail, and the trail here can be overgrown. Its 10.8 miles traverse a series of washes and ridges offering panoramic views before descending into the Joshua tree groves of Juniper Flats and then the Lost Horse Valley to end at Keys View trailhead. Nearby Ryan Campground also provides trail access on the eastern end of this section.

- Section 3: **Ryan Ranch to Geology Tour Road.** This 6.5-mile section of the trail veers close to the ruins of Ryan Ranch and the Lost Horse Well south of Ryan Mountain before climbing to the Geology Tour Road trailhead.

- Section 4: **Geology Tour Road.** From Geology Tour Road, the next section is the shortest, clocking in at 4.4 miles to end up at the Pinto Basin Trailhead (Twin Tanks parking between Belle and White Tank Campground). Its manageable distance and light elevation gain make it a candidate for a day hike. Views of Jumbo Rocks and the Pinto Basin make it worth the effort.

- Section 5: **Pinto Basin to North Entrance.** The final 7.3-mile stretch skirts Belle Campground and offers sweeping views of Twentynine Palms as it continues north to end just south of the north park entrance.

Cottonwood Spring
MASTODON PEAK

Distance: 3 miles round-trip
Duration: 1.5-2 hours
Elevation gain: 375 feet
Effort: Moderate
Trailhead: The trail begins at a nature trail a few

49 Palms Oasis

Cottonwood Spring

yards east of the Cottonwood Spring sign and staircase; campers follow a signed trail from the eastern end of Loop A.

Directions: From the Cottonwood Visitors Center continue 1.2 miles southeast on the Cottonwood Campground road until it dead-ends at Cottonwood Spring.

Mastodon's rocky peak crowns this loop hike and affords dramatic desert views stretching toward the Eagle Mountains, San Jacinto Mountains, and as far as the Salton Sea. On the way, the preserved remains of the Mastodon Mine add some historical spice to the trail. The peak was named by miners for its resemblance to the prehistoric creature. If you spend enough time in the desert sun, it's possible you'll start to see dubious shapes in the rocks too.

The Mastodon Peak loop is very well-signed and clearly established. It begins on a nature trail that leaves from the parking area and heads northwest to a junction at 0.5 mile.

Turn right (left leads to the campground) to continue toward the base of the foothills. Just past the junction, concrete foundations mark the site of the old **Winona Mill.** From the base of the mountains, the trail climbs toward the peak and remains of the **Mastodon Mine,** clinging to the hillside below the peak at 1.4 miles. From the mine there are sweeping views toward the west and the Cottonwood Mountains. George Hulsey operated the gold mine from 1919 to 1932. He was also responsible for building the Winona Mill, used to process ore from the Mastodon Mine and other claims to the north in the Dale Mining District. Continue the loop down the mountain. At the base of the hills the trail forks. To complete the loop, turn right. (A left turn will take you to the Lost Palms Oasis in approximately 3 miles.) The loop has a strong finish at scenic **Cottonwood Spring.** From the spring, follow the staircase up to the parking lot.

For a longer hike, combine a trip to the Lost Palms Oasis for a spectacular 9.5-mile trek.

★ LOST PALMS OASIS

Distance: 7.5 miles round-trip
Duration: 4-5 hours
Elevation gain: 460 feet
Effort: Moderate
Trailhead: The trail begins at a staircase leading down to Cottonwood Spring; campers follow a signed trail from the eastern end of Loop A.
Directions: From the Cottonwood Visitors Center continue 1.2 miles southeast on the Cottonwood Campground road until it dead-ends at Cottonwood Spring.

This trail undulates through striking desert scenery before dropping down to a secluded canyon and the largest collection of fan palms in the park.

The trail is straightforward, making a beeline to the southeast along a very well-marked and signed route. It starts from scenic **Cottonwood Spring** and ripples over an up-and-down landscape dominated by a series of ridges and washes. The trail is almost completely exposed, flanked by interesting desert gardens including barrel cacti, ocotillo, and desert willows.

The trail edges into the foothills of the Eagle Mountains before emerging to overlook a steep canyon and the Lost Palms Oasis, tucked on a rugged canyon hillside. The name makes sense in this remote place. The **Lost Palms Oasis** is a watering hole for bighorn sheep and other wildlife. A steep trail continues to the boulder and palm-strewn canyon floor. Shaded and peaceful, this is a great place to take a break before your return. If you're still feeling like exploring, continue to follow the trail down the canyon. One mile of picking your way and rock scrambling will bring you to another fan palm stand—the **Victory Palms.**

For a longer hike, add the loop to Mastodon Peak and the Mastodon Mine (adds two miles) for a total 9.5-mile hike.

BIKING

Biking within Joshua Tree National Park is confined to roads that are open to vehicles, but there are some good rides along the park's paved and backcountry roads. For road biking, **Park Boulevard** offers a great route through the park's most spectacular scenery. The paved road runs 25 miles from the West Entrance in Joshua Tree to the North Entrance in Twentynine Palms, with many opportunities for shorter stretches in

a steep trail into Lost Palms Oasis

Quail Springs is a popular place to watch climbers.

Tree, **Joshua Tree Bicycle Shop** (6416 Hallee Rd., Joshua Tree, 760/366-3377, www. joshuatreebicycleshop.com, 10am-6pm Mon.-Sat., $20 per hour, $65 per day) is a full-service bike shop that rents bikes and offers repairs and ride recommendations.

★ ROCK CLIMBING

Joshua Tree's unique desert landscape drives thousands of visitors a year to tackle its signature monzogranite boulders and striking rock formations. From rock stars to beginners, climbers of all levels are drawn to the park's traditional-style crack, slab, and steep-face climbing and its vast array of climbs. More than 400 climbing formations and more than 8,000 recognized climbs make it a world-class destination. When other climbing meccas like Yosemite are covered in winter snow and ice, climbers flock to the scene in "J-Tree" (as it's called by this adventure-driven subculture).

With so many tempting rocks everywhere, it's hard to go anywhere in the northwestern section of the park without seeing someone rock climbing, which is good not only for climbers but also for camp chair enthusiasts. Some good places to watch climbers in action are the **Quail Springs** picnic area, **Hidden Valley Campground**, the **Wonderland of Rocks, Cap Rock, Jumbo Rocks, Indian Cove, Ryan Campground, Split Rock,** and **Live Oak.**

To keep an ear to the ground about closed routes and any other climbing info, **Climber's Coffee** (Hidden Valley Campground, 8am-10am Sat.-Sun. mid-Oct.-Apr.) offers the opportunity to meet Joshua Tree's climbing ranger and share information with other climbers.

There are many great rock climbing guides sold in the park's visitors centers, as well as outfitters outside the park. Classic guides include *The Trad Guide to Joshua Tree* by Charlie and Diane Winger and a number of guides by rock climber and author Randy Vogel (*Rock Climbing Joshua Tree, Rock Climbing Joshua Tree West*). More recent books on the market include *Joshua Tree*

between. **Pinto Basin Road,** the other main park road, cuts through the Pinto Basin's open desert with scenery that's less rewarding than Park Boulevard, but also more lightly traveled. It runs 30 miles from its start four miles south of the North Entrance.

For mountain biking, the short series of dirt roads crossing the **Queen Valley** (the Hidden Valley area between Barker Dam and the Pine City backcountry board) totals 13.4 miles and offers scenic rides through large stands of Joshua trees. The **Geology Tour Road** stretches slightly downhill for its first 5.4 miles to Squaw Tank; beyond this, it loops six miles through Pleasant Valley. Be cautious as the road is sandy and rutted at points. Other backcountry roads, such as **Black Eagle** (9 miles one-way) and **Old Dale Road** (23 miles one-way), are possible for mountain biking, but sand can make either a difficult trek.

There are no bike rentals available in Joshua Tree National Park. Located near the West Entrance in the town of Joshua

Rock Climbs by Robert Miramontes and Bob Gaines' *Best Climbs Joshua Tree National Park.*

Outfitters

To get in on the action as a first-timer or experienced climber looking to hone your skills, you may want to take a group class or a private, guided climb through one of several outfitters in the area. **Joshua Tree Rock Climbing School** (760/366-4745, www.joshuatreerockclimbing.com) offers year-round rock climbing classes and private guided outings. **Cliffhanger Guides** (209/743-8363, www.cliffhangerguides. com) specializes in custom guided rock climbing adventures with half-day and full-day rates for up to 10 people. **Vertical Adventures** (800/514-8785, www.vertical-adventures.com) is available for one- to five-day courses, as well as private instruction and guided climbing in Joshua Tree National Park and Idyllwild's Tahquitz and Suicide Rocks. **Climbing Life Guides** (760/780-8868, www.joshuatreeclimbinglifeguides. com) are available for guiding rock climbing and technical climbing instruction for up to six people.

Gear

To gear up for your rock climbing (or other) adventures, check out one of the three outfits located on the main drag in Joshua Tree, close to the intersection of Park Boulevard and Highway 62.

Nomad Ventures (61795 Twentynine Palms Hwy., Joshua Tree, 760/366-4684, www.nomadventures.com, 8am-6pm Mon.-Thurs., 8am-8pm Fri.-Sun., summer hours vary) is the most extensively stocked of the Joshua Tree outfitters, with a huge selection of climbing gear, an assortment of camping and hiking gear, and a wide selection of guidebooks (including rock climbing guides).

Coyote Corner (6535 Park Blvd., Joshua Tree, 760/366-9683, www.joshuatreevillage. com, 9am-7pm daily) is eclectically stocked with gifts and gear ranging from T-shirts,

jewelry, novelty items, and books to camping, hiking, and rock climbing gear. The best part? Showers! For about $5, you can buy a hot shower, quite a bonus considering none of Joshua Tree's campgrounds have showers.

Joshua Tree Outfitters (61707 Twentynine Palms Hwy., Joshua Tree, 760/366-1848, 9am-5pm Thurs.-Tues.) mainly specializes in camping gear rentals, including tents, sleeping bags, coolers, camp stoves, water containers, and lanterns. They also rent rock climbing guides and bouldering pads and offer gear repair. Their retail space is sparsely stocked, but it has a few high-quality clothing items and miscellaneous gear, maps, and books.

HORSEBACK RIDING

With more than 250 miles of equestrian trails and trail corridors, horseback riding is a great way to experience Joshua Tree National Park if you bring your own horse. Two campgrounds offer equestrian camping with overnight areas for stock animals: **Ryan Campground** (760/367-5545, $15, no water), in centrally located Hidden Valley, and **Black Rock Canyon** (877/444-6777, www.recreation.gov, $20, water available) in Joshua Tree's northwest corner. Reservations are required.

Both campgrounds lie along the continuous 36-mile **California Riding and Hiking Trail** that extends through Joshua tree forests, washes, canyons, and open lands from northwestern Black Rock Canyon east to the North Entrance. Popular areas for equestrian users include trails near the West Entrance and Black Rock Canyon. Horse trail maps are available for download from the park website (www.nps.gov/jotr). Special **permits** (760/367-5545) are required for camping with stock in the backcountry.

If you're not bringing your own horse, **Joshua Tree Ranch** (760/366-5357, www. joshuatreevillage.com, $35 per hour pp) offers guided private and group trail rides from their ranch, located less than two miles from the park's West Entrance.

CAMPING

There are no accommodations inside the park boundaries. The closest lodgings are just outside the park in the gateway towns of Joshua Tree, Yucca Valley (both via the West Entrance), and Twentynine Palms (at the North Entrance).

Inside the Park

There are seven NPS campgrounds located within the park boundaries, two of which—**Black Rock Campground** and **Indian Cove Campground**—accept seasonal reservations October through May. The other five campgrounds are first-come, first-served year-round. Campgrounds in Joshua Tree start to fill up on Thursday mornings most weekends **October through May,** beginning with the more popular and centrally located campsites like Hidden Valley, Jumbo Rocks, and Ryan Campground, which have sites tucked in among Joshua Tree's famous boulders and Joshua trees. By Thursday evening, your options are limited. If you can't make it into the park by Thursday afternoon, and you don't have a reservation, better have a contingency plan. Fortunately, there is overflow camping and private camping available outside the park boundaries. In summer, all campgrounds are first-come, first-served.

Only three campgrounds—Black Rock, Indian Cove, and Cottonwood—have **drinking water.** Even if you are staying at one of these campgrounds, it is wise to bring at least two gallons of water (per person per day) with you into the park.

There are no RV hookups at any of the park campgrounds. Black Rock and Cottonwood Campgrounds have RV-accessible potable water and dump stations, and there are spaces that can accommodate trailers under 25 feet at Hidden Valley and White Tank Campgrounds.

BLACK ROCK CANYON CAMPGROUND

Black Rock Canyon Campground (99 sites, 877/444-6777, www.recreation.gov, $20) is in the northwest corner of Joshua Tree, just south of the town of Yucca Valley. Black Rock Canyon has a distinct geographic feel; instead of boulder jumbles, you'll find rolling hills dotted with Joshua trees and yuccas. This is a good campground for first-time visitors, as **drinking water** is available and the location offers easy access to Yucca Valley for supplies. This campground also offers limited equestrian sites (by reservation only), and trailer and RV sites with water fill-up and dump stations are also available. Campground amenities include drinking water, flush toilets, picnic tables, fire rings, and a small visitors center with maps and guides.

The road in dead-ends at the campground, and there is no driving access into the rest of the park. A series of hiking trails, including the short Hi-View Nature Trail, the view-filled Eureka Peak, Panorama Loop, and Warren Peak trails, leave from the campground and offer access into the park by foot. The trailhead for the 35-mile California Riding and Hiking Trail also starts at the campground.

Reservations are accepted online (www.recreation.gov) from October through May up to six months in advance. To get there from Highway 62 in Yucca Valley, turn south on Joshua Lane and drive five miles into the park.

HIDDEN VALLEY

Central **Hidden Valley** (44 sites, first-come, first-served year-round, $15) tends to be the most difficult campground to get a spot in. On the southern end of the Wonderland of Rocks, the campground is popular with rock climbers … and everyone else. Its sites are picturesquely set amidst Joshua Tree's signature boulders, and you are right in the heart of the park. The campground can accommodate trailers and RVs (under 25 feet), and amenities include vault toilets, fire rings, and picnic tables. There is **no drinking water.**

Reservations are not accepted. To reach Hidden Valley from the Joshua Tree Visitors Center on Highway 62, turn south onto Park Boulevard and continue 14 miles

Campgrounds At-a-Glance

	Location	Sites	Reservations	Amenities
Black Rock Canyon	Black Rock Canyon	99	accepted Oct.-May; first-come, first-served June-Sept.	tent, RV, and equestrian sites; drinking water, flush toilets, dump station
Hidden Valley	Hidden Valley	44	first-come, first-served year-round	tent and RV sites; vault toilets; no drinking water
Ryan	Hidden Valley	31	first-come, first-served year-round	tent and equestrian sites; vault toilets; no drinking water
Sheep Pass	Hidden Valley	6	required year-round	group tent sites; vault toilets; no drinking water
Jumbo Rocks	Hidden Valley	124	first-come, first-served year-round	tent and RV sites; vault toilets; no drinking water
Belle	Hidden Valley	18	first-come, first-served Oct.-May	tent sites; vault toilets; no drinking water
White Tank	Hidden Valley	15	first-come, first-served year-round	tent and RV sites; vault toilets; no drinking water
Indian Cove	Indian Cove	101	accepted Oct.-May; first-come, first-served June-Sept.	tent and RV sites; access to drinking water; vault toilets
Cottonwood	Cottonwood Spring	62	first-come, first-served year-round	tent, RV, and group sites; drinking water, flush toilets, dump station

to the intersection with Barker Dam Road. The campground will be to the left.

RYAN CAMPGROUND

Ryan Campground (31 sites, first-come, first-served year-round, $15) is a scenic campground centrally located between Hidden Valley and Jumbo Rocks with campsites interspersed among boulders and Joshua trees. The adjoining **Ryan Horse Camp** (760/367-5545, $15) offers four equestrian sites by reservation only from October through May. Amenities include vault toilets, fire rings, and picnic tables. There is **no drinking water.**

Reservations are not accepted. To reach Ryan Campground from the Joshua Tree Visitors Center on Highway 62, follow Park Boulevard south for 27 miles, passing the Hidden Valley Campground. Immediately past the Keys View Road turn-off, the campground will appear on the right.

SHEEP PASS GROUP CAMP

Towering rock formations and Joshua trees surround **Sheep Pass Group Camp** (6 sites, 877/444-6777, www.recreation.gov, $35-50), a tent-only group campground centrally located off of Park Boulevard in between Ryan and Jumbo Rocks Campgrounds. Amenities include vault toilets, fire rings, and picnic tables. There is **no drinking water.**

Reservations are required and can be made up to one year in advance. The campground is 18 miles south of the West Entrance and 16 miles south of the North Entrance.

JUMBO ROCKS

Jumbo Rocks (124 sites, first-come, first-served year-round, $15) is the largest campground in the park. Despite its size, sites fill up quickly thanks to a convenient location along Park Boulevard and access to plentiful rock climbing opportunities, as well as the Skull Rock Nature Trail. Popular sites are scenically tucked into the large rock formations for which the campground is named, but the sheer volume of sites leaves little privacy. This lends the place the feel of a small village, which may be good for families or groups. Amenities include vault toilets, fire rings, and picnic tables. There is **no drinking water.**

Reservations are not accepted. To reach Jumbo Rocks from the North Entrance in Twentynine Palms, follow Utah Trail south as it becomes Park Boulevard and continue southwest for eight miles. From the West Entrance in Joshua Tree, it is a drive of about 24 miles.

BELLE CAMPGROUND

Belle Campground (18 sites, first-come, first-served Oct.-May, $15) is a small, low-key campground with cozy sites tucked amid a pile of rock formations. Amenities include vault toilets, fire rings, and picnic tables. There is **no drinking water.**

Reservations are not accepted. To reach Belle from the North Entrance in Twentynine Palms, follow Utah Trail south as it becomes Park Boulevard and continue about 5 miles to the junction with Pinto Basin Road. Follow Pinto Basin Road 1.5 miles south, turning left onto Belle Campground Road.

WHITE TANK

The smallest campground in the park, **White Tank** (15 sites, first-come, first-served year-round, $15) is a laid-back campground with sites tucked in amid scattered rock formations. Sites can accommodate trailers and RVs (under 25 feet). Amenities include vault toilets, fire rings, and picnic tables. There is **no drinking water.**

Reservations are not accepted. White Tank is located just south of Belle Campground along Pinto Basin Road, about 7.4 miles south of the North Entrance.

INDIAN COVE

Indian Cove (101 sites, first-come, first-served June-Sept., $20) is one of two campgrounds in the park that **accepts reservations** (877/444-6777, www.recreation.gov, Oct.-May) *and* it has **drinking water available** at the ranger station just

Jumbo Rocks

two miles away. The sites are tucked into spectacular boulder formations and offer both group and RV (under 25 feet) camping options. Indian Cove sits on the northern edge of the Wonderland of Rocks and is popular with rock climbers; the north end of the popular Boy Scout Trail also begins here. Amenities include vault toilets, fire rings, and picnic tables, and access to drinking water.

The campground is located off Highway 62, between the towns of Joshua Tree and Twentynine Palms, and is accessed via Indian Cove Road South. The road dead-ends at the campground, so there is no vehicle access into the rest of the park. The nearest park entrance is the North Entrance in Twentynine Palms.

COTTONWOOD CAMPGROUND

The area around **Cottonwood Campground** (62 sites, first-come, first-served year-round, $20) is much more lightly visited than the Hidden Valley region, which makes finding a site here slightly less competitive. Still, you should plan to be here by Friday morning on weekends from October through May. The campsites are scattered across an open desert dotted with creosote.

Though there is little to divide them, the sites are nicely spaced and offer some privacy. The nearby Cottonwood Visitors Center is a fully stocked visitors center and bookstore, while hiking trails to scenic Lost Palms Oasis and Mastodon Peak depart directly from the campground. There are also trailer and RV sites with water fill-up and a dump station. The **Cottonwood Group Campground** (3 sites, 877/444-6777, www.recreation.gov, $35-40) provides tent-only sites by reservation. Amenities include flush toilets, fire rings, picnic tables, and **drinking water.**

Reservations are not accepted. Cottonwood Campground is located in the Pinto Basin at the South Entrance to the park. From I-10 south of the park, take Cottonwood Spring Road north for about 10 miles. At the Cottonwood Visitors Center, turn right onto Cottonwood Oasis Road and continue 7.5 miles to the campground on the left.

Outside the Park

Campgrounds in the park fill quickly October through May. Outside the park, options include backcountry camping on BLM land or at a privately owned RV park in Joshua Tree.

Cottonwood Campground

BLM CAMPING

Overflow camping is available on **Bureau of Land Management** (BLM, www.nps.gov/jotr) land both north and south of the park. Note that BLM camping includes no amenities (toilets, water, fire pits, or drinking water). Fires are allowed in self-contained metal fire pits (provide your own) in the overflow camping south of the park, but are not allowed on BLM camping north of the park. Bring your own firewood.

For camping **north of the park:** Drive four miles east of Park Boulevard on Highway 62 and turn left (north) on Sunfair Road. Continue two miles to Broadway, then turn right (east) on Broadway, where the pavement ends. Drive one mile to a one-lane, unmarked dirt road (Cascade) at a line of telephone poles running north and south. Turn left (north) onto Cascade, and drive 0.5-mile until you pass a single-lane, unmarked dirt road. Camping is allowed on the right (east) side of that road for 0.5-mile beginning with the unmarked dirt road.

For camping **south of the park:** Drive six miles south of the Cottonwood Visitors Center, passing the park boundary sign. Just beyond the aqueduct, turn right or left on the unmarked water district road. Camping is allowed south of the water district road west and east of the Cottonwood Road. South of I-10, Cottonwood Road turns into Box Canyon Road; camping is allowed south of I-10 on both the east and west sides of Box Canyon Road.

JOSHUA TREE

Joshua Tree Lake RV and Campground (2601 Sunfair Rd., Joshua Tree, 760/366-1213, www.joshuatreelake.com, first-come, first-served, $10 pp tent sites, $4 children 12 and under; $20-30 RV sites) is 14 miles north of the West Entrance. The property offers tent and RV camping on exposed desert. Sites include picnic tables and fire pits, and the campground has a small fishing lake, a camp store with firewood and basic supplies, RV hookups, hot showers, flush toilets, and a playground.

TRANSPORTATION AND SERVICES

The West Entrance to Joshua Tree National Park is located 40 miles north of Palm Springs (about an hour's drive) and 145 miles east of Los Angeles (plan 3-4 hours for the drive from LA). The North Entrance near Twentynine Palms is 16 miles further east along Highway 62. The South Entrance is located about 60 miles (one hour) east of Palm Springs along I-10 and 160 miles (four hours) east of Los Angeles. All roads and entrance stations are open year-round, weather permitting.

Car

For exploring Joshua Tree National Park, it is vital to **have your own vehicle;** there is no transportation available inside the park. To reach the **West Entrance** from I-10 near Palm Springs, head north on Highway 62 for about 30 miles to the town of Joshua Tree. Turn south on Park Boulevard and follow the road into the park. To reach the **North Entrance** near Twentynine Palms, continue east on Highway 62 for 16 more miles and turn south on Utah Trail. To reach the **South Entrance,** follow I-10 east for 60 miles to Cottonwood Spring Road and turn north.

Several major car rental agencies are available in Yucca Valley: **Enterprise** (57250 29 Palms Hwy., 760/369-0515, www.enterprise.com, 8am-6pm Mon.-Fri., 9am-noon Sat.), **Avis** (56309 29 Palms Hwy., 760/365-4723, 8am-4:30pm Mon.-Fri., 8am-1pm Sat.), and **Budget** (56307 29 Palms Hwy., 760/365-0560, www.avis.com, 8am-4:30pm Mon.-Fri., 8am-1pm Sat.).

Yucca Valley is also the best place to fuel up before entering the park. Within the park, there are frequent, free parking areas near sights and major trailheads.

Air

The closest airport is the **Palm Springs Airport** (PSP, 3400 E Tahquitz Canyon Way,

Palm Springs, 760/318-3800, www.palm-springsca.gov) served by 11 airlines. The major car rental carriers are located here, including Enterprise, Hertz, Dollar, and Alamo.

Services

Services are more conspicuous in their absence. There is no food available inside the park. There are good dining options in the gateway towns along the edge of the park, including Yucca Valley, Joshua Tree, and Twentynine Palms. There are also full, chain grocery stores in the towns of Twentynine Palms and Yucca Valley.

Water is not widely available within the park; bring at least two gallons per person per day with you. Within the park, water may be available at the West Entrance ($0.25 fee), the Black Rock Campground, the Indian Cove Ranger Station, the Oasis Visitors Center in Twentynine Palms, and Cottonwood Campground at the south end of the park.

There is limited cell service in the park. Emergency phones are located at the Indian Cove Ranger Station and at the Hidden Valley Campground. In the event of an emergency, dial 911 or call 909/383-5651.

Ranger Programs

Park rangers offer guided hikes, evening programs, and patio talks—many geared toward families—to connect you with Joshua Tree's geography and history. Locations, subject matter, and times vary seasonally. The ranger program schedule is available for download on the park website (www.nps.gov/jotr), or you can pick up a copy at any visitors center.

The Yucca Valley

Dotting the northern border of Joshua Tree National Park are several small towns and sights worthy of a visit in their own right. Creative and unusual works of outsider art here express the desert's remoteness and wild freedom, all of which is accompanied by a "desert rock" soundtrack composed of talented musicians performing nightly on stages across the scenic valley.

Orientation

The town of Yucca Valley, located 13 miles west of the park's main West Entrance, is the largest town in this area. Funky boutiques and vintage stores compete with the big box stores, grocery stores, and chain hotels for the character of the place. These reminders of 21st-century suburban living feel strangely out of place against the timeless beauty of the desert. However, if you need services, Yucca Valley will likely have what you need. Its proximity to Pappy & Harriet's make it a magnet for artists and musicians.

The town of Joshua Tree, seven miles to the east, is a small artsy outpost that welcomes visitors through the park's main West Entrance, which is located five miles south. A cluster of charming restaurants (and a saloon) as well as outfitters, gift shops, and hotels offer a picturesque getaway with a laid-back desert vibe.

Fifteen miles east of Joshua Tree, the town of Twentynine Palms is the most remote, giving passage to Joshua Tree National Park's North Entrance. The historic 29 Palms Inn anchors the tourism experience here. The small town is scattered across open desert. It's home to a military base and a few functional businesses, including inexpensive motels, a grocery store, and gas stations.

SIGHTS
The Integratron

George Van Tassel (1910-1978) held respectable jobs as an aeronautical engineer for Lockheed Douglas Aircraft and as a test pilot for Hughes Aviation, but arguably his real life's work was as an inventor and UFO advocate.

Van Tassel was the engineer behind **The Integratron** (2477 Belfield Blvd., Landers, 760/364-3126, www.integratron.com, $25-250 by appointment only), a spherical, all-wood dome originally intended as an electrostatic generator to promote cellular rejuvenation and time travel. An avowed alien contactee, Van Tassel claimed that extraterrestrials from Venus gave him the formula to build the structure. The building's ship-tight wood construction and dome shape imbued it with an amazing sound resonance.

The current owners of The Integratron haven't yet figured out how to tap into the structure's time travel aspects, but they are intent on rejuvenation (at least for the soul). The only way to visit The Integratron is by reserving a private or "pop-up" **sound bath** (by appointment only). Sound baths last one hour and include 25 minutes of crystal bowl harmonies followed by recorded music for relaxation and meditation. Reserving a sound bath also gives you access to the structure's grounds and a display about the history of The Integratron.

GIANT ROCK

Tens of thousands of people attended George Van Tassel's annual Spacecraft Conventions held at **Giant Rock** (three miles north of The Integratron), the largest freestanding boulder in the world coming in at seven stories high and covering 5,800 square feet of ground. The spiritually powerful place was a sacred Native American site and meeting place for local tribes until the 1900s.

Van Tassel used to hold weekly meditations in rooms underneath Giant Rock that had originally been dug by a local prospector. From the 1950s to the 1970s, Val Tassel used these meditations to try to attract UFOs. He was eventually successful (according to him) in 1953, when a saucer from the planet Venus landed and he was invited onto the ship and given the formula for The Integratron. Sadly, a visit to Giant Rock today shows a sad disrespect for nature and history: broken glass litters the ground and graffiti detracts from the impressive landmark.

GETTING THERE

The Integratron is located in Landers, north of the town of Yucca Valley. From the intersection of Highways 62 and 246 (Old Woman Springs Rd.), turn left onto Highway 247 and head north for 10.6 miles. Turn right (west) onto Reche Road and continue 2.3 miles. Turn left (north) onto Belfield Boulevard and continue 2 miles to The Integratron.

Noah Purifoy Outdoor Desert Art Museum

Artist Noah Purifoy (1917-2004) used found items to create assemblage sculpture that was dubbed "Junk Dada." The title feels dead-on. In the surreal **Noah Purifoy Outdoor Desert Art Museum** (63030 Blair Ln., Joshua Tree, www.noahpurifoy.com, sunrise-sunset daily, free but donations appreciated), metal, plywood, porcelain, paper, cotton, and glass are twisted and stacked into sculptures spread across 10 acres of an otherworldly artscape.

Born in 1917 in Snow Hill, Alabama, Purifoy was almost 40 when he received his BFA from Chouinard Art Institute (now California Institute of the Arts). He was the school's first full-time African American student. He spent much of his life in Los Angeles working in public policy and cofounding the Watts Towers Art Center. Using found objects to create sculpture, Purifoy devoted himself to art and social change to become a pivotal American artist.

Purifoy launched his career as a sculptor with his collection *66 Signs of Neon* (1966), assembled from the charred wreckage of debris he collected from the 1965 Watts Riots in Los Angeles. In the late 1980s, he moved to Joshua Tree full-time, creating large-scale art on the Mojave Desert floor.

The sculptures in this outdoor desert museum are whimsical, political and comical with broken pieces and discarded junk mended into recognizable shapes. Made

The Yucca Valley

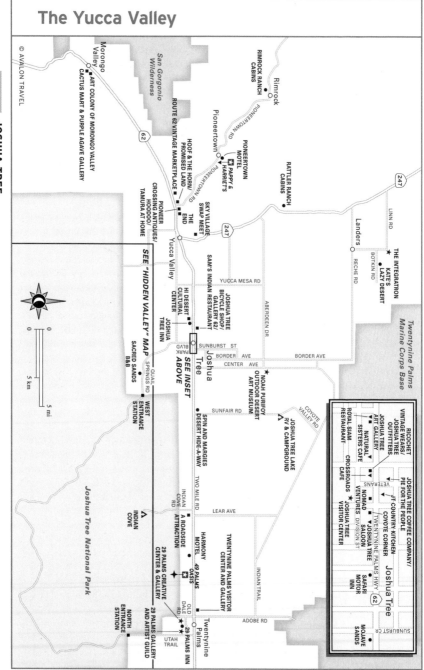

© AVALON TRAVEL

CACTUS MART & PURPLE AGAVE GALLERY
ART COLONY OF MORONGO VALLEY
Morongo Valley

San Gorgonio Wilderness

Rimrock
RIMROCK RANCH CABINS

Pioneertown
PIONEERTOWN RD

PIONEERTOWN MOTEL
PAPPY & HARRIET'S

RATTLER RANCH CABINS

HOOF & THE HORN/ PROMISED LAND
ROUTE 62 VINTAGE MARKETPLACE
PIONEERTOWN RD
THE END
SKY VILLAGE SWAP MEET

PIONEER CROSSING ANTIQUES/ HOODOO/ TAMURA AT HOME

Yucca Valley

247

247

LINN RD
Landers
BOTKIN RD
RECHE RD

THE INTEGRATRON
KATE'S LAZY DESERT

YUCCA MESA RD

ABERDEEN DR

HI DESERT CULTURAL CENTER
SAM'S INDIAN RESTAURANT

JOSHUA TREE BICYCLE SHOP/ GALLERY 62/
JOSHUA TREE INN

PARK BLVD
SUNBURST ST
Joshua Tree

SEE "HIDDEN VALLEY" MAP

SEE INSET ABOVE

SACRED SANDS B&B
QUAIL SPRINGS RD

BORDER AVE
CENTER AVE
BORDER AVE

NOAH PURIFOY OUTDOOR DESERT ART MUSEUM

SUNFAIR RD

COYOTE VALLEY RD

JOSHUA TREE LAKE RV & CAMPGROUND

SPIN AND MARGIE'S DESERT HIDE-A-WAY

WEST ENTRANCE STATION

INDIAN COVE RD
INDIAN COVE

A ROADSIDE ATTRACTION

LEAR AVE

TWO MILE RD

HARMONY MOTEL
49 PALMS OASIS

Twentynine Palms Marine Corps Base

Twentynine Palms

Joshua Tree National Park

29 PALMS CREATIVE CENTER & GALLERY

29 PALMS GALLERY AND ARTIST GUILD
29 PALMS INN

NORTH ENTRANCE STATION
UTAH TRAIL

OLD DALE RD
ADOBE RD

INDIAN TRAIL

TWENTYNINE PALMS VISITOR CENTER AND GALLERY

0   5 km
0   5 mi

RICOCHET VINTAGE WEARS/ JOSHUA TREE
JOSHUA TREE COFFEE COMPANY/ PIE FOR THE PEOPLE
JT COUNTRY KITCHEN
COYOTE CORNER
JOSHUA TREE OUTFITTERS
JOSHUA TREE ART GALLERY
NATURAL SISTERS CAFE
CROSSROADS CAFE
ROYAL SIAM RESTAURANT
VETERANS
NOMAD VENTURES
JOSHUA TREE SALOON
JOSHUA TREE VISITOR CENTER
TWENTYNINE PALMS HWY
TWENTYNINE PALMS DIVISION ST
SAFARI MOTOR INN
MOJAVE SANDS
SUNBURST CR
Joshua Tree
62

from cheap plywood and gaudy paint, the interior of the brightly colored *Carousel* is jammed with computer monitors, discarded office machinery, and analog artifacts. Other sculptures, such as *Shelter* and *Theater,* are reminiscent of abandoned mining camps and Wild West towns, resuscitated once again into a cobbled together reminder of the American Dream scattered across rocky desert.

In 2015, several of Purifoy's sculptures were featured in an exhibition at the Los Angeles County Museum of Art. It's a testament to the strength of his sculpture that the pieces held their own even when removed from their desert context and featured in a more sterile museum space.

GETTING THERE

From Highway 62 in the town of Joshua Tree, turn north onto Yucca Mesa Road and drive four miles to Aberdeen Drive. Turn right (east) and continue another four miles to Center Street. Turn left (north) onto Center Street, and make the next right onto Blair Lane (dirt road).

Pioneertown

Created as a Wild West movie set in 1946, **Pioneertown** (Pioneertown Rd.) was founded by Hollywood investors as a frontier town that served as a backdrop for Western movies. Some of the big names that helped establish Pioneertown included Roy Rogers, Gene Autry, Russell Hayden, and the Sons of the Pioneers (which gave Pioneertown its name). The 1940s and 1950s saw Pioneertown as a popular filming destination, with more than 50 films and television shows featuring the stables, saloons, jails, and shops of the main street. As part of the set-up, a functioning motel provided quarters for the Hollywood set who were there for filming. When not filming, Pioneertown did double duty as a roadside attraction and tourist spot. Visitors came for an ice cream parlor, bowling alley, and the motel.

The adjacent **Pappy & Harriet's Pioneertown Palace** (53688 Pioneertown Rd., 760/365-5956, www.pappyandharriets. com) was originally part of the set as a dusty cantina facade. It was eventually turned into a functioning cantina that served as a biker burrito bar from 1972 to 1982. In 1982, the cantina debuted as "Pappy & Harriet's Pioneertown Palace."

Today Pioneertown continues as a family-friendly attraction. Visitors can wander the main street, taking in the frontier buildings.

Noah Purifoy Outdoor Desert Art Museum

The original sound stage has been restored and now features live music some weekend afternoons. Visitors can also browse a handful of **retail shops** (open weekends) that feature gifts, soap, and pottery. And of course, no Wild West town would be complete without a staged **gunfight,** available on Mane Street most weekends.

GETTING THERE

Pioneertown is located four miles north of Yucca Valley. From the intersection of Highway 62 and Pioneertown Road, turn left to head north for four miles. Pioneertown's Mane Street is located adjacent to Pappy & Harriet's Pioneertown Palace, and the two share parking.

ENTERTAINMENT AND EVENTS
Live Music

"The Desert is Freedom, Music is Power, & Community is Crucial" reads the tagline for the **Joshua Tree Music Festival** (www. joshuatreemusicfestival.com, May and Oct., $60-180), a four-day, outdoor, independently produced music festival held twice yearly at the **Joshua Tree Lake RV and Campground** (2601 Sunfair Rd., Joshua Tree, 760/366-1213, www.joshuatreelake.com). This musical carpet ride takes place in an intimate setting outside the park boundary with the open desert as backdrop to an eclectic mix of up-and-coming bands. There are two alternating stages, so you don't have to make any tough decisions. The spring festival in May features a groovier vibe with dance, world, electro-funk, and groove artists. The fall in October gets rootsier dipping into folkadelic, raw rock and roll, space rock, newgrass, and rootsicana realms. Communal, festival tent camping is included with the price of a ticket. Cozy vintage trailers and limited RV spaces are also available. The all-ages festival is family-friendly, with a designated Kidsville for entertainment and activities. Festival amenities include organic food and bevvy vendors, yoga classes, a saloon, an espresso bar, a world market, bathrooms, showers, and free drinking water.

There are many good reasons to go to the **Joshua Tree Saloon** (61835 29 Palms Hwy., Joshua Tree, 760/366-2250, www. thejoshuatreesaloon.com, 7am-midnight Sun.-Thurs., 7am-2am Fri.-Sat.). The fact that they have live music to accompany their well-executed menu, good service, and array of cold bevvies adds another reason to the list. From open-mic and karaoke on the weekdays to live bands rocking out on weekends to mellow acoustic accompaniment at brunch, the Joshua Tree Saloon knows how to make the atmosphere festive.

You're never sure what you're going to get at the weather-beaten roadhouse that is **The Palms Restaurant** (83131 Amboy Rd., Wonder Valley, 760/361-2810, 3pm-6pm Fri.-Sat., 3pm-8pm, 9am-6pm Sun.), but it won't be boring. Whether you're sipping icy cold, dirt-cheap PBR (think $2 drafts) with the locals on a laid-back Sunday or there for a weekend festival held out back on the rickety stage in the scrubby, open desert, there's a certain charm to this dusty outpost with the out-of-tune piano.

Live music is on the weekends, but music and events are sporadic; check the Facebook page or call if seeing music is your main goal. Their biggest music event is **Deserted at the Palms** (http://desertedparty.tumblr.com, May), a one-day camping event featuring a serious lineup of bands in the neo-psychedelic vein. Be advised: They're not afraid of the experimental and music that tends toward the out-there.

The limited menu features bar food (with veggie options) that's better than it has any right to be considering this place looks like the patron saint of abandoned homesteads.

★ PAPPY & HARRIET'S

You don't need a festival to hear great live music at **Pappy & Harriet's** (53688 Pioneertown Rd., Pioneertown, 760/365-5956, www.pappyandharriets.com, 11am-2am Thurs.-Sun., 5pm-2am Mon., cover charge varies). Set amid historic Pioneertown, originally built as a Wild West movie set, the saloon, venue, and restaurant boast an impressive music lineup that stands up to offerings in Los Angeles and San Diego. Weekends bring heavy-hitting bands in rock 'n roll genres from sludgy desert rock to Americana-influenced. Sundays (no cover) are chill with The Sunday Band, a rotating star-studded mix of local musicians and the occasional surprise guest. Musicians are excited to play here, and you can feel that energy in this intimate space.

The annual **Desert Stars Festival** (www. desertstarsfestival.com, Sept., $100-150) is a heavy-hitting micro-fest at Pappy & Harriet's. The two-day (Fri.-Sat.) festival includes three stages featuring well-known bands. They play both kinds of music here: rock and roll (from heavy, psychedelic rock to alternative shoe-gaze) and all the raw, polished, desert, space, pop, folk nuances in between. Tickets give you access to the litany of impressive sounds set against the desert sky. Camping is available on-site at the **Corral Campground** (http://pioneertowncorrals.biz, open year-round, cash only, no water) next to the Pioneertown Motel. There are also limited RV spaces. Nearby Yucca Valley hotels are a good bet also.

Art Galleries and Events

Joshua Tree's reputation as a haven for creative types means that it has a robust visual arts scene. For two weekends every October, the arts community across the Morongo Basin is galvanized by the **Route 62 Open Studio Art Tours** (www.hwy62arttours. org, Oct.), sponsored by the Morongo Basin Cultural Arts Council. Artists (literally) open their studio doors to an art-thirsty public, showcasing the vibrant pieces available in the desert communities adjacent to Joshua Tree National Park. As diverse and compelling as its desert backdrop, works feature painting, sculpture, metal work, ceramics, assemblage, photography, textiles, illustration, conceptual art, jewelry, and more. Visitors and locals get the chance to view the art and meet the artists in their studios where all the magic happens.

With nearly 100 participating artists and artist studios scattered up and down the Morongo Basin, you'll want to plan your art tour according to what speaks most to you. Highway 62 Open Studio Art Tours pamphlets and maps are available for free in local businesses. If you can't make the October exhibition, you can take in work by artists in the Morongo Basin at a few galleries open year-round or most of the year.

Pioneertown was built as a Wild West movie set.

A Rock-and-Roll Pilgrimage

Joshua Tree's mystical piles of boulders, spiky, lonely Joshua trees, and vast sky have long been a mecca for musicians from LA and elsewhere seeking inspiration. Musicians grow up here, creating a distinct sound to try to fill the open spaces and spare landscape that can make humans take stock of their place in the cosmos. Any way you look at it, Joshua Tree has a serious rock-and-roll résumé.

Follow this pilgrimage through Joshua Tree, by starting at Room 8 in the Joshua Tree Inn (61259 29 Palms Hwy.). On the night of September 18, 1973, country rocker **Gram Parsons** overdosed on alcohol and morphine at age 26. Parsons has since attained cult status for his timeless music, as well as the strange events following his death. His body was on its way to Louisiana for burial in the family plot when friends, acting on Parsons' pre-death request to have his body set on fire in the desert, managed to follow-through on a drunken plan that involved borrowing a hearse and stealing his body and coffin off the tarmac at the Los Angeles International Airport. Hightailing it to then Joshua Tree National Monument, they promptly doused his body with gasoline and lit it on fire near Cap Rock. There is a small shrine at the Joshua Tree Inn and at the site of the "cremation."

Dublin-based **U2**'s cinematic, chart-topping album *Joshua Tree* evoked the open spaces of the American West with its iconic cover. The Joshua tree on display was actually closer to Death Valley, but you can still follow in their footsteps with a visit to the funky, low-key **Harmony Motel** (71161 29 Palms Hwy., Twentynine Palms) where they stayed during their desert sojourn.

U2's 1987 album, distinctive as it was, fit squarely into a long line of musicians trying to connect with the quintessential American West experience. **The Eagles** shot their 1972 debut album cover in what was then Joshua Tree National Monument, tripping out around a campfire in a band-bonding visit to the desert. In the 1970s, **John Lennon** recorded the rare *Joshua Tree Tapes* including "Imagine" and "Come Together." In a faded 1960s video, Doors front man **Jim Morrison** drove his Shelby GT500 Mustang, dubbed "The Blue Lady," through Joshua Tree as the desert highway flashed by.

The stoner rock scene was born in the 1990s pioneered by the band **Kyuss,** a crew of kids (Josh Homme, Brant Bjork, John Garcia, Nick Oliveri) who grew up in Palm Desert. It was the low desert as opposed to the high desert elevation near Joshua Tree, and their grittier sound was cre-

MORONGO VALLEY

Located on Highway 62, 11 miles west of Yucca Valley, Morongo Valley is a tiny outpost with a café, gas station, saloon, and combination cactus mart, gift shop, and art gallery. While many people stop into the **Cactus Mart & Purple Agave Gallery** (49889 29 Palms Hwy., 760/363-6076, www.cactusmart. net, 8am-5pm Mon.-Sat., 9am-5pm Sun.) for its array of irresistible cacti and succulents, their **Purple Agave Gallery** and gift shop also offers fine art originals and prints, pottery, metal sculptures, posters, greeting cards, hardware, hiking guides, gifts, and other sundries.

Support local art, the Big Morongo Canyon Preserve, and the Morongo Valley when you visit the **Art Colony of Morongo Valley Gift Shop** (11165 Vale Dr., www.artcolonyofmorongovalley.com, 10am-3pm Wed. and Sat.), featuring fine art, photography, jewelry, books, cards, and T-shirts. The Art Colony also holds monthly art shows.

JOSHUA TREE

Gallery 62 (61607 29 Palms Hwy., www.hwy62arttours.org, 11am-5pm Fri.-Sun.), in the main hub of Joshua Tree, offers a rotating series of gallery exhibits of different media as well as openings and art crawls. **Joshua Tree Art Gallery** (JTAG, 61607 29 Palms Hwy., 760/366-3636, www.joshuatreeartgallery.com, 10am-3pm Sat., noon-3pm Sun. June-Sept.), a cooperative fine art gallery, features the work of painters, photographers, and sculptors. JTAG has opening

Harmony Motel, where U2 stayed while shooting photos for their *Joshua Tree* album

ated at live shows out in the washes and canyons. These now-infamous "generator parties" were fueled by beer, psychedelics, and a single, hardworking generator. Members of the band went on to notable projects including Queens of the Stone Age, Fu Manchu, Dwarves, Eagles of Death Metal, and Mondo Generator.

The music scene is still alive and well. A smattering of recording studios, like the notable **Rancho de la Luna** (www.ranchodelaluna.com, closed to the public) in Joshua Tree, draw artists from all over the world including Kurt Vile, Arctic Monkeys, The Duke Spirit, Mark Lanegan, Foo Fighters, and The Melvins. Drive through the national park and surrounding desert on any given day and you're likely to see a chicly clad poncho wearer posing photogenically against the iconic boulders, looking like they're shooting a music video. Pay attention—they probably are.

receptions the second Saturday (6pm-8pm) of each month.

The **Hi-Desert Cultural Center** (61231 29 Palms Hwy., 760/366-3777, www.hidesertculturalcenter.org, box office open 11am-4pm Mon.-Fri.) is a multi-theater complex that promotes the performing and visual arts in Joshua Tree and surrounding desert communities. In addition to theater and comedy offerings, the center includes mini-galleries on its campus with visual arts exhibitions that change three times a year.

TWENTYNINE PALMS

Since 1963, the **29 Palms Gallery and Artist Guild** (74055 Cottonwood Dr., 760/367-7819, www.29palmsartgallery.com, noon-3pm Wed.-Sun., summer hours noon-3pm Fri.-Sun.) has been a nexus for high desert art. The well-established historic adobe gallery at the Oasis of Mara features ongoing exhibits as well as opening receptions and events, art classes, and social painting events.

Just a few blocks west of National Park Drive and the Oasis Visitors Center, **Twentynine Palms Visitors Center and Gallery** (73484 29 Palms Hwy., 760/367-6197, http://visit29.org, 10am-4pm daily; summer hours 9am-3pm Mon.-Fri., 9am-2pm Sat.-Sun.) offers local books, maps, local information, souvenirs, and an art gallery featuring local artists. Themed group exhibitions are on public display, highlighting the area's natural beauty and history.

The gallery offerings for the **29 Palms Creative Center and Gallery** (6847 Adobe

Rd., Twentynine Palms, 760/361-1805, www.29palmsart.com, 10am-6pm Mon.-Sat., 10am-3pm Sun.) range widely and include painting, pottery, jewelry, furniture, and collage. Many of the sales benefit the Mojave Desert Land Trust. The center also offers a variety of art classes and activities for all ages on subjects such as pottery, stained glass, oil painting, drawing, tile mosaics, and bookmaking.

A Roadside Attraction (69197 29 Palms Hwy., 760/401-8038, 11am-5pm Wed.-Sun.) is the studio and showroom of artist Douglas O Smith, who specializes in the creation of fine art prints with a cosmic aesthetic.

WONDER VALLEY

Locals from Joshua Tree and other communities farther west joke that the wonder of Wonder Valley is that anyone would live there at all. But don't tell that to the artists, desert dreamers, and others who call this austere desert valley home. The region took hold with passage of the Small Tract Act in 1938; would-be homesteaders flocked here in the 1940s to build tiny "jackrabbit" homesteads and eke out a living. Today you can still see the old homesteads scattered across the desert scrub—tiny wooden dwellings, some inhabited, some in disrepair. Artists seeking both refuge and inspiration have made a small arts community in this neck of the desert. Wonder Valley is about 13 miles east of Twentynine Palms, along Highway 62.

The **Glass Outhouse Gallery** (77575 Hwy. 62, Twentynine Palms, 760/367-3807, 1pm-5pm Tues.-Sun.) is one display of the visual arts scene in Wonder Valley, featuring gallery exhibits and opening receptions for local valley artists in a range of media.

Casino

Spotlight 29 in the Coachella Valley has a sister establishment, **Tortoise Rock Casino** (73829 Baseline Rd., Twentynine Palms, 760/367-9759, www.tortoiserockcasino.com, 24 hours), located north of Joshua Tree

National Park in the town of Twentynine Palms. The large casino offers slots and table games plus a lounge, live entertainment, and a casual eatery.

SHOPPING

The two main hubs for shopping in the area are in the gateway towns of Yucca Valley and Joshua Tree. Yucca Valley is best for vintage and boutique browsing. The town also has big-box stores for supplies. Joshua Tree offers limited boutique shopping and several outdoors outfitters.

Yucca Valley

Most of the shops are clustered at the intersection of 29 Palms Highway and Pioneertown Road in Old Town Yucca Valley; an historic, curved stucco building (a former pharmacy) marks the distinct junction. There's enough unique boutique clothing, vintage, antique, and lifestyle shops to easily fill an afternoon browsing.

Local tastemakers Adam and Jen preside over the impossibly hip (but not impossibly priced) retail shop **Hoof and the Horn** (55840 29 Palms Hwy., Yucca Valley, www.hoofandthehorn.com, 10am-6pm Sun.-Fri., 10am-7pm Sat.), stocking it with a carefully curated selection of women and men's new clothing, graphic tees, hats, jewelry, gifts, and housewares (plus some select vintage clothing and vinyl). The perfect leather boots for kicking around in the desert? Check. Flannel shirts to keep you warm and cool at the same time? Check. Tapping into Joshua Tree's reputation as a haven for rock and roll, art, and a bohemian lifestyle, Hoof and the Horn provides your desert chic trappings.

Newcomer on the scene **Promised Land** (55838 29 Palms Hwy., Yucca Valley, 760/853-0252, www.visitpromisedland.com, 11am-6pm daily or by appointment), established 2015, features 20th-century vintage designer fashion. Owners Anessa and Paul recently relocated their shop from Los Angeles and brought their style game with them to the desert. They stock an impeccably curated collection of clothing and shoes, from classic to cosmic, reclaimed from the past for your fashion-forward future.

Pioneer Crossing Antiques (55854 29 Palms Hwy., Yucca Valley, 760/228-0603, www.pioneercrossingantiques.com, 10am-5pm Sun.-Mon. and Thurs.-Fri., 10am-6pm Sat.) is a charming old-school antiques mall with multiple vendors featuring antiques, collectibles, furniture, knickknacks, and art. The highlight may be their new offerings of sleek and festively colored Bauer pottery made in Los Angeles.

The vintage designer clothing and accessories at **The End** (55872 29 Palms Hwy., 760/418-5536, 11am-5pm daily) are the stylish beginning for savvy shoppers who dig a vibrant, retro clothing score. It's a colorful stop chock-full of funky patterns, art, jewelry, and housewares.

Whether the store's name of **Hoodoo!** (55866 29 Palms Hwy., 760/365-9505, www.shophoodoo.com, 11am-7pm daily) refers to the system of folk magic or the spires of rock that protrude from desert soil, it is into the mystical things in life. Specializing in rock and roll, comics, and tiki, this curiosity shop for the desert wanderer features graphic tees, tiki wares, and gifts—where it really shines

is in its unique collection of vinyl records, comics, and graphic novels.

As its name suggests, **Tamura at Home** (55870 29 Palms Hwy., Yucca Valley, 760/369-3900, www.tamuraathome.com, 10am-6pm Tues.-Fri., 10am-4pm Sat.) features home design accessories, from anchor pieces and statement furniture spanning contemporary, old-world, and ethnic design sensibilities to home accents including candles and home fragrances. Beautify your space or shop for gifts.

A trove of antique wares, **Route 62 Vintage Marketplace** (55635 29 Palms Hwy., 760/365-4330, 10am-5pm Mon.-Sat., 10am-4pm Sun.) features several vendors who provide a revolving supply of upcycled housewares and furniture ranging from vintage Coleman lanterns and suitcases to dressers, lamps, and art.

Located at the old Sky Drive-in Theater, the weekly **Sky Village Swap Meet** (7028 Theatre Rd., Yucca Valley, 760/365-2104, www.skyvillageswapmeet.com, 6am-2pm Sat., 7am-2pm Sun.) is a Yucca Valley institution with junk, gems, and everything in between. Permanent vendors and a variety of day sellers offer art, new and vintage jewelry, gifts, recycled housewares, Western Wear boots,

Boutique retail shops line downtown Yucca Valley.

hats, belts, and buckles and random sundries set amid seven acres of recycled junk turned art.

Joshua Tree

The main hub of Joshua Tree is at the intersection of Highway 62 and Park Boulevard, leading to the main (west) park entrance. Anchored by the Joshua Tree Saloon and three outdoors outfitters offering rock climbing, camping, and other outdoor gear, the area also has a modest selection of shopping for vintage clothing and gifts.

Stop into **Ricochet Vintage Wears** (61731 29 Palms Hwy., Joshua Tree, 760/366-8822, 11am-3pm Mon., 11am-5pm Fri., 10am-5pm Sat.-Sun.) for their selection of groovy American threads for men and women. They also offer boots, handbags, belts, jewelry, and more.

Coyote Corner (6535 Park Blvd., Joshua Tree, 760/366-9683, www.joshuatreevillage.com, 9am-7pm daily) is the place to go if you're looking for a souvenir, gift, or novelty item for yourself or the unlucky person who didn't get to come out to Joshua Tree. The store's eclectic inventory ranges from T-shirts, jewelry, and vintage clothing to novelty items, books, and gifts. The store also stocks camping and rock climbing gear.

BKB Ceramics (61705 29 Palms Hwy., Joshua Tree, 760/821-3765, www.bkbceramics.com, 11am-3pm Sat.-Sun.) features rustic modern ceramics handcrafted by potter Brian Bosworth. His simple, textured, geometric patterns are available in several West Coast boutique retail outlets, his Joshua Tree shop, or in limited quantities from his online store.

FOOD
Yucca Valley

People drive many desert miles to the food, drink, and culture oasis that is ★ **Pappy & Harriet's Pioneertown Palace** (53688 Pioneertown Rd., Pioneertown, 760/365-5956, www.pappyandharriets.com, 11am-2am Thurs.-Sun., 5pm-2am Mon., lunch and dinner served until 9:30pm, $7-30).

Originally built in the 1940s as part of the Pioneertown Wild West film set, the barbecue restaurant and saloon, which also triples as a music venue, packs in die-hard fans and first-timers every night, managing to stay on the fun side of controlled chaos. The food (burgers, sandwiches, salads, Tex-Mex, steaks, chili, and veggie options) is legitimately good, far surpassing run-of-the-mill bar food. Reservations for dinner are highly recommended two weeks in advance (two seatings 5pm-5:30pm and 7pm). Wait times without a reservation can be staggering (2-3 hours). Pappy & Harriet's lineup is impressive, snagging groups you might only expect to see in a big city, and gives the whole place a honky-tonk vibe. Lunches are more mellow, and the back patio is a great place for a weekend brunch.

Joshua Tree

The burgers are hot and the beers are cold at the ★ **Joshua Tree Saloon** (61835 29 Palms Hwy., Joshua Tree, 760/366-2250, www.thejoshuatreesaloon.com, 7am-midnight Sun.-Thurs., 7am-2am Fri.-Sat., $8-22). As the go-to place in a small town with limited options, the Joshua Tree Saloon does a surprisingly good job of obliging a steady stream of hungry tourists and locals with consistently good food and service amid weathered Wild West decor. The bar and grill is open daily, dishing out well-executed burgers, salads, sandwiches, and solid veggie options as well as a full bar.

Crossroads Café (61715 29 Palms Hwy., Joshua Tree, 760/366-5414, www.crossroadscafejtree.com, 7am-9pm Mon.-Sat., 7am-8pm Sun., $8-12) is a Joshua Tree institution, offering reimagined diner fare with a Southwest hippie bent and lots of vegetarian options. Knotty pine walls and reclaimed wood touches bring warmth to the small contemporary diner space, which bustles with hungry hikers as well as locals. Breakfast and lunch are the most popular times, but they have a simple dinner menu as well. Beer and wine are served.

The tiny **Natural Sisters Café** (61695 29 Palms Hwy., Joshua Tree, 760/366-3600, www.thenaturalsisterscafe.com, 7am-7pm daily, $6-14) serves organic, vegan, and vegetarian breakfast and lunch, coffee, smoothies, and made-to-order fresh juices in a casual spot. They also offer tempting pies and pastries. Hey, they're vegan, so they must be good for you! Lines can get long on busy weekends in the park.

If it was good enough for Anthony Bourdain, it's good enough for me. **JT Country Kitchen** (61768 29 Palms Hwy., 760/366-8988, 6am-3:30pm daily, $8-10 cash only) is a down-home café serving tasty American diner-style breakfast and lunch. Presided over by owner Mareine Yu, it's like eating in your grandma's living room. Positive karmic notes and other shrine-style knickknacks dot the walls. The basic diner fare is very well executed and served with a side of sweet-spicy pico de gallo. Try the sausage breakfast burrito or pancakes.

The **Joshua Tree Coffee Company** (61738 29 Palms Hwy., 760/974-9272, www.jtcoffeeco.com, 7am-6pm daily) may be exaggerating slightly when they claim to serve the most delicious coffee on the planet, but it is pretty good. This is organic, locally roasted coffee made by people who are super into coffee in a hip space tucked behind the yoga studio and Pie for the People. The delicious vegan pastries and an outdoor patio are a plus.

Pie for the People (61740 29 Palms Hwy., 760/366-0400, www.pieforthepeople.net, 11am-9pm Mon.-Thurs., 11am-10pm Fri.-Sat., 11am-8pm Sun., $10) tosses up very respectable thin-crust New York-style pizzas with a myriad of toppings as well as specialty pizzas. Dine in their casual contemporary space or call for delivery, something almost unheard of in this area.

While **Sam's Indian Restaurant** (61380 29 Palms Hwy., 760/366-9511, www.joshuatreevillage.com, 11am-8pm Mon.-Thurs., 11am-7pm Fri.-Sat., 3pm-8pm Sun., $10-15) primarily serves heaping plates of authentic Indian classics, they ingeniously appropriate some of their fluffy naan into pizza and subs, making for a diverse menu that totally makes sense once you think about it. Situated in a strip mall, the casual, cozy space serves satisfying food and beer that hits the spot after a day in the park.

If you can tough it out through the often erratic service, the **Royal Siam Restaurant** (61599 29 Palms Hwy., 760/366-2923, 11:30am-9pm Wed.-Mon., $10-16) has tasty

JT Country Kitchen serves up a tasty breakfast and lunch.

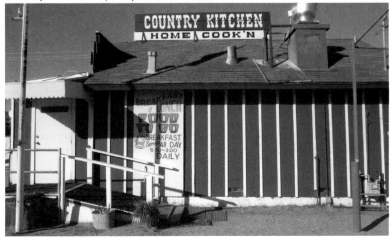

Thai food, even by Los Angeles standards. Crunchy vegetables, sticky noodles, and savory soups can make it worth your while. Tucked in a strip mall, the casual atmosphere tends toward the brightly lit.

Twentynine Palms

The ★ **29 Palms Inn** (73950 Inn Ave., 760/367-3505, www.29palmsinn.com, lunch 11am-2pm Mon.-Sat., 9am-2pm Sun., $7-16; dinner 5pm-9pm daily, $15-32) is the charming center of the desert inn's 70-acre universe, offering dining room and poolside dining for lunch and dinner daily. The eclectic menu pulls off classic steaks, seafood, and pastas with a fresh touch. They bake their own sourdough bread and source fresh veggies and herbs from the inn's garden when they can. Acoustic music accompanies dinner nightly. If you're staying here, it's a no-brainer. If not, it's worth the drive.

ACCOMMODATIONS

There's great lodging with character as well as more basic choices (read: chain motels) in the gateway towns of Joshua Tree, Twentynine Palms, and Yucca Valley. In addition to inns, motels, and hotels, there are also many unique rental lodgings in the area (rehabbed homestead cabins, stucco ranch-style homes, sleek modern dwellings, re-minted house trailers, etc.) available. Many of these private rentals in the Yucca Valley neighborhoods of Pipes Canyon, Pioneertown, and Rimrock are collected online at **Destination Pipes Canyon** (www.destinationpipescanyon.com).

Yucca Valley

The artfully furnished, solar-powered **Rattler Ranch Cabins** (Joshua Tree, 909/224-8626, www.rattlerjoshuatree.com, $140-160) are homestead bungalows near the west park entrance. Two one-bedroom cabins are available with wood-burning stoves, kitchen or kitchenettes, outdoor patios, and desert views.

Built in the 1940s as part of a permanent Wild West town film set, the

★ **Pioneertown Motel** (5240 Curtis Rd., Pioneertown, 760/365-7001, www.pioneertown-motel.com, $175) offers 17 desert lodge-style rooms. The motel is in the process of a welcome overhaul, and behind the rustic log cabin facade you'll find sparely styled rooms (queen, king, and twin beds) with exposed concrete floors, reclaimed wood, and a Wild West chic aesthetic (no televisions or coffeemakers). The motel is situated between the rustic main street of the Pioneertown tourist attraction and the wildly popular **Pappy & Harriet's** restaurant and saloon. Rooms book quickly with guests coming to see live music at Pappy & Harriet's, and it can be a bit of a party spot depending on what's happening that weekend. Rooms on the back of the property are quieter. Pro tip: On busy weekends, put your name on the Pappy & Harriet's dinner wait list then kick back in your room.

Tucked away in Rimrock Canyon near Pioneertown, the **Rimrock Ranch Cabins** (50857 Burns Canyon Rd., Pioneertown, 760/369-3012, www.rimrockranchcabins. com, $130-175) offer pitch-perfect 1940s-style cabins on 10 acres of grounds with hiking trails, a fire pit, and a summer plunge pool. Choose from a refurbished Airstream, a cabin, or a lodge.

The brightly restored Airstreams of **Kate's Lazy Desert** (58380 Botkin Rd., Landers, 845/688-7200, www.lazymeadow.com, $200) offer a kitschy retreat in the open desert of Landers near The Integratron. The six vintage Airstreams have been artistically restored and have full beds, bathrooms, kitchenettes, air-conditioning, and space heaters for winter. The grounds feature a "hobo hottie" fire pit and aboveground pool for relaxing. This is a fun place for a weekend getaway or as a base camp for exploring Joshua Tree, a 20-minute drive away.

The romantic **Sacred Sands B&B** (63155 Quail Springs Rd., Joshua Tree, 760/424-6407, www.sacredsands.com, $330-360) is a luxury retreat poised on a hill with sweeping desert views just 1.3 miles from the park's West

Entrance. Each of the two serene guest rooms offers an indoor shower with river-rock floors, and an outdoor shower, a private terrace with hot tub, and a meditation platform round out the amenities. Stays require a two-night minimum and include a complimentary gourmet breakfast.

Joshua Tree

The 1950s hacienda-style ★ **Joshua Tree Inn** (61259 29 Palms Hwy., 760/366-1188, www.joshuatreeinn.com, office open 3pm-8pm daily, $89-164) offers funky courtyard rooms and rock-and-roll history. With eclectic furniture, Spanish tile floors, and outdoor patios in its 11 rooms, as well as a huge seasonal pool, landscaped courtyard, and fire pit, they've tapped into a formula that keeps a dedicated following coming back. Speaking of dedicated followings, room number 8 is where country rocker Gram Parsons spent his last days, going from rock star to cult status rock legend. Pay your respects at a small shrine in the landscaped desert courtyard.

There's no way to tell from the unassuming outside of this 1950s desert hideaway that the ★ **Mojave Sands** (62121 29 Palms Hwy., 760/550-8063, www.mojavesandsatjoshuatree. com, $150-300) is an impeccably renovated, industrial-chic desert modern retreat with an emphasis on the *treat*. Its five rooms and suites faced with glass and steel beams look over common grounds brought to life with a reflecting pool, reclaimed wood, and metal. The rooms feature polished concrete floors, open showers, locally made bath products, vintage turntables, and mini record collections. The two suites add kitchens and living areas. Suite 5 has an outdoor clawfoot tub and shower. They're tapped into some deep feng shui here. Do yourself a favor.

Both secluded and colorful, **Spin and Margie's Desert Hide-A-Way** (64491 29 Palms Hwy., www.deserthideaway.com, $145-185) is a Southwestern-themed inn with Americana road trip-inspired grounds tucked away on the outskirts of Joshua Tree. Four suites and a cabin feature tile floors, fully equipped kitchens or kitchenettes, dining areas, outdoor courtyard and lounge areas, and flat-screen televisions.

For the price, the **Safari Motor Inn** (61959 29 Palms Hwy., 760/366-1113, www. joshuatreemotel.com, $49-69) is a good base camp for exploring Joshua Tree. This basic budget motel has drive-up motel rooms with single king, single queen, or two queen beds, coffeemakers, mini-fridges, and a swimming

rustic-chic lodging at the Pioneertown Motel

pool on the property. It's the closest motel to the west park entrance and walking distance to food and drinks.

Twentynine Palms

The ★ **29 Palms Inn** (73950 Inn Ave., 760/367-3505, www.29palmsinn.com, $165-215) is so great that I once stayed there for a weekend and never left the premises, not even to visit Joshua Tree National Park just a few minutes away. Drive onto the grounds and you'll be greeted by a glass-lined, art-filled lobby and funky wooden signs that direct you over the inn's 70 palm-dotted acres. The eclectic lodging includes nine 1930s adobe bungalows with tile floors, fireplaces, and private sun patios, eight wood frame cabins with private decks, and seven two-bedroom guesthouses. Stroll the grounds past the Oasis of Mara, a 9,000-year-old palm oasis used as a settlement by the Serrano and Chemehuevi Indians into the 1900s. The on-site **29 Palms Inn Restaurant** serves up lunch, dinner, and daily specials and draws inn guests as well as other visitors and locals to its dining room and bar. A charming swimming pool allows for poolside dining and great lounging.

The **Harmony Motel**'s (71161 29 Palms Hwy., 760/367-3351, www.harmonymotel.com, $75-95) claim to fame is that U2 stayed here when making their iconic album *Joshua Tree*. The colorful 1950s motel is set on a hilltop above Twentynine Palms, six miles from the north park entrance. The grounds have a pool, hot tub, and nice views of the Little San Bernardino Mountains. The hotel offers seven cheerful, homey rooms and one cabin. Some rooms have kitchenettes, and a common dining room with coffee is available to guests. This place is a great value.

TRANSPORTATION AND SERVICES
Car

For getting around and between the gateway communities of Yucca Valley, Joshua Tree, and Twentynine Palms, having a car is highly preferable since distances are far between businesses and towns. Gas up in Yucca Valley before heading south into the park or farther east along Highway 62, where services become sparse and the stretches between them greater.

The town of **Yucca Valley** is located at the junction of Highways 63 and 247, approximately 28 miles north of Palm Springs. From I-10, take Highway 62 north for 20 miles. Access to the Black Rock Canyon area of

the historic 29 Palms Inn

Joshua Tree National Park is via Joshua Lane south (about five miles).

The town of **Joshua Tree** lies seven miles east of Yucca Valley along Highway 62. To enter the park through the West Entrance, follow Quail Springs Road as it heads south, becoming Park Boulevard at the park boundary. The sights of Hidden Valley can be reached in 14 miles.

The town of **Twentynine Palms** sits 15 miles east of Joshua Tree along Highway 62 in a remote section of the valley. The Oasis Visitors Center and the North Entrance to the park are accessed by heading south on Utah Trail, which becomes Park Boulevard in about four miles.

Taxi

There are two taxi companies in the Yucca Valley region. **Lucky 777 Cab** (760/660-9115, www.lucky777cab.com) is based in Yucca Valley and serves the communities of Twentynine Palms and Joshua Tree. They have six cabs and accept reservations. The **American Cab Company** (760/368-1000, www.callamericancab.com) is available 24/7 and also accepts reservations. Wait times for a taxi can be long, so plan to book ahead. There are no ride-sharing services available in the area.

Public Transit

Limited public transportation is available in Morongo Basin (which includes the communities of Joshua Tree, Twentynine Palms, Yucca Valley, Morongo Valley, and Landers) in the form of the **Morongo Basin Transit Authority** (760/366-2395, www.mbtabus.com, $1.25-2.50 exact fare only). However, bus service is limited in its destinations and mainly geared toward local commuters. Schedules are available online.

Background

The Landscape

GEOGRAPHY
Mojave and Sonoran Deserts

Joshua Tree National Park straddles the Mojave and Sonoran Desert ecosystems. The Mojave Desert covers an area of 35,0000 square miles and extends into Nevada and southern Utah. It encompasses the northwest section of Joshua Tree National Park, the most popular and heavily visited, for good reason. A drive through Joshua Tree's Mojave Desert reveals a surreal landscape of shattered boulder piles, fields of spiky Joshua trees, and broken mountains ringing broad valleys. The Mojave is characterized by higher elevations (3,000-5,000 feet) and cooler temperatures than its neighboring Sonoran Desert ecosystem, which spans elevations below 3,000 feet. The Mojave Desert is marked by distinct vegetation, including large swatches of Joshua trees. Above 4,000 feet, juniper and piñon pine woodlands take over, lending a more forested feel. Desert gardens that blend yucca plants, Joshua trees, junipers, and piñons are not unusual. On the lower end of the elevation range, cacti such as barrel cactus dot the rocky hillsides.

The Coachella Valley lies south of Joshua Tree National Park, and encompasses Palm Springs. The valley extends northwest-southeast for approximately 45 miles, outlined on the west by the San Jacinto Mountains and then the Santa Rosa Mountains continuing south. On the north and east, the Little San Bernardino Mountains frame the valley. The San Andreas fault follows the foothills of the Little San Bernardino Mountains, spouting up at major fissures in a series of hot springs. The Coachella Valley lies within the Sonoran Desert system, which covers southeastern California, much of Arizona, and northwestern Mexico. This "low desert" encompasses the eastern section of Joshua Tree National Park as well as Palm Springs. It is lower and hotter than the neighboring Mojave, with elevations below 1,000 feet and more stark landscape. The plants that grow here are hearty, able to withstand searing heat and a lack of water. Spindly ocotillos resemble fingered sticks until they bloom with flame-like flowers in wet springs, while fuzzy cholla cactus spread out into strange armies of plants. Bushy creosote, an indicator of the Sonoran Desert, does well here too.

The section of the Sonoran Desert that blankets eastern Joshua Tree National Park and the Coachella Valley is also referred to as the Colorado Desert. A subregion of the Sonoran Desert, the Colorado falls south of the Mojave Desert extending east to the Colorado River, which marks the boundary between California and Arizona. The Colorado Desert covers more than seven million acres, spanning the Coachella Valley and the heavily irrigated agricultural Imperial Valley (location of the Salton Sea) to the south.

Joshua Tree Geology

The strange, jumbled rock formations that make up the labyrinthine Wonderland of Rocks and other striking formations in the northwest of Joshua Tree National Park are captivating. The cracked granite is strangely contorted: giant piles of melted rock are somehow thrown together in otherworldly piles. They rise up in seemingly random clusters, massive sculptures with rocks that resemble skulls or hollowed-out space stations.

The forces that sculpted the monzogranite boulders, peaks, and domes date back two

---

billion years, about half the present age of Earth. Eroded sediment washed off of ancient continents into the ocean, forming thick layers that fused into sedimentary rock. Around one billion years ago, fragments of ancient continents collided to form a massive supercontinent, Rodinia. As mountain chains rose from the collision, some of the offshore sedimentary rock was buckled by heat and pressure, causing it to metamorphose into granitic gneiss. Joshua Tree has gneiss similar to types found in Australia and Antarctica, suggesting that a mountain chain once connected the three continents. When Rodinia broke apart, the North American continent drifted toward the equator. Likely part of a continental shelf, Joshua Tree lay underwater for 250 million years.

Another supercontinent formation (Pangaea) and breakup 210 million years ago finally forced Joshua Tree above water as North America drifted west and collided with the massive Pacific tectonic plate. The shifting plates caused an intense friction, and rising magma bubbled up, reaching the gneiss layer (Pinto Gneiss) before cooling into granite.

The rock formations you see in the park are this bubbling magma, turned into granite after millions of years of erosion of the overlying rock—sediment, volcanic ash, and metamorphic rock. Their cracked and sculpted shapes are the result of upheaval as rocks were squeezed to the surface and expanded as top layers eroded. When Joshua Tree was much wetter, trickling groundwater also eroded the granite along the crisscrossed fissures that had been formed during the tectonic plate shifts. As the climate in Southern California became drier, this type of erosion slowed, and surface erosion increased, revealing the surreal formations we see today.

San Andreas Fault and Transverse Mountain Ranges

The famous San Andreas fault extends 800 miles from the Salton Sea (south of Palm Springs in Imperial County) to Cape Mendocino in Northern California's Humboldt County. The fault marks the zone where two massive tectonic plates—the North American Plate and the Pacific Plate—come into contact. These plates, mostly rigid slabs of rock that make up the earth's mantle, are generally stable, but when they shift, they cause earthquakes. (The North American Plate is slowly drifting south and the Pacific Plate is creeping north). The most famous shift was the 1906 San Francisco earthquake.

Sonoran Desert landscape

for some of the natural beauty of Coachella Valley as well as its profusion of natural hot springs. The fault runs 10 miles deep, connecting the surface with geothermal activity and underground water. (You can see the fault as a dark green line of native California fan palm trees running along the foot of the Little San Bernardino Mountains.) At times, these fan palms are clustered around surface pools and oases, such as the shaded pools in the Thousand Palms Oasis of the Coachella Valley Preserve.

Hot springs are largely responsible for making Palm Springs the destination it is. In particular, hot springs abound in Desert Hot Springs, feeding the mineral pools of the area's many resorts. Palm Springs' history as a resort town began around these natural mineral springs that bubbled up to the surface.

CLIMATE

When distinguishing between Joshua Tree National Park (and surrounding towns) and Palm Springs (and the Coachella Valley), locals refer to the "high desert" and "low desert." These designations actually refer to their respective elevations and the two different desert zones that encompass them. The elevation is the largest factor on the two region's very different climates.

Joshua Tree mostly lies within the Mojave Desert, a transition desert between the hot Sonoran Desert to the south, and the cold Great Basin Desert to the north. The Joshua Tree section of the Mojave has elevations generally between 3,000 and 5,000 feet. The highest point in Joshua Tree National Park is Quail Mountain at 5,816 feet. At these elevation levels, the Mojave is considered a high desert, cooler than the neighboring low desert. Joshua Tree's climate is characterized by wild temperature swings, and the region experiences cold winters and blazing hot summers. Rainfall in the area is generally only about 3-5 inches per year, but Joshua Tree can receive late summer storms that produce flash floods. Occasionally, Joshua Tree receives a very light blanketing of snow in winter.

Upheaval and erosion created Joshua Tree's distinct rock formations.

The San Andreas fault is also responsible for the unique transverse mountain system that dominates the Joshua Tree and Coachella Valley regions. The east-west trending mountain ranges are a geologic anomaly in North America, where most ranges are oriented north-south. This is because the San Andreas fault is not completely straight; north of the Coachella Valley (near the coastal town of Santa Barbara), the fault line makes a clear-cut east-west bend. This bend concentrated geologic pressure and forced up the transverse ranges in Southern California. These east-west trending ranges form the boundaries of the Coachella Valley—the San Jacinto Mountains and Santa Rosa Mountains on the west and Little San Bernardino Mountains to the north. In Joshua Tree National Park, the transverse formations are reflected in the Little San Bernardino Mountains that run along the park's southern border as well as the remote Eagle Mountains in the eastern wilderness of the park.

The San Andreas fault is also responsible

Below 3,000 feet, the Sonoran Desert encompasses the eastern part of the park as well as the Coachella Valley and Palm Springs to the south. With its lower elevation, it is significantly hotter than the Mojave (depending where you are, this can be up to 10-15 degrees hotter). Palm Springs is only 479 feet above sea level. This low elevation means that temperatures are fairly mild in the winter. Summers, however, can be brutally hot with temperatures holding fast in the triple digits for much of June, July, August, and September. October through April are the most temperate months, with temperatures ranging from the high 60s to the low 90s during the day.

In the desert, there is also the wind to contend with; the San Gorgonio Pass on the northern end of the valley is one of the windiest places on earth. (The vast wind farms there give testament to this claim.) Temperatures in the Coachella Valley drop at night due to the dry air and lack of cloud cover, which allows temperatures to plummet with the sunset. However, plummeting from 115 degrees during the day in summer to 90 degrees at night is still pretty warm. In contrast, the towering peaks of the San Jacinto Mountains to the south and San Bernardino Mountains to the west are often snowcapped through late spring, offering a dazzling contrast to the sometimes hairdryer-like heat below. This snowmelt feeds the streams in the Indian Canyons and percolates into ravines, natural rock tanks, and springs.

ENVIRONMENTAL ISSUES
Air Quality

In 2015, Joshua Tree National Park earned the dubious distinction of being one of four national parks to receive a failing grade on its air pollution report card. The ranking, conducted by the National Parks Conservation Association, surveyed 48 national parks. Joshua Tree was the fourth worst, in company with the popular Sequoia and Kings Canyon National Park in the southern Sierra Nevada and iconic Yosemite.

Population growth in the Coachella Valley, as well as pollution coming from the Los Angeles Basin, has created reduced air quality, affecting views and quality of life. In addition to being unhealthy, smoggy and hazy air can diminish the park experience. People come for the area's beauty and sweeping views, which can stretch for 200 miles on a clear day. That natural visibility has been seriously impacted with poor air quality that has limited views to about 90 miles on average.

Adding to the problem are dust particulates from the Salton Sea at the southern end of the Coachella Valley. The 350-square-mile Salton Sea is shrinking due to rapid evaporation in the region's high summer temperatures and a decrease in the agricultural runoff that supplied the water. The agricultural water source contains pesticides, which makes the dust blowing in from the Salton Sea even more polluted. Without an environmental intervention, the Salton Sea has the potential to become a huge dust bowl as the playa becomes more and more exposed.

Overuse and Vandalism

Though the desert may seem impervious to visitors, it is a delicate and fragile ecosystem relying on tiny amounts of rainfall to sustain life in extreme conditions. Of 59 national parks in the United States, Joshua Tree is one of the most popular, welcoming 1.6 million visitors annually, making it one of the top 10 most heavily visited parks in the country. The park spans just under 800,000 acres (approximately 1,200 square miles), and while it is twice as big as the median size for U.S. national parks, most of its traffic is concentrated in the popular western section. This is partially because this is where the striking rock formations and Joshua trees for which the park is known are concentrated, and partially because the only developed roads run through this section. This is not by accident—most of the remote eastern (Pinto Basin) section of the park is being preserved as wilderness.

At its most benign the park's heavy

visitation numbers can translate into crowded park entrances, a lack of solitude on trails and at picnic areas, and a dearth of camping spots during the busy fall and spring seasons. At its most hostile, a higher incidence of visitors can mean a higher likelihood of vandalism, graffiti, and general abuse of the land and cultural resources. Vandalism and graffiti has become an increasing problem in Joshua Tree and other national parks. We like to think of our national parks as a place to be wild and free, but a lack of oversight in some areas may leave space for vandalism and graffiti. In 2016, the park service had to shut down two sensitive, cultural sites, both linked to Joshua Tree's mining history, due to looting and vandalism. Social media can also play a role in the increase in graffiti; people graffiti to be seen, and often post graffiti pics on Instagram and other online venues. In 2015, a well-known street graffiti artist was caught leaving his signature tag on rocks within Joshua Tree National Park.

Water and Drought

The Coachella Valley is one of the fastest-growing regions in the state of California, and it is also one of the driest places in North America, receiving only 3-4 inches of rain annually. This tension surrounding competition for resources is growing in a region that is known for luxury resorts, golf courses, and swimming pools. In 2015 the state ordered the region to cut water use by 36 percent, and resort cities like Palm Springs and Rancho Mirage have adopted strict conservation measures. For now, the region continues to take full advantage of its water rights, receiving billions of gallons annually from the Colorado River and other sources to replenish its underwater aquifer and feed the growing number of housing developments as well as the recreation industry. The valley's population continues to grow even as resources shrink into a hotter and drier future, representing the challenges that California faces as a whole.

Plants and Animals

Joshua Tree and the Coachella Valley are home to a wide range of desert plants and animals including 700 plant species, more than 50 mammal species, and 40 reptile species, a thriving ecosystem existing within the seemingly stark landscape.

MOJAVE DESERT FLORA

Referred to as piñon-juniper woodland or piñon-juniper forest, a mix of low, bushy evergreens occurs at higher desert elevations above 4,000 feet. The woodlands span regions of the Southwest including northern Arizona and New Mexico, the Canyonlands region of Utah, and the Sierra Nevada. A good place to find this piñon-juniper forest mix in Joshua Tree is along the Pine City Trail in the Queen Valley.

Joshua Trees

The signature plant of the Mojave Desert and

Joshua Tree National Park, the spiky Joshua tree (*Yucca brevifolia*) favors the higher elevations. You can find them in large stands on the western side of Joshua Tree National Park. With their sharp demeanor, these specimens resemble cacti but are actually members of the agave family. They were named by Mormon explorers who thought their jaunty shapes resembled the upstretched arms of the prophet Joshua pointing them toward the promised land. Joshua trees can reach more than 40 feet and, although dating is difficult due to their fleshy interior (no tree rings), several hundred years old.

Mojave Yucca

The bayonet-like Mojave yucca (*Yucca schidigera*) thrives at elevations from 1,000 to 4,000 feet and is often found mixed in with Joshua trees in transition zones leading to the higher

154

BACKGROUND
PLANTS AND ANIMALS

elevation piñon-juniper forests, creating a desert garden feel. The fibers of the yucca were a staple Native Americans used to weave rope, sandals, baskets, and other items.

SONORAN DESERT FLORA

There are clear contrasts between the Mojave and Sonoran Deserts as vegetation shifts at the lower elevations on the desert valleys and floors.

Smoke Trees

Ephemeral in appearance, smoke trees inhabit low washes, their gray-green leaves puffing from spindly branches. These natives of the eastern Mojave Desert and Colorado subsection of the Sonoran Desert are most prevalent in Joshua Tree National Park. The best place to find them is along the Pinto Basin Road north of Cottonwood Spring.

Mesquite

If you're wandering in the low desert and see a plant that you want to identify, mesquite is a good guess. Mesquite is the most common shrub of the Southwest, not to take away its power. This drought-tolerant plant survives in harsh environs via its long taproot, which it can use to suck water out of a very low water

table. It was an integral resource for Native Americans who ground the mesquite pods and seeds into flours that were turned into cakes. Hard-up settlers ate the beans roasted or boiled.

Ocotillo

The whip-like funnel-shapes of the ocotillo dot the low-desert landscape, its spindly branches bare for most of the year but flaming out in red bloom each spring. It favors the Sonoran Desert of southeastern California, extending to Texas and Mexico.

Creosote

The creosote bush can be found in ranges from California to West Texas and Mexico, dominating the Mojave, Sonoran, and Chihuahuan Deserts. The creosote is hardy, surviving in regions with temperatures more than 120 degrees Fahrenheit and surviving through periods of intense drought with waxy leaves that maintain moisture and roots that choke off the water supply of surrounding plants by releasing toxins. The creosote was valued by Native Americans for its medicinal properties; indeed, it emits a medicinal smell when slightly wet. Maybe the strangest thing about the creosote is its propensity for longevity. To reproduce,

Spindly ocotillos favor the lower Sonoran Desert.

plants originate from a single progenitor. The creosote ring dubbed King Clone in the Mojave Desert is thought to be 11,700 years old, making it one of the oldest living organisms on earth.

Cholla

The cholla cactus, also known as the jumping cholla, may look fuzzy and cuddly, but it is known for its spiny stems, which easily detach when brushed, clinging to unsuspecting visitors who have gotten too close. If you see one cholla cactus, you will likely see them all since new plants grow from stems that have fallen from an adult. Their bristly ranks extend across the desert in mini-cactus gardens.

WILDFLOWERS

Spring wildflowers begin to color the lower elevations of the Pinto Basin in February, climbing to higher elevations in March and April. Above 5,000 feet, desert regions may see blooms as late as June. The colorful display varies each year depending on winter precipitation and spring temperatures. Optimal conditions include a good soaking of rain and warm spring temperatures.

The staunchly shaped barrel cactus offers beautiful blooms in spring; pink and yellow crowns form at the top of the cactus. Barrel cactus are highly ornamental, cultivated by nurseries for their symmetric and easy-growing properties; but they are also dangerous, easily puncturing skin. The beavertail has broad flat stems growing in clusters and can be identified by its vivid magenta flowers.

Brittlebush is ubiquitously cheerful across the lower elevations. Vibrant yellow flowers bloom on the silvery gray bushes that dot washes and hillsides. The tiny purple flowers of the sand verbena have been known to quilt large areas favoring dunes, washes, and sandy areas.

MAMMALS
Bighorn Sheep

The most dramatic sight in Joshua Tree may be bighorn sheep. Three herds (about 250 animals total) of bighorns live in the park. The largest herd (about 120 animals) ranges through the remote Eagle Mountains in the southeastern section of the park. The second largest (about 100 animals) lives in the Little San Bernardino Mountains along the park's western boundary. The smallest herd (only about 30 animals) lives in the Wonderland of Rocks. Bighorn sheep prefer steep, rocky terrain in order to elude predators, as they are able to navigate canyons and cliffs, bounding as far as 20 feet from ledge to ledge. Their distinctive concave hoofs have a hard outer shell and a softer interior sole, perfect for gripping the steep canyon walls. Scan the hillsides to make a sighting; male sheep in particular have impressively curved horns and can weigh more than 220 pounds.

Mountain Lions

Mountain lions, also known as cougars or pumas, are the second-largest wildcats in the Western Hemisphere (jaguars are the largest). Mountain lions historically ranged across all of the contiguous 48 states, but were hunted almost into extinction. Conservation efforts have brought their populations back in the west. Mountain lions are lethal hunters; they often stalk animals before they pounce, which can be more than 30 feet in one leap. Solitary hunters, mountain lions range far over a home territory and generally go out of their way to avoid humans. If you do happen to encounter a mountain lion, maintain eye contact, back away slowly, make yourself appear larger; make loud noises and speak slowly, firmly, and loudly.

Coyotes

Coyotes roam all across Joshua Tree and are common wildlife sightings. Even if you don't see one, you may hear their howling at night—a diabolical-sounding series of yips and yaps when they are in a pack. Coyotes mainly eat small mammals and rodents, but they are scavengers that have been known to get into trash receptacles looking for food.

Jackrabbits

Another commonly spotted animal in Joshua Tree is the jackrabbit, originally called the "jackass rabbit." It is distinguished by its long ears, which give it exceptional hearing to protect it from predators.

REPTILES

Joshua Tree abounds with reptiles, which are well suited to the dry climates of the desert.

Desert Tortoise

The largest reptile in the Mojave and Sonoran Deserts is the desert tortoise, which can weigh up to 50 pounds. Desert tortoises were plentiful until the 1950s; since then, populations have drastically declined due to several factors, including development and habitat loss, and speeding and off-road vehicles. Studies estimate that up until the 1950s, the desert tortoise population maintained at least 200 adults per square mile; these numbers have dropped to only 5-60 adults per square mile. The desert tortoise is on both the California and Federal Endangered Species list. Desert tortoises survive the heat by staying cool in burrows and rehydrating after a rainstorm. If you come across a desert tortoise do not disturb it—even getting close can stress a tortoise, causing it to void vital water stored in its bladder.

Chuckwalla

The chuckwalla is an iguana distinctive for its potbelly. After the Gila monster, it is the second-largest lizard in North America. The chuckwalla inflates when frightened, puffing up its lungs to three times their normal capacity. Desert Indians hunted them for food, and there is at least one account of a later settler serving up chuckwalla. "Chuckwalla Bill," a would-be miner who lived in a canyon south of Desert Hot Springs in the 1930s, earned his nickname by serving chuckwalla to a priest and trying to pass it off as fish. The priest was not fooled, and the nickname stuck.

INSECTS AND ARACHNIDS

Hairy tarantulas are the largest spiders in the world, and while they may look creepy, the reality is that their venomous bites, which paralyze insects, lizards, and small mammals, are harmless to humans. Also misunderstood is the giant hairy scorpion, with its famous stinger. Although stings are painful, they are generally harmless to humans (approximate to a bee sting). The giant hairy scorpion is the largest in the United States and common in the Joshua Tree region. However, because it is nocturnal, it is rarely seen.

Rattlesnakes

The Mojave and Sonoran Deserts have their share of venomous creatures, although only the rattlesnake poses a real health threat. Of the 11 rattlesnake species in North America, six reside in the region around Joshua Tree National Park, including the Mojave rattlesnake—one of the most toxic of all rattlesnakes. Fortunately, it is highly unlikely you will encounter a rattlesnake as they prefer open rocky habitat with crevices to hide in and plentiful rodents. Still, if you do hear the rattle of a snake, consider it a warning and back away, giving it a wide berth.

BIRDS

Joshua Tree and the Coachella Valley are in the direct path of the Pacific Flyway, a major north-south flight path for migratory birds, extending from Alaska to Patagonia in South America. The Salton Sea, at the south end of the Coachella Valley, is a notable stop on the migratory path. Joshua Tree National Park and the surrounding desert are also home to many nesting bird species, including the golden eagle. This predatory bird has an eight-foot wingspan, which makes it the largest bird of prey in North America. You may also see the long-legged roadrunner dashing across roads (seriously!) and the desert floor in Joshua Tree National Park and Coachella Valley neighborhoods. What they lack in flying abilities, they make up for with ground speed and maneuverability.

History

PALM SPRINGS
Agua Caliente Band of Cahuilla Indians

The first inhabitants came to Palm Springs 2,000 years ago, establishing complex communities in the well-watered canyons at the base of the San Jacinto Mountains. These people fished, trapped, and gathered as well as developed agricultural systems by diverting streams to irrigate crops. Named after the natural hot springs in the canyons, the Agua Caliente (hot water) Band of Cahuilla Indians still owns these canyons. You can see evidence of the ancient habitation in Tahquitz Canyon, Chino Canyon, and the Indian Canyons. Indian artifacts including baskets and pottery can be viewed at the Palm Springs Art Museum.

In 1876, the federal government deeded land to both the Southern Pacific Railroad and the Cahuilla Indians in a checkerboard of alternating tracts. The Indians' land turned out to be highly valuable real estate. The next year the Southern Pacific Railroad built a line linking Yuma, Arizona, with Los Angeles and running through the Cahuilla reservation.

The Birth of Tourism

The presence of water is what set Palm Springs' course. In the mid-19th century, there was a plan to irrigate the area around Palm Springs to create an agricultural valley, but grander things were in store. A railroad engineer "discovered" mineral springs in 1853, calling them "Agua Caliente." With the railroad in place, tourists began to visit the hot climate for their health, hiking the canyons, and learning about Native culture. The first structures were canvas and wood huts clustered together.

In 1884, pioneer settler "Judge" John Guthrie McCallum built the first permanent structure. McCallum had come seeking a climate to aid his young son's tuberculosis. His adobe homestead is still standing, now home to the Palm Springs Historical Society. Right next door is the Cornelia White House, built entirely of railroad ties. The White House was part of the first hotel, the Palm Springs Hotel, built in 1893 by Welwood Murray. He drummed up business by having a local Indian dress in Arabic clothing and ride a camel to the railroad station to greet passengers as they stopped at the railroad watering stop. The timing of the hotel was a rough one, coinciding with a drought that lasted until 1905.

Palm Springs as a destination didn't take off until 1915 when "Mother" Nellie Coffman built the Desert Inn across the street. Stars of the silent screen, including Fatty Arbuckle and Rudolph Valentino, spent winter months at her hotel for their health, triggering Palm Springs as a destination for desert and Wild West-themed movies.

Another game changer, the Oasis Hotel, was built in 1928 and had the first swimming pool in Palm Springs. The building of the luxurious, Spanish-Moorish-style El Mirador, as well as the opening of the ranch-style accommodations at Smoke Tree Ranch, ushered in the Palm Springs era as a glitterati destination, hosting stars like Marlene Dietrich, Clark Gable, Bette Davis, and Errol Flynn and Hollywood moguls such as Samuel Goldwyn and Walt Disney.

Palm Springs' Heyday

Following World War II, tastes moved from the traditional adobe and stucco construction into a more futuristic style. Palm Springs has an astonishing concentration of first tier modernist architecture, one of the highest concentrations in the world. The sleek lines and use of glass, concrete, and metal distinguish hotels, public buildings, and private homes throughout the chic resort town. Beginning in the 1930s, Hollywood began decamping to the desert; the 1950s and 1960s were the zenith of the legendary Hollywood party scene as well as architectural style.

Noted architects Albert Frey, E. Stewart Williams, William Cody, Donald Wexler, John Lautner, Richard Neutra, John Porter Clark, and others literally shaped the town, commissioned to build celebrity homes, businesses, civic buildings, and stylish and affordable tract homes.

Many of these houses were second homes, thus architects did not have to adhere so much to the daily functionality required of a main residence. The architectural lines, like the lifestyle out in Los Angeles' desert backyard, were freer. The optimism of the 1950s also inspired creative risk-taking, and architectural designers began playing with the modern form. Modernism was an international trend, but it was a brilliant match with the austere landscape and sun-soaked climate of the California desert. Architects were able to erase barriers between indoors and outdoors, opting for open spaces that integrated with the landscape. Palm Springs' magnificent scenery, such as the striking escarpment of the San Jacinto Mountains, inspired clean lines and low designs that deferred to the views, creating a harmony of nature and culture.

Soon iconic celebrities like Frank Sinatra, Marilyn Monroe, Sammy Davis Jr., Bing Crosby, and Bob Hope were regulars in Palm Springs. Frank Sinatra and Bob Hope even built houses here.

The 1970s and 1980s were a low point for Palm Springs, as modernist designs (and as a result, the town) fell out of fashion and celebrities and vacationers gravitated toward luxurious resorts in Rancho Mirage and farther south. Palm Springs limped along as a seedy spring break destination, much of its downtown shuttered. As a resort town Palm Springs stagnated, and developers did not care enough to even raze and rebuild it to conform with newer ideas of luxury (ahem, Las Vegas). It was this apathy that saved Palm Springs. When members of the fashion world started to buy properties in the late 1990s, it turned out

that the town was a trove of architectural treasure waiting to be rediscovered and rehabbed.

JOSHUA TREE
Ancient Culture

The first known culture to inhabit Joshua Tree was the Pinto Culture, dating as far back as 8,000 years. The Pinto occupied today's Pinto Basin, the stark rolling landscape in the southern part of the park. At the end of the Ice Age, roughly 10,000 years ago, California's deserts had been lush and filled with rivers, lakes, and large mammals such as mastodons, camels, and mammoths wandering the grassy landscape. A river flowed through Pinto Basin, but by the time the Pinto Culture arrived, many of the Ice Age mammals had gone extinct and the river was dry. Still, the Pinto Culture persisted for as long as 4,000 years. Though very little is known about them, what we do understand is based on archaeological finds from the 1930s, which include stone tools and spear points. These artifacts suggest that the Pinto Culture was mobile, mostly dependent on large game for survival.

Serrano and Cahuilla Indians

The Serrano and Cahuilla Indians moved into the region several thousand years after the Pinto Culture left. They used the park seasonally, moving to where food sources were plentiful. The largest village was at the Oasis of Mara (near the Oasis Visitor Center), the winter home of the Serrano Indians. In summer the Serrano moved west to the pine forests of the San Bernardino Mountains. The Cahuilla Indians occupied the southern reaches of the park (their northernmost boundary) and regions farther south, into Palm Springs and the Indian Canyons.

The harsh landscape and climate dictated the daily activities of the desert Indians. They were primarily hunters and gatherers living in seasonal, small villages of 25-100 individuals. The most important food sources were pine nuts, acorns, and mesquite beans as well as small animals like jackrabbits and rodents.

Villages consisted of communal structures for storage, a sweat house, and a ceremonial room; family houses were circular thatched huts made of palm fronds. Serrano and Cahuilla women were expert weavers, crafting baskets, netting, rope hats, sandals, and other items from palm trees and yuccas. Pottery made by desert Indians included earthenware vessels called ollas for food and water storage.

The Mission Era

The 1771 construction of the Spanish Mission San Gabriel Archangel in present-day Los Angeles marked the start of a land and power shift away from the native tribes in the California desert to European control, although it would be another 100 years before the full impact was felt. The mission was just one of the 21 Spanish officials had ordered to be constructed along the California coast. The Spanish largely avoided the deserts, seeing them as remote and dangerous. With the dominance of Spanish missions on the coast, Native Americans fled inland, sharing the land with groups who were already living in the Joshua Tree region. The Spanish built a second chain of missions inland. The closest to Joshua Tree National Park was erected in 1819 in Redlands, less than 40 miles away, impacting Serrano and Cahuilla Indians within its reach. More far-flung villages like the one at Oasis of Mara evaded the mission's control.

Miners, Ranchers, and Homesteaders

The year 1848 was eventful for California. It had became a U.S. state, handed over from Mexico, and the gold rush started in Northern California. As goldfields tapped out, prospectors chased the precious metal farther afield into California's deserts, which until this point had been mostly untouched. Gold was discovered near the Oasis of Mara in 1863. This discovery plus a smallpox epidemic that swept east from Los Angeles, decimating whole villages of the Indian population, marked the breakdown of traditional Indian

life including political and social structure, and shifted the culture of the desert. Indians at the Oasis of Mara hung on for several decades, sharing their precious water resources with the Chemehuevi who had been driven from their traditional lands to the east as well as gold prospectors, all the while locked in a land dispute with the Southern Pacific Railroad. By 1912 the last holdouts were gone, and there were no Indians remaining at the oasis.

Prospectors had been poking around Joshua Tree for decades, but 1883 marked the defining moment for mining when one discovered rich deposits in the Pinto Mountains east of the Oasis of Mara. Prospectors flocked to the boomtown named Dale that, at its peak, claimed over 1,000 citizens. Over time, the town moved, following the gold. Other mines sprang up. Today the region, called the Old Dale Mining District, is located just north of the Joshua Tree National Park boundary. It is littered with old mining camps and crisscrossed by a series of rugged roads.

It may be easy to think of Joshua Tree National Park as a pristine land, preserved in its natural state, but the reality is that ranching, mining, and homesteading were deeply entrenched in the region in the 1900s. The area was a stretch used for ranching; the sparse landscape required 17 acres per animal for grazing. The presence of concrete dams at places like Barker Dam and Twin Tanks are reminders of Joshua Tree's halcyon ranching days.

The most notable settler was resourceful homesteader, rancher, and miner Bill Keys who arrived in 1910 and thrived for de-cades on his property within the Joshua Tree National Park boundary. He got his start as supervisor of the Desert Queen Mine. When the mining company he worked for went bankrupt, Keys gladly accepted their offer of a deed to the mine. From there he settled a 160-acre homestead and built a ranch. On a trip to Los Angeles he met his future wife, and they raised a family on the ranch. Keys was a legendary scavenger, collecting machinery and spare parts from abandoned mines and other desert sites. His resourcefulness served him well in this hardscrabble desert environment. The couple lived at the ranch until well into the 1960s when Joshua Tree had already become a national monument. It is possible to tour the still-standing Desert Queen Ranch via tours offered by the park service.

Joshua Tree National Monument

The 1930s brought the seemingly conflicting goals of settlement and preservation to Joshua Tree. In many of the Western states including Arizona, California, Nevada, New Mexico, and Utah, the federal government was promoting development of "useless" lands unsuitable for ranching or farming; the 1938 Small Tract Act offered dirt-cheap land to individuals for settlement. To earn a right to purchase at the government's rates, applicants had to build a simple dwelling within three years. This homestead act tapped into a deep American desire to claim a piece of territory, even if the land was deemed unprofitable. Some of these "jackrabbit homesteads" are evident north of the park, particularly in the area of Wonder Valley, east of Twentynine Palms. In this scrubby desert, the tiny shacks stand in various degrees of preservation and decay, some housing a burgeoning artist community. The homestead program was not disbanded until 1976.

While the federal government was encouraging settlement, activists were calling for the preservation of Joshua Tree's unique geography. Beginning in the 1920s, Minerva Hoyt, a rich Pasadena widow, led the conservation effort to protect Joshua Tree. Following the untimely death of her husband and infant son, she made frequent trips to the California desert, taking solace there. While Joshua Tree had caught on as a tourist destination, the prevailing mentality was that the desert was indestructible. Landscapers catering to a desert garden craze in Los Angeles looted the area, uprooting plants by the acre and doing lasting damage to the ecosystem. Travelers setting up camp routinely set fire to Joshua trees at night to guide motorists coming in after dark. Hoyt, an active gardener, designed desert conservation exhibits that were showcased in New York and London to address the ecological damage she had witnessed on her trips. This got her elected as president of the newly created Desert Conservation League through which she campaigned for protected lands to encompass the Southern California deserts. In 1936 President Roosevelt signed a proclamation that established Joshua Tree National Monument. It spanned privately owned land including massive swatches owned by the Southern Pacific Railroad and more than 8,000 existing mining claims, some operating and profitable, within its boundaries.

Joshua Tree National Park

Over the next decades, the park service negotiated and maneuvered, obtaining deeds and purchasing real estate. In 1964 Congress authorized the Wilderness Act, protecting federally managed lands from mechanized vehicles and equipment. In 1994, President Bill Clinton signed the Desert Protection Act, upgrading Joshua Tree to national park status and transferring three million acres for protection in Joshua Tree, Death Valley National Park, and the Mojave National Preserve. Joshua Tree National Park is wildly popular and receives more than one million visitors a year.

Local Culture

PALM SPRINGS AND THE COACHELLA VALLEY

Palm Springs began its current incarnation as a seasonal resort town in the 1920s. The 1930s to the 1970s mark the halcyon years for Palm Springs as Hollywood celebrities and others flocked to the stylish resorts springing up. In the 1970s, the city of Palm Springs began its fall from favor as visitors gravitated to increasingly grandiose resorts in Rancho Mirage and farther south in the Coachella Valley. As Palm Springs languished, the Coachella Valley became known as a golfing and retirement destination. Palm Springs itself veered into a seedy spring break destination and many of its downtown businesses were boarded shut. In the 1990s, some of the fashionable set began buying up the area's mid-century architectural gems, breathing new life into Palm Springs as a resort destination.

Today, the town of Palm Springs is a connected community of entrepreneurs with a forward-looking vision and passionate interest in the town's history. Palm Springs has a vested interest in preserving its mid-century architectural heritage while refreshing its hotels and businesses to be current and chic. New retail shops and restaurants continue to pop up in the town's stylish Uptown Design District. It's hard to keep up with the burgeoning business scene. Old hotels and residences are continually being shined and styled. Once a seasonal destination, the town is on the upswing as a year-round resort destination that attracts a wide variety of visitors. You may still see caftan-wearing golden-agers dining on shrimp cocktail and martinis or golfers whiling away the mornings on the greens, but there's also been an infusion of newer generations visiting Palm Springs. Hip hotels like the Ace Hotel draw a stylish millennial set (as well as the young at heart) to deejay and craft cocktail-fueled pool parties. Palm Springs is again a celebrity destination, with the Hollywood set buying homes (Leonardo DiCaprio purchased entertainer Dinah Shore's old mansion) or hiding out at desert retreats like the Korakia Pensione.

The gay community is hugely represented in Palm Springs' year-round residents, with many gay-owned hotels and retail shops. Palm Springs is also an international LGBT destination. Visitors come here for resorts that cater specifically to men or women, as well as destination parties like the all-male White Party and the all-female The Dinah, the largest gay and lesbian music festival parties in the world.

Native American groups in Palm Springs and the Coachella Valley have the corner on some of the region's stunning natural beauty as well as resort casinos. The Agua Caliente Band of Cahuilla Indians owns their land and allows visitors access (for a fee) to the gorgeous, palm-tree and stream-filled Indian Canyons, as well as Tahquitz Canyon's creek and waterfall. The tribe also owns and manages several casinos in the Coachella Valley. The Morongo Band of Cahuilla Mission Indians operates a casino at the foot of the San Gorgonio and San Jacinto Mountains west of Palm Springs.

JOSHUA TREE AND THE YUCCA VALLEY

Like many desert regions, the land around Joshua Tree National Park has grappled with competing visions for its use. In the 1930s when the park was made a national monument, the monument status blanketed a patchwork of homesteads and mining claims. It took the better part of the 20th century to fold these tracts into what was eventually Joshua Tree National Park. If you look at a map even now, you will see the strategically excluded district east of Twentynine Palms where the Dale Mining District once thrived.

Native American groups were not

considered in the national monument status effort, having been driven out of the region in the early part of the 20th century amidst pressure from the Southern Pacific Railroad and other hardships.

The region's identity as an outdoors destination was emphasized in 2016 by conservation efforts resulting in three newly established national monuments to protect desert lands. The 154,000-acre Sand to Snow National Monument (www.fs.fed.us) links Joshua Tree National Park to the east and the Santa Rosa and San Jacinto Mountain National Monument to the south with several preserves by folding in previously unprotected land.

The gateway towns of Yucca Valley, Joshua Tree, and Twentynine Palms draw a wide cast of characters, each town with its own distinct vibe. Joshua Tree is funky, artsy, and outdoorsy, luring park visitors, locals, and seasonal rock climbers. It's a tiny town with a saloon, outdoor outfitters, and a few small hotels to anchor its small main street. It functions as the main gateway to Joshua Tree National Park (the popular West Entrance is accessed via Joshua Tree), but feels like an authentic town instead of a tourist trap. Yucca Valley is more suburban, home to big-box stores and chain restaurants. It does not have a direct entrance to the park, but it does give access to the Black Rock Canyon Campground as well as the Covington Flats area of the park, making it a strange mix of suburban and natural beauty. Yucca Valley also supports a burgeoning boutique and vintage shopping market. For a visitor to the area, Yucca Valley is not without its charms. Twentynine Palms operates as the eastern gateway to the park with its Oasis Visitor Center and North Entrance. There are a few excellent hotels, but the town is not the gateway tourist destination that Joshua Tree, or even Yucca Valley, is. The town of Twentynine Palms is home to a Marine base, which forms the backbone of the community here.

The region around Joshua Tree National Park has long been a haven for musicians and artists. Musicians from Los Angeles and other locations come out here to record albums, shoot music videos, and soak up the silence and stunning landscape. The music scene is alive and well with small music festivals drawing some big names throughout the year. Many visual artists are also based here, showcasing their work in galleries across the Morongo Basin and in yearly open studio art tours every October.

The communities in the region of Joshua Tree are slowly growing as escapees from urban centers like Los Angeles find their way here. There is even a growing homestead movement in which people are attempting to rehab old homesteads, sometimes even creating permaculture systems.

Essentials

Transportation

GETTING THERE

Air

The **Palm Springs International Airport** (PSP, 3400 E Tahquitz Canyon Way, Palm Springs, 760/318-3800, www.palmspringsca. gov) is in metro Palm Springs, less than three miles from downtown. The airport provides service via 10 major airline carriers. It is also convenient to the Joshua Tree area, 40 miles (less than a one-hour drive) from Palm Springs. Several Palm Springs hotels offer airport shuttle service. The major car rental carriers are located here, including Enterprise, Hertz, Dollar, and Alamo.

Ontario International Airport (ONT, 2500 Terminal Way, Ontario, 909/937-2700, www.lawa.org) is another good option. It is located off I-10 in the city of Ontario, about 90 miles southwest (a 1.75-hour drive) from Joshua Tree and 70 miles west of Palm Springs (a one-hour drive via I-10). Ontario Airport has all the major rental car companies on-site.

The two closest major cities to Palm Springs are Los Angeles to the west and San Diego to the southwest. Both airports provide options, though a car rental will be required to reach the Palm Springs area.

Los Angeles International Airport (LAX, 1 World Way, Los Angeles, 424/646-5252, www.lawa.org) is a major international airport with many carriers and flight options, as well as car rentals. Airport shuttles, hotel shuttles, long-distance vans, ride-share vans, and taxis can all be accessed at the lower Arrivals Level outside of the baggage claim area; median waiting platforms are marked by overhead signs. A **FlyAway Bus** service (no reservations, 24 hours daily) offers the best public transportation from LAX to destinations around the city, including Union Station (downtown), Van Nuys, Westwood, Santa Monica, and Hollywood. The drive from LAX to Palm Springs takes 2-4 hours, as traffic congestion can increase travel time significantly.

The **San Diego International Airport** (SAN, 3225 N Harbor Dr., San Diego, 619/400-2404, www.san.org) is the farthest option, located 140 miles (about a 2.5-hour drive) south in the city of San Diego. Major airline carriers include Southwest, American, United, Alaska, and Delta, and there is a consolidated rental car center on-site.

Car

A car is necessary to visit Joshua Tree National Park and any towns in the Coachella or Yucca Valleys. Within the town of Palm Springs, it is easier to get around without a car, although the blocks between neighborhoods can be long and desert heat may be a factor.

FROM LOS ANGELES

If you're lucky and time your trip outside of rush hour, the drive from Los Angeles can take less than two hours via I-10. (Getting out of LA can be a slog, though, so you may need to factor in extra time.) From Los Angeles, take I-10 east for approximately 100 miles to the town of Palm Springs. Take Exit I-10 and then Highway 111 south toward Palm Springs. Highway 111B continues south to reach the Palm Springs city limit in just over 10 miles, turning into N Palm Canyon Drive, the main road through Palm Springs.

The I-210 and Highway 60 freeways can sometimes provide good eastbound alternatives if I-10 is jammed. Both I-210 and Highway 60 join up with I-10 west of Palm Springs.

Previous: San Gorgonio wind farm; palm trees line Indian Wells.

To reach the West Entrance to Joshua Tree National Park, take Exit 117 north from I-10 for 56 miles. In the town of Joshua Tree, follow Highway 62 southeast into the park.

FROM SAN DIEGO

From San Diego, take I-15 North for about 50 miles. When I-15 splits off with I-215, follow I-215N and signs for Riverside/San Bernardino. Continue north on I-215N for 30 miles until it intersects with Highway 60. Take the exit for Highway 60, heading east for 18 miles. Merge onto I-10 E and continue east for another 18 miles until reaching the Highway 111 exit toward Palm Springs. Highway 111B continues south to reach the Palm Springs city limit in just over 10 miles, turning into N Palm Canyon Drive, the main road through Palm Springs.

To reach the West Entrance to Joshua Tree National Park, take Exit 117 north from I-10 for 56 miles. In the town of Joshua Tree, follow Highway 62 southeast into the park

Car Rental

Car rentals are available from all area airports. Approximately 40 car rental companies operate at Los Angeles International Airport; all vehicle rental companies are located off-site. Several companies offer courtesy shuttles that pick up customers at the lower Arrivals Level of all terminals.

To reach other car rental agencies, take the LAX Bus C to reach the **Off-Airport Rental Car Terminal** to meet the rental car courtesy shuttle. Many of these rental car companies provide phone links inside or near the baggage claim areas on the lower Arrivals Level of the terminals so travelers can request a free shuttle pickup to reach the rental car sites. Check with your car rental agency when making a reservation to make sure you know how to get there.

In addition to Palm Springs and LAX, several major car rental agencies are available in the gateway town of Yucca Valley including **Enterprise Rent-A-Car** (57250 29 Palms Hwy., 760/369-0515, www.enterprise.com,

8am-6pm Mon.-Fri., 9am-noon Sat.), **Avis Car Rental** (56309 29 Palms Hwy., 760/365-4723, www.avis.com, 8am-4:30pm Mon.-Fri., 8am-1pm Sat.), and **Budget Car Rental** (56307 29 Palms Hwy., 760/365-0560, 8am-4:30pm Mon.-Fri., 8am-1pm Sat.).

RV Rental

A few RV rental agencies have offices in Los Angeles, including **Cruise America** (310/522-3870 or 800/671-8042, www.cruiseamerica.com). Camper van rentals are available through **Escape Campervans** (4858 W Century Blvd., Inglewood, 877/270-8267 or 310/672-9909, www.escapecampervans.com), **Lost Campers** (8820 Aviation Blvd., Inglewood, 415/386-2693 or 888/567-8826, www.lostcampersusa.com), and **Jucy Rentals** (15318 Hawthorne Blvd., Lawndale, 800/650-4180, www.jucyrentals.com).

Train and Bus

It's possible to take **Amtrak** (800/872-7245, www.amtrak.com) from Los Angeles to Palm Springs to arrive at one of three stations in Palm Springs: North Palm Springs Train Station (PSN), Airport Bus Station (PSP), and Downtown Palm Springs Bus Station (PSS). The Amtrak routes have travel times ranging between 2.5 and 4 hours, not a bad deal when considering the drive time from downtown Los Angeles to Palm Springs is just under two hours and can be far worse (upward of 3-4 hours, especially on Fridays or holidays). Most of the train commutes are a combination train and bus with a transfer.

Your best bet is to travel on the *Pacific Surfliner* ($19-29) from downtown LA's **Union Station** (800 N Alameda St.) to arrive at the Palm Springs **Airport Bus Station** (PSP, 3400 E Tahquitz Canyon Way) or **Downtown Bus Station** (PSS, 190 N Indian Canyon Dr.), both about five minutes apart. This route offers a civilized timetable that would work with any vacation timing. (The hitch is that this is a two-part trip involving a train, one transfer, and the Thruway Bus, the majority of your trip). The train leaves Union

Station daily at 9:55am and 11:15am with one bus transfer to arrive in Palm Springs around 2pm. An evening option leaves at 5:10pm getting visitors to Palm Springs just after 8pm. Return times are equally reasonable with two daily routes. Consider returning on the 3:05pm bus to arrive in Los Angeles at 6:55pm with one train transfer. Morning commutes leave at 9am, arriving in Los Angeles at 12:10pm with one train transfer. Tickets are available online and at Union Station.

Traveling between Los Angeles Union Station and the North Palm Springs Train Station (PSN) involves only one train with no bus or transfers. That's the good news. The bad news is the timetable. From Union Station in Los Angeles, trains leave daily at 10pm, arriving after midnight at 12:36am. The reverse trip is even more inconvenient. Trains leave weekdays only (no Fri. or Sat.)

from the North Palm Springs Train Station at 2:02 am for a 3.5-hour trek to Los Angeles. This means that if you are returning from a weekend in Palm Springs, your best option would be to take the Sunday night/Monday morning train leaving Palm Springs at 2am.

GETTING AROUND

Palm Springs is immensely walkable; however, there is a free and convenient shuttle for getting around. The **Buzz Bus** (www.buzzps. com, 11am-1am Thurs.-Sun.) runs every 15 minutes with stops along Palm Canyon Drive and Indian Canyon Drive.

In and around Joshua Tree National Park, the towns of Yucca Valley, Joshua Tree, and Twentynine Palms are all accessed off Highway 62. Public transit in this area is limited to nonexistent. Travel in this region requires that you have your own vehicle.

Travel Hub: Los Angeles

Los Angeles has a lot to offer as a gateway hub to Palm Springs and Joshua Tree, including a thriving downtown, beaches, a wealth of foodie neighborhoods, shopping, and cultural sightseeing. However, LA's reputation as a difficult driving destination precedes it. The number of freeways crossing the city, a rush hour that never ends, and the sheer sprawl of the metro region mean that it's best to come to Los Angeles with a plan. If you only have a day or two, set up your base camp in one of three major areas.

The official visitor website for **Los Angeles** (www.discoverlosangeles.com) is an excellent resource.

DOWNTOWN LOS ANGELES

Los Angeles' newly restored historic downtown has turned it into a vibrant destination for food, culture, and events. Located on the northeast side of Los Angeles, downtown is an excellent jumping-off point

for exploring and continuing east to Palm Springs and Joshua Tree.

Sights and Activities

Los Angeles has a wealth of outstanding architecture. Downtown is home to notable landmarks such as the **Walt Disney Concert Hall** (111 S Grand Ave.) designed by Frank Gehry. This distinct building, home to the Los Angeles Philharmonic, draws focus with the striking stainless steel curves of its exterior. The **Bradbury Building** (304 S Broadway) is an architectural landmark built in 1893, commissioned by gold mining millionaire Lewis L. Bradbury. The Broadway Theater District stretches for six blocks from 3rd Street to 9th Street along South Broadway and includes 12 movie theaters built between 1910 and 1931, many of them in the process of being restored. Walking tours are available through the **Los Angeles Conservancy** (www.laconservancy.org).

A Mexican marketplace that is part of the

El Pueblo de Los Angeles Historic Monument, **Olvera Street** (www.olvera-street.com, hours vary) features historic structures, restaurants, and shopping along the oldest street in Los Angeles. The Museum of Contemporary Art (MOCA) has three distinct locations in the great Los Angeles Area. **MOCA Grand Avenue** (250 S Grand Ave., 213/626-6222, 11am-6pm Mon., Wed., and Fri., 11am-8pm Thurs., 11am-5pm Sat.-Sun., $12, students and seniors $6, children under 12 free) is the main branch in downtown Los Angeles on Grand Avenue near the Walt Disney Concert Hall. It features a prominent collection of post-1940s works.

The **Broad Museum** (221 S Grand Ave., 213/232-6200, www.thebroad.org, 11am-5pm Tues.-Wed., 11am-8pm Thurs.-Fri., 10am-8pm Sat., 10am-6pm Sun., free) was financed by philanthropists Eli and Edyth Broad to house their prominent and world-renowned collection of postwar and contemporary art in a newly designed, stunning $140 million building.

Griffith Park spans 4,310 acres of surprisingly rugged landscape in the hills of northeast Los Angeles, nine miles north of downtown. Its 53 miles of trails are popular as well as its acres of picnic and recreation areas. Hiking trail maps are available from the **Griffith Park Ranger Station** (4730 Crystal Springs Dr.) as well as online (www.modernhiker.com). Griffith Park also features the **Los Angeles Zoo and Botanical Gardens** (5333 Zoo Dr., 323/644-4200, www.lazoo.org, 10am-5pm daily, $20 adults, $17 seniors, $15 children 2-15, children under 2 free), a 133-acre zoo that's home to 1,100 animals and a botanical collection that features more than 800 different plant species. The **Griffith Observatory** (2800 E Observatory Rd., 213/473-0800, www.griffithobservatory.org, sunrise-10pm daily) is an art deco landmark with a planetarium and grounds that feature stunning views of the city. The instantly recognizable Hollywood Sign became part of Griffith Park to protect the area from development.

Hikes lead to the views of the city from above the sign.

The **Autry Museum of the American West** (4700 Western Heritage Way, www.theautry.org, 323/667-2000, 10am-4pm Tues.-Fri., 10am-5pm Sat.-Sun., adults $10, students and seniors $6, children 3-13 $4, children under 3 free) features exhibits that tell the stories of the peoples and cultures of the American West. **Travel Town Museum** (5200 Zoo Dr., 323/662-5874, www.traveltown.org, 10am-4pm Mon.-Fri., 10am-6pm Sat.-Sun., free) highlights railroad history in the western United States from 1880s to the 1930s. A miniature train once owned by Gene Autry takes passengers on a loop around the museum grounds.

The only horse ranch in Los Angeles, **Sunset Ranch Hollywood** (3400 N Beachwood Dr., 323/469-5450, www.sunsetranchhollywood.com, $40-95) offers a unique Griffith Park outing in the form of one- and two-hour trail rides featuring spectacular views of the Hollywood sign, Griffith Observatory, and downtown Los Angeles.

Accommodations

The boutique **Ace Hotel** (929 S Broadway, 213/623-3233, www.acehotel.com/losangeles, $250-300) has been stylishly renovated in the onetime location of the 1927 United Artists Theater and Tower. Amenities include a gym and rooftop bar and pool. The home of old Hollywood glamour, the historic 1923 **Millennium Biltmore Hotel** (506 S Grand Ave., 213/624-1011, www.millenniumhotels.com, $200-300) is a cultural landmark with 683 guest rooms and amenities including a Roman-style pool.

The boutique **O Hotel** (819 S Flower St., 213/623-9904, www.ohotelgroup.com, $200-250) features 67 contemporary-functional rooms in a unique, historic setting built in 1925. Also on-site is the rustic-chic, lobby-level **Orchid Bar Kitchen** (11:30am-11pm Mon.-Thurs., 11:30am-midnight Fri., 5pm-midnight Sat., 5pm-10pm Sun., $14-36).

The historic **Hotel Figueroa** (939 S Figueroa St., 213/627-8971, www.hotelfigueroa.com, $200-250) was renovated in 2016 to restore it to its original Spanish Colonial beauty. The hotel offers 285 guest rooms, lobby bar, and a veranda pool. Located in the Little Tokyo Historic District, **Miyako Hotel** (328 E 1st St., 213/617-2000, www.miyakoinn.com, $175-200) is a contemporary hotel offering 173 Asian-inspired guest rooms and amenities including on-site fitness room and a cocktail and karaoke lounge.

The contemporary **Luxe City Center Hotel** (1020 S Figueroa St., 213/748-1291, www.luxehotels.com/luxecitycenter, $200-250) sits on a busy corner opposite the L.A. Live entertainment venue. The hotel features 178 guest rooms, on-site restaurant, and outdoor lounge overlooking the lively street scene.

Food

A landmark food and retail emporium established in 1917, **Grand Central Market** (317 S Broadway, 213/624-2378, www.grandcentralmarket.com, 8am-6pm Sun.-Wed., 8am-9pm Thurs.-Sat.) is an incredible mix of old classics and exciting new chef-driven fare. Eateries include the rustic Italian menu at **Knead & Co Pasta Bar & Marketplace** (213/223-7592), the traditional Jewish **Wexler's Deli** (213/620-0633, www.wexlersdeli.com, 8am-4pm daily), breakfast-centric **Eggslut** (www.eggslut.com, 8am-4pm daily), and seasonal Thai street fare at **Sticky Rice** (213/621-2865, 11am-6pm Sun.-Wed., 11am-9pm Thurs.-Sat.). Several stalls pour a range of craft beers and fine wines in addition to tasty eats: **Olio GCM Wood Fired Pizzeria** (www.oliowfp.com, 10am-5:30pm Sun.-Thurs., Fri.-Sat.), Texas-inspired **Horse Thief BBQ** (213/625-0341, www.horsethiefbbq.com, 11am-4pm Mon.-Wed., 11am-9pm Thurs.-Fri., 9am-9pm Sat., 9am-6pm Sun.), **Madcapra Falafel** (213/357-2412, www.madcapra.com, 10am-4pm Sun.-Wed., 10am-9pm Thurs.-Sat.), **Oyster Gourmet** (theoystergourmet.com, 11am-6pm Sun.-Wed., 11am-9pm Thurs.-Sat.) and local favorite **Golden Road Brewing Company** (11am-6pm Sun.-Wed., 11am-9pm Thurs.-Sat.).

Historic, restored **Clifton's Cafeteria** (648 S Broadway, 213/627-1673, www.cliftonsla.com) features three dazzling floors of glamorous California redwoods and gothic-themed decor. Dining options include first-floor **Cafeteria** (11am-9pm Mon.-Thurs., 11am-10pm Fri., 10am-10pm Sat., 10am-9pm Sun.), second-floor **Monarch Bar** (11am-2am Mon.-Fri., 10am-2am Sat.-Sun.), and the third-floor **Gothic Bar** (6pm-2am Thurs.-Sat.).

Phillipe the Original (1001 N Alameda St., 213/628-3781, www.philippes.com, 6am-10pm daily, $7-9 cash only) serves up signature French dips and deli sides in this historic space (established in 1908) with sawdust-covered floors and communal tables. An old-school diner that has been operating since 1924, **The Original Pantry** (877 S Figueroa St., 213/972-9279, www.pantrycafe.com, 24 hours daily, cash only) serves American classics and all-day breakfast.

Marble floors and high ceilings are the backdrop for the bustling **Bottega Louie** (700 S Grand Ave., 213/802-1470, www.bottegalouie.com, 6:30am-11pm Mon.-Thurs., 8am-midnight Fri.-Sun., $16-30), serving up pizzas, pastas, and small plates as well as weekend brunch and patisserie items.

A destination restaurant that feels like your favorite neighborhood hang, **Baco Mercat** (408 S Main St., 213/687-8808, www.bacomercat.com, 11:30am-2:30pm and 5:30pm-11pm Mon.-Thurs., 11:30am-3pm and 5:30pm-midnight Fri.-Sat., 11:30am-3pm and 5pm-10pm Sun., $12-28) pulls in Western and Eastern influences for its tasty dishes including the signature bäco flatbread sandwich.

Yxta Cocina Mexicana (601 S Central Ave., 213/596-5579, www.yxta.net, 11:30am-9pm Mon.-Tues., 11:30am-10pm Wed.-Fri., 4pm-10pm Sat., $12-20) serves updated

Mexican classics in a vibrant, airy space plus delivers a great daily happy hour.

B.S. Taqueria (514 W 7th St., 213/622-3744, www.bstaqueria.com, lunch 11:30am-2:30pm Mon.-Fri., dinner 5:30pm-11pm daily, $8-16) offers innovative tacos and refreshing beverages in a colorful, stylish space.

Little Sister (523 W 7th St., 213/628-3146, www.littlesisterla.com, 10am-10pm daily, $8-28) has a sleekly warm bistro setting and features contemporary Vietnamese small plates, craft beer, and wine.

Pok Pok Phat Thai (978 N Broadway, 213/613-1831, www.pokpokla.com, noon-10:30pm Mon.-Thurs., noon-midnight Fri.-Sat., noon-9:30pm Sun., $11-16) serves signature chicken wings and noodle-focused Thai dishes in a bustling space in historic Chinatown's Mandarin Plaza.

Family-run **Yang Chow** (819 N Broadway, 213/625-0811, www.yangchow.com, 11:30am-9:30pm Sun.-Thurs., 11:30am-10:30pm Fri.-Sat., $12-18) is a Chinatown fixture, serving authentic Mandarin and Szechwan cuisine in a stripped-down space. Try the signature slippery shrimp.

HOLLYWOOD AND MID-CITY

Centrally located between the beaches and downtown, mid-city gives the easiest access to famous Hollywood and Museum Row.

Sights and Activities

Museum Row, a walkable stretch of Wilshire Boulevard between Fairfax Avenue and La Brea Avenue, is home to four main Los Angeles museums. Visit the **Los Angeles County Museum of Art** (LACMA, 5905 Wilshire Blvd., 323/857-6000, www.lacma.org, 11am-5pm Mon.-Tues. and Thurs., 11am-8pm Fri., 10am-7pm Sat.-Sun., $15 adults, $10 seniors and students, children 17 and under free) for the largest collection of art spanning ancient to contemporary in the western United States. The **Petersen Auto Museum** (6060 Wilshire Blvd., 323/930-2277, www.petersen.org, 10am-6pm daily,

$15 adults, $12 seniors and students, $7 children, children under 3 free) celebrates the automobile with over 25 exhibitions including automobiles in the movies, hot rods, and more than cars for the road. Kids and adults alike will love the **LaBrea Tar Pits** (5801 Wilshire Blvd., 323/857-6300, www.tarpits.org, $12), a museum and archaeological excavation where extinct animals were captured and preserved in tar. With a focus on the edge of craft and design, **Craft and Folk Art Museum** (5814 Wilshire Blvd., 323/937-4230, www.cafam.org, 11am-5pm Tues.-Fri., 11am-6pm Sat.-Sun., $7 adults, $5 students and seniors) cycles exhibitions in a range of media including glass, metal, paper, ceramics, photography, and textiles.

Originally established in 1934, the **Original Farmer's Market** (6333 W 3rd St., 323/933-9211, www.farmersmarketla.com, 9am-9pm Mon.-Fri., 9am-8pm Sat., 10am-7pm Sun.) is a destination gourmet market with more than 100 grocers and restaurants. It is adjacent to **The Grove** (189 The Grove Dr., 323/900-8080, www.thegrovela.com, 10am-9pm Mon.-Thurs., 10am-10pm Fri.-Sat., 10am-8pm Sun.), an upscale shopping, entertainment, and dining complex.

The highlight of Hollywood is the star-studded sidewalks of the **Hollywood Walk of Fame.** Beginning at La Brea Avenue (to the west), the famous pavement runs for 18 blocks to Gower Street on the east. You can also find the sidewalk stars along three blocks of Vine Street (running north and south of Hollywood Boulevard). Two historic cinema palaces, **Grauman's Chinese Theater** (6925 Hollywood Blvd.) and **Grauman's Egyptian Theater** (6706 Hollywood Blvd., www.tclchinesetheatres.com) are cultural landmarks worth a stop on your walking tour. The intricately designed Grauman's Chinese Theater opened to celebrity fanfare in 1927 and is still sought after for movie premieres and events. Its renovated theater has a regular movie schedule. The iconic 1922 Grauman's Egyptian Theater is operated by American

Cinematheque and screens indie, classic, and rare movies. The newer **ArcLight Hollywood** (6360 W Sunset Blvd., 323/464-1478, www.arclightcinemas.com) is a 14-screen multiplex located along Sunset Boulevard, offering online tickets, reserved seats, a café, and concessions. The world's largest independent record store, **Amoeba Records** (6400 Sunset Blvd., 323/245-6400, www.amoeba.com, 10:30am-11pm Mon.-Sat., 11am-10pm Sun.) is a bustling outlet with a massive collection of vinyl records as well as CDs, videos, and live shows. If you're in town on a Sunday, the **Hollywood Farmer's Market** (www.hollywoodfarmersmarket.net, 8am-1pm Sun.) is an outdoor street market offering impressively stacked blocks of fresh produce and goods from local farmers, ranchers, and vendors.

Accommodations

Hotel Wilshire (6317 Wilshire Blvd., 323/852-6000, www.hotelwilshire.com, $250-350) is a sleekly contemporary, glass and steel boutique hotel with a rooftop pool, restaurant, and bar near Museum Row.

California-country chic **Farmer's Daughter** (115 S Fairfax Ave., 323/937-3930, www.farmersdaughterhotel.com, $220-270) is a boutique hotel offering retro rooms, an outdoor pool, and on-site restaurant and bar. It's convenient to The Original Farmer's Market and The Grove complex.

The glamorous **Roosevelt Hotel** (7000 Hollywood Blvd., 323/856-1970, www.thehollywoodroosevelt.com, $300-350), established in 1927, is located along the Walk of Fame offering a stunning pool and on-site restaurants and bars.

The family-friendly **Magic Castle Hotel** (7025 Franklin Ave., 323/851-0800, www.magiccastlehotel.com, $189-349) offers rooms and suites and a ton of amenities including a 24-hour heated pool, complimentary continental breakfast, snacks, and robes. Rooms book fast.

The **Redbury** (1717 Vine St., 323/962-1717, www.theredbury.com, $350-450) is an all-suite

luxury hotel in the heart of Hollywood offering on-site dining and cocktails.

Food

At Hollywood's oldest eatery, **Musso and Frank's** (6667 Hollywood Blvd., 323/467-7788, www.mussoandfrank.com, 11am-11pm Tues.-Sat., 4pm-9pm Sun., $15-49) tuxedoed waiters serve steaks, pastas, and American specialties in a classic setting.

Canter's Deli (419 N Fairfax Ave., 323/651-2030, www.cantersdeli.com, 24 hours daily, $11-16) is an iconic Jewish deli serving up a vast menu of sandwiches and deli fare. The adjacent **Kibbitz Room** (323/651-2030, 10:30am-1:40am daily) offers an old-school cocktail lounge with a full bar and small stage.

The lines at **Pink's Hot Dogs** (709 N La Brea Ave., 323/931-4223, www.pinkshollywood.com, 9:30am-2am daily, $4-10) attest that it is worth the wait at this landmark 1939 roadside stand.

Celebrity-owned **Trejo's Tacos** (1048 S La Brea Ave., 323/938-8226, www.trejostacos.com, 11am-4pm) is a casual taqueria offering meat and vegan specialty tacos with kombucha, *aguas frescas,* and beer and wine on tap in a bright, industrial-sleek setting.

Jon & Vinny's (412 N Fairfax Ave., 323/334-3369, www.jonandvinnys.com, 8am-10pm daily, $10-24) features Italian-inspired fare including creatively topped pizzas and pasta in a relaxed, contemporary setting.

Rustic-chic **Birch** (1634 N Cahuenga Blvd., 323/960-3369, www.birchlosangeles.com, 5pm-10pm Mon.-Thurs., 5pm-11pm Fri.-Sat., noon-9pm Sun., $7-24) offers new American refined, seasonal small plates and larger format options.

SANTA MONICA AND VENICE

Los Angeles' beaches are a destination in and of themselves, and they're a great place to visit if you only have a day or two. The beach cities are also conveniently located near the Los Angeles International Airport.

Sights and Activities

Along the coastal towns of Venice and Santa Monica, **Venice Beach** and **Santa Monica Beach** (www.venicebeach.com) offer a gorgeous, recreational three-mile stretch of coastline along the Pacific Ocean with the Santa Monica Mountains creating a dramatic backdrop. Soaking up the sea, sand, and sun should be your major activity here. In the immediate vicinity, the funky **Venice Beach Boardwalk** is good for a stroll and people watching. An oceanfront skate park, the **Venice Skate Park** (www.veniceskatepark.com) has a fun vibe, and is a great place to watch the talented kids. The **Santa Monica Pier** (www.santamonicapier.org) has an amusement park and good strolling on its weathered timbers. Rent bikes at one of several beach bike rental shops along the boardwalk connecting Venice and Santa Monica. A paved bike path connecting the two communities makes for an easy ride with gorgeous oceanfront views. Downtown Santa Monica offers retail shopping and dining on its **3rd Street Promenade** (www.3rdstreetpromenade.com), a few blocks from the beach.

For exploring Venice, check out the cool **Abbott Kinney** (www.abbotkinneyblvd.com) neighborhood. This walkable one-mile stretch between Westminster and Venice Boulevard is a hub of fashionable retail shopping, restaurants, art galleries, and nightlife. If you're in town on Sunday, don't miss the weekly **Santa Monica Farmer's Market** (2640 Main St., 9:30am-1pm Sat.) where local chefs regularly shop. It's a great place to grab coffee and breakfast and be dazzled by the array of seasonal produce, meats and dairy, artisanal goods, and flowers.

Accommodations

A contemporary boutique hotel near Venice Beach, **The Inn at Marina Del Rey** (737 Washington Blvd., Venice, 310/821-4455, www.pacificahotels.com/innatmarinadelrey, $200-300) offers 68 well-appointed guest rooms as well as an outdoor patio and Jacuzzi. Sister hotel **Inn at Venice Beach** (327 W Washington Blvd., Venice, 310/821-2557, $240-280) has a bohemian vibe with chic digs (43 guest rooms) set in a residential neighborhood on the border of Venice Beach and Marina Del Rey.

Venice on the Beach Hotel (2819 Ocean Front Walk, Venice, 310/429-0234, www.veniceonthebeachhotel.com, $215-275) provides a low-key stay in a 1950s style beachfront hotel. Contemporary, eco-conscious **The Shore Hotel** (1515 Ocean Ave., Santa Monica, 310/458-1515, www.shorehotel.com, $369-529) overlooks the beach opposite the Santa Monica Pier, with a heated outdoor pool and hot tub, and on-site Mexican restaurant.

The upscale, beachfront **Loews Santa Monica** (1700 Ocean Ave., Santa Monica, 310/458-6700, www.santamonicaloewshotel.com, $425-475) is centrally located and offers an outdoor heated pool and two-tier pool deck with beach views.

Food

The laid-back **Venice Ale House** (2 Rose Ave., Venice, 310/314-8253, www.venicealehouse.com, 10am-midnight Mon.-Thurs., 10am-2am Fri., 9am-2am Sat., 9am-midnight Sun., $7-19) offers American gastropub fare on the Venice boardwalk.

The German-themed beer garden **On the Waterfront Café** (205 Ocean Front Walk, Venice, 310/392-0322, www.waterfrontcafe.com, 11am-11pm Mon.-Fri., 9:30am-11pm Sat.-Sun., $10-22) is a great place for pints, bar food, ocean views, and people watching on the Venice boardwalk.

Opened in 1934, **The Galley** (2442 Main St., Santa Monica, 310/452-1934, www.thegalleyrestaurant.net, $13-44) is Santa Monica's oldest restaurant, serving seafood and steaks amidst nautical decor.

At **Gjusta** (320 Sunset Ave., Venice, 310/314-0320, www.gjusta.com, 7am-9pm daily, $11-16), choose from the mouthwatering sandwiches, breakfasts, and cases of freshly made salads and sides at this artisanal, gourmet bakery housed in a hip, industrial space.

Upscale and cool **Cassia** (1314 7th St., Santa Monica, 310/393-6699, www.cassiala. com, 5pm-10pm daily, $18-46) brings a California sensibility to French-Asian dishes with their seafood-focused menu.

Milo and Olive (2723 Wilshire Blvd., Santa Monica, 310/453-6776, www. miloandolive.com, 8am-11am daily, $14-20)

elevates everyday food with small plates, pastas, salads, wood-fired pizzas, and fresh baked goods served in a communal space.

The Tasting Kitchen (1633 Abbot Kinney Rd., Venice, 310/392-6644, www. thetastingkitchen.com, dinner 5:30pm-midnight daily, brunch 10:30am-2:30pm Sat.-Sun., $13-40) is a hip and charming setting for creative Mediterranean comfort fare and cocktails.

Travel Tips

WHAT TO PACK

It's possible to pack lightly for the resort town of Palm Springs. Temperatures are usually mild year-round, if cooler at night and subject to cooler weather and temperature fluctuations in winter. Pack for poolside and dress up for dinners or brunch. Most hotels provide pool towels and some provide sunscreen, water, snacks, or other amenities.

Temperatures are cooler in Joshua Tree, with cold winters (it's been known to snow) and hot summers (over 100 degrees). Always carry layers, and be prepared for temperature fluctuations throughout the day. Nighttime temperatures can drop as much as 40 degrees. For hiking and touring around the desert, wear sturdy shoes, a brimmed hat, and sunglasses. The gateway towns around Joshua Tree are very casual; no formal attire required.

INTERNATIONAL TRAVELERS

The closest gateway city for international travelers to fly into is **Los Angeles.** The drive from Los Angeles to Palm Springs takes 2-4 hours depending upon traffic. There are no stops, checkpoints, or special concerns along this route, which sticks to I-10.

Visas and Passports

Visitors from most other countries must have a valid passport and a visa to enter the United States. You may qualify for the Visa Waiver

Program if you hold a passport from one of the following countries: Andorra, Australia, Austria, Belgium, Brunei, Czech Republic, Denmark, Estonia, Finland, France, Germany, Greece, Hungary, Iceland, Ireland, Italy, Japan, Latvia, Liechtenstein, Lithuania, Luxembourg, Malta, Monaco, the Netherlands, New Zealand, Norway, Portugal, San Marino, Singapore, Slovakia, Slovenia, South Korea, Spain, Sweden, Switzerland, Taiwan, and the United Kingdom. To qualify, apply online with the **Electronic System for Travel Authorization** (http://esta.cbp.dhs.gov/esta) and make sure you have a return plane ticket to your country of origin dated less than 90 days from your date of entry. Holders of Canadian passports do not need visas or visa waivers. To learn more about visa and passport requirements, visit http://travel.state.gov.

In most countries, the local U.S. embassy or consulate should be able to provide a **tourist visa.** The average fee for a visa is US$160. While a visa may be processed as quickly as 24 hours on request, plan at least a couple of weeks, as there can be unexpected delays, particularly during the busy summer season (June-Aug.).

Los Angeles is home to **consulates** from many countries around the globe. If you should lose your passport or find yourself in some other trouble while visiting California, contact your country's offices for assistance. To find a consulate or embassy, check online (www.state.gov) for a list of all foreign countries represented in the United States. A representative will be able to direct you to the nearest consulate.

Customs

Before entering the United States from another country by air, you'll be required to fill out a customs form. Check with the U.S. embassy in your country or the **U.S. Customs and Border Protection** (www.cbp.gov) for an updated list of items you must declare. If you require medication administered by injection, you must pack syringes in a checked bag; syringes are not permitted in carry-ons coming into the United States. Also, pack documentation describing your need for any narcotic medications you've brought with you. Failure to produce documentation for narcotics on request can result in severe penalties in the United States. For information about current regulations on domestic flights, visit the **Transportation Security Administration website** (www.tsa.gov).

If you are driving into California along I-5 or another major highway, prepare to stop at **Agricultural Inspection Stations** a few miles inside the state line. You don't need to present a passport or a driver's license; instead, you must be prepared to present any fruits and vegetables you have in the vehicle. California's largest economic sector is agriculture, and a number of the major crops grown here are sensitive to pests and diseases. In an effort to prevent known pests from entering the state and endangering crops, travelers are asked to identify all the produce they're carrying in from other states or from Mexico. If you are carrying produce, it may be confiscated on the spot. You'll also be asked about fruits and veggies on the U.S. Customs form that you fill out on the plane before reaching the United States.

Money

California and Nevada businesses use the U.S. dollar ($). Most businesses also accept the major credit cards Visa, MasterCard, Discover, and American Express. ATM and debit cards work at many stores and restaurants, and ATMs are available at banks and in some local businesses like convenience or grocery stores. Within the Joshua Tree area and Yucca Valley, ATMs are limited. Currency exchange offices are available at any international airport.

TOURIST INFORMATION

Entering the city of Palm Springs from the north via I-10, you will be greeted by the **Palm Springs Visitor Center** (2901 N Palm Canyon Dr., 760/778-8418, www.visitpalmsprings.com, 9am-5pm daily), a good stop for books and information.

When visiting the Joshua Tree area, make sure to stop into one of the park's four visitor centers for maps and information. Three of these correspond to the park entrances: The **Joshua Tree Visitor Center** (6554 Park Blvd., Joshua Tree, 760/366-1855, 8am-5pm daily) is located in the town of Joshua Tree near the West Entrance to the park. The **Oasis Visitor Center** (74485 National Park Dr., Twentynine Palms, 760/367-5500, 8:30am-5pm daily) is en route to the park's North Entrance in the gateway town of Twentynine Palms. The **Cottonwood Visitor Center** (Cottonwood Spring Rd., 8:30am-4pm daily) is at the remote southern entrance to the park. In addition, the **Black Rock Nature Center** (9800 Black Rock Canyon Rd., Yucca Valley, 760/367-3001, 8am-4pm Sat.-Thurs., 8am-8pm Fri. Oct.-May) is a small visitor center used primarily as a check-in for campers to the Black Rock Canyon Campground. Other area visitor centers include the **Twentynine Palms Visitor Center and Gallery** (6847 Adobe Rd., Twentynine Palms, 760/361-1805, 10am-4pm daily fall-spring, 9am-3pm Mon.-Fri., 9am-2pm Sat.-Sun. in summer) en route to the North Entrance in the gateway town of Twentynine Palms.

ACCESS FOR TRAVELERS WITH DISABILITIES

Palm Springs

The Palm Springs Aerial Tramway is fully ADA compliant, including the rotating tram cars and both tram stations. At the Valley Station on the desert floor, an outdoor lift takes visitors from the parking area to the ground floor station. There is an accessible viewing area outside the back of the station giving a look at tram cars as they ascend and descend Chino Canyon. At Mountain Station, there is an accessible outdoor patio and viewing area. From the back of Mountain Station, a paved path leads down to forest level; however, this path is steep and not necessarily appropriate for all wheelchairs.

The Living Desert Zoo and Gardens, in the Coachella Valley, has paved paths meandering through the main exhibits of the park.

While none of the trails in the Indian Canyons are accessible, there is a beautiful picnic area in the parking area at the head of Andreas Canyon set next to a stream and palm groves.

Joshua Tree

An **Access Pass** (https://store.usgs.gov, free) permits free entrance to Joshua Tree National Park for U.S. citizens and/or permanent residents with permanent disabilities. Passes can be obtained online or in person at the park.

All Joshua Tree National Park **visitor centers** are ADA complaint, and all have accessible ranger desks. The Joshua Tree Visitor Center and the Oasis Visitor Center have low displays in their natural history areas. At the Oasis Visitor Center, there is an accessible sidewalk and garden area.

There are also several **accessible nature trails.** The Bajada Trail (near the South Entrance) is a 0.3-mile loop with a packed dirt and gravel surface that leads through exposed Colorado Desert featuring interpretive panels. The trail is 5.6 miles south of the Cottonwood Spring Ranger Station and 0.5 mile north of the south park entrance. The Cap Rock Nature Trail leads 0.4 mile along packed dirt and gravel through eroded boulder formations. Parking is available at the junction of Park Boulevard and Keys View Road. At the end of Keys View Road, Keys View Nature Trail is a paved 0.2-mile wheelchair-accessible trail offering sweeping views of Palm Springs, Coachella Valley, and the San Jacinto Mountains. At the historic Oasis of Mara, a 0.5-mile boardwalk trail winds through native vegetation and fan palms in an area that was used extensive by Native American groups.

A bounty of paved **pullouts** along Park Boulevard also offer close-up views of boulder piles, rock formations, and other spectacular scenery. A few sites worth admiring include: Skull Rock (located on Park Boulevard near the Jumbo Rocks Campground entrance) and the Cholla Cactus Garden along the Pinto Basin Road. At the Intersection Rock parking area and the Hidden Valley picnic areas, sidewalks give access to wayside exhibits and vault toilets. Intersection Rock parking area also has an accessible sidewalk for access to wayside exhibits and pit toilets.

ADA-compliant **campground** sites include Jumbo Rocks Campground (site 122) and Black Rock Campground (site 61).

TRAVELING WITH CHILDREN

While it is possible to have a great family vacation in Palm Springs, many hotels are adults-only and do not allow guests under age 21. Be sure to check the individual policy of any hotel when booking a room. The Parker Palm Springs and the Ace Hotel are two hotels that welcome children and offer separate swimming pools geared toward families.

Joshua Tree is a great family destination. Children will enjoy being able to clamber around on the rocks and boulders, and there are a number of easy, short hikes that families can enjoy. The Junior Ranger Program allows young visitors (typically between ages

Desert Survival Tips

Vast spaces, remote roads, and weather extremes can create potentially risky situations, but traveling is not any more dangerous than in other national parks if you are prepared for the unique environment. Know what weather to expect and where you're going, and be prepared for the unexpected.

TELL SOMEONE WHERE YOU ARE GOING

Whether you're hiking, driving, or a combination, make sure you tell someone where you are going and when to expect your return. The desert covers a huge area, and in the event that you are stranded, the search effort can be pinpointed. For hiking or backcountry camping, obtain a backcountry permit from one of 13 backcountry registration boards located throughout Joshua Tree National Park.

BRING SUPPLIES

Temperatures can fluctuate 40 degrees between day and night. Bring a sleeping bag or emergency blanket even if you do not plan to be out overnight. Pack appropriate clothing for a range of temperatures, and be prepared for cold temperatures at night. Always bring extra water and extra nonperishable food that does not have to be cooked. GPS navigation is notoriously unreliable in the park. Be prepared with a paper map or an electronic offline map and a charger. Cell phones do not work in the park. Be prepared to survive until help arrives if you are stranded.

VEHICLE BREAKDOWNS

Sharp rocks, long bumpy roads, and heat can cause your vehicle to break down on backcountry roads. Always drive with a full-size spare tire. A fix-a-flat tire kit may also be helpful. If you are stranded, stay with your car until help arrives. It is much easier to spot a big metal car that flashes in the sunlight than a person walking. Also, it is dangerous to overexert yourself in the heat of the valley, so hiking out to safety is not generally the best option. Be prepared with extra supplies including food, water, and warm clothes.

WINDSTORMS

The wind can be a relentless companion in Joshua Tree, especially in spring, with nights generally windier than days. Wind can be a minor irritant or it can seriously impact your visit and create potentially dangerous situations. At times, wind can descend in the form of a windstorm preceded by a cold front. There may be very little warning, and a dark cloud may be the only indication that a windstorm is approaching. Always stake tents and secure other camp belongings such as camp chairs. Windstorms can create whiteout conditions with serious visibility limitations. If you are driving, use headlights and be prepared to pull over if visibility becomes limited to the degree that driving is dangerous.

5 and 13) to earn a badge by completing a series of activities including drawing, writing, attending a ranger program, and picking up trash in the park. Ranger programs such as the Discovery Walks are geared toward families and can help kids earn a Junior Ranger badge. Joshua Tree also participates in national Junior Ranger programs including Junior Paleontologist, Junior Ranger Night Explorer, and Wilderness Explorer. Booklets are available at park visitor centers.

SENIOR TRAVELERS

A **Senior Pass** (https://store.usgs.gov, $10) is available to U.S. citizens/permanent residents over age 62 who are visiting Joshua Tree National Park. The Senior Pass is available online or in person at park visitor centers.

GAY AND LESBIAN TRAVELERS

Palm Springs is an international gay-friendly resort destination and a mecca for gay and lesbian travelers. Many accommodations cater exclusively to gay travelers (only one accommodation caters exclusively to lesbian travelers); however, all lodging in Palm Springs are open to gay and lesbian visitors. In addition to a range of gay bars and clubs, the spring festival season draws thousands of visitors annually to the all-male music and dance party weekend (White Party, www.jeffreysanker.com) and the all-female music and party weekend (The Dinah, www.thedinah.com).

TRAVELING WITH PETS

Many hotels in Palm Springs accept well-behaved pets for a fee; check with each individual hotel when booking. However, it is best to leave your pet at home when visiting Joshua Tree National Park. Pets are allowed in Joshua Tree, but they are not allowed on any trails and cannot be left unattended in a car, since desert temperatures can soar. Pets must be on a leash at all times and cannot be more than 100 feet from a picnic area, road, or campground.

HEALTH AND SAFETY

As a desert park, Joshua Tree National Park is no more dangerous than any other national park. However, there are a few extra precautions you should take to stay safe.

Heat

Heat is the biggest health threat in the desert. The hottest conditions occur at the lower elevations during summer and can be dangerously hot **May-October.** Many visitors choose to visit the park in summer, and it is possible to do so safely if you take some precautions. *Avoid hiking or other outdoor exertion at low elevations during summer.* In summer, confine hiking to high elevations, or, go out early in the morning or late in the

evening; stick to paved roads for touring at low elevations. When hiking or exploring outdoors, wear a wide-brimmed hat, sunglasses, and proper sun protection. Lightweight, light-colored breathable clothing can offer better protection than sunscreen—wear both.

Dehydration

Dehydration is the biggest threat to health in Joshua Tree. Daytime temperatures can soar. Always carry plenty of water—at least two gallons per person per day (and more than you think you will need)—especially when hiking or engaging in other physical activity. Signs of heat exhaustion include dizziness, nausea, and headaches. If these occur, get into the shade and drink plenty of water or sports drinks.

Getting Lost

With its wide network of popular trails, it is easy to underestimate potential dangers when hiking in Joshua Tree National Park. Attempt to keep track of distant landmarks when hiking; the landscape can be extremely disorienting with its sweeping boulder piles and Joshua trees. This is especially important since trails in Joshua Tree's sandy soil are easily erased with wind and water, making them hard to follow across open landscape. Watch for trail markers, such as a row of rocks or downed Joshua tree marking trail boundaries. Also because of the sandy soil, trails and washes can look alike. It is easy to get off course and follow a wide, sandy wash instead of a trail. This may account for the prevalence of social trails (informal trails established by use) in Joshua Tree. Often these trails are made by people who have gotten off course or are attempting a short cut. Avoid social trails if possible; they have the potential to get you lost, and they damage the landscape.

Resources

Suggested Reading

GUIDEBOOKS

Kaiser, James. *Joshua Tree: The Complete Guide,* 5th edition. Chicago, IL: Destination Press, 2014. This colorful guide covers Joshua Tree's recreation highlights, geology, ecology, and history.

MacKay, Pam. *Mojave Desert Wildflowers: A Field Guide to Wildflowers, Trees, and Shrubs of the Mojave Desert.* Guilford, CT: Morris Book Publishing, 2013. An excellent field guide to Mojave flora.

HIKING

Cunningham, Bill, and Polly Cunningham. *Hiking Joshua Tree National Park: 38 Day and Overnight Hikes.* Guilford, CT: Falcon Guides, 2008. This classic hiking guide provides detailed trail descriptions for a wide range of hikes for hikers of all abilities and interests in Joshua Tree National Park.

Ferranti, Philip, and Hank Koenig. *140 Great Hikes in and near Palm Springs.* Golden, CO: Colorado Mountain Club, 2013. This hiking guide offers a thorough overview of hiking near Palm Springs including trail descriptions of hikes in the Coachella Valley, San Jacinto Mountains, Santa Rosa Mountains, and Palm Springs and the Indian Canyons.

ROCK CLIMBING

Miramontes, Robert. *Joshua Tree Rock Climbs.* Silt, CO: Wolverine, 2014. An in-depth guide to rock climbing the entire park, this guide features 3,000 of Joshua Tree's easy and moderate routes and recommended bouldering circuits.

Vogel, Randy. *Rock Climbing Joshua Tree West.* Guilford, CT: Falcon Guide, 2006. Focusing on the popular western part of the park, this guide covers climbs from Quail Springs to Hidden Valley Campground.

Winger, Charlie, and Diane Winger. *The Trad Guide to Joshua Tree: 60 Favorite Climbs from 5.5 to 5.9.* Golden, CO: Colorado Mountain Club Press, 2004. This classic rock climbing guide details climbs for a moderate, trad climber in Joshua Tree National Park.

CULTURE AND HISTORY

Shulman, Julius, Michael Stern, and Alan Hess. *Julius Shulman: Palm Springs.* New York: Rizzoli, 2008. This photography book captures more than 60 iconic Southern California modernist buildings by 15 notable mid-century architects through the lens of photographer Julius Shulman.

Stringfellow, Kim. *Greetings from the Salton Sea: Folly and Intervention in the Southern California Landscape, 1905-2005.* Santa Fe, NM: Center for American Places, 2005. An artistic mix of cultural geography, history, and photography, this book provides a fascinating glimpse into the dissolution of California's Salton Sea.

Stringfellow, Kim. *Jackrabbit Homestead: Tracing the Small Tract Act in the Southern California Landscape, 1938-2008*. Chicago, IL: Center for American Places at Columbia College Chicago, 2009. This book glimpses the history of the homesteads in Wonder Valley near Joshua Tree through a mix of cultural geography and photography.

NONFICTION

Nyala, Hannah. *Point Last Seen: A Woman Tracker's Story*. New York: Simon & Schuster, 1997. A compelling story of a woman who fled personal danger to become a tracker in Joshua Tree National Park. The author describes her time spent as a tracker and its intersection with her personal narrative.

MAPS

Joshua Tree National Park. San Rafael, CA: Tom Harrison Maps, 2013. A shaded-relief topographic map of Joshua Tree National Park with detailed hiking trails including mileages, road networks, campgrounds, picnic areas, and ranger stations. This map can be the backbone for hiking and driving tours.

Joshua Tree National Park Trails Illustrated Topographic Map. Evergreen, CO: National Geographic, 2005. A topographic map that details hiking trails with mileages, paved and dirt roads, campgrounds, picnic areas, and ranger stations in Joshua Tree National Park.

A Map of Modern Palm Springs. Palm Springs Modern Committee. This foldout map to mid-century modern landmarks includes location, address, architect, and the year built. The map is available for download in app form as well, with a ton of mid-century architecture information including additional listings, photos, history, and architect information. The user-friendly listings allow you to take a self-guided tour.

Santa Rosa & San Jacinto Mountains National Monument. Palm Desert, CA: Wilderness Society, 2008. A detailed topographic trail map that covers extensive ground, including trails near the town of Idyllwild in the Mount San Jacinto State Park and Wilderness, the Agua Caliente Indian Reservation and Indian Canyons, Palm Springs, and sections of the Pacific Crest Trail. This useful and comprehensive map includes mileages as well as trail listings with distances.

Internet Resources

Coachella Valley Preserve
www.coachellavalleypreserve.org
The website includes preserve information, including hours, location, history, and flora and fauna as well as downloadable trail maps for the preserve's 25 miles of hiking trails.

Joshua Tree National Park
www.nps.gov/jotr
The main park website is a good resource for planning your visit, including up-to-date visitor center hours and event calendars, an overview of the park's main sights, campgrounds, and climate as well as information about permits, fees, and park rules.

Visit Gay Palm Springs
www.visitgaypalmsprings.com
The official gay and lesbian guide to hotels, resorts, nightlife, clubs, bars, and events that cater to a gay and lesbian clientele, as well as attractions and activities that may be appealing for all visitors. This

information is also available in downloadable app form.

Visit Palm Springs
www.visitpalmsprings.com
The official visitor website provides recommendations for where to dine, stay, shop, and
explore as well as event listings and basic visitor information on traveling to Palm Springs.

The information is also available in helpful
downloadable app form.

Whitewater Preserve
www.wildlandsconservancy.org
The website lists visitor information, including trail map and descriptions, hours, program information, and plant and animal
checklists.

Index

List of Maps

Photo Credits

Title page photo: © Laina Babb

All photos © Jenna Blough except page 3 © Chon Kit Leong | Dreamstime.com; page 6 © Nyker1 | Dreamstime.com; page 7 © Greg Epperson | Dreamstime.com; page 8 © William Perry | Dreamstime.com; page 9 (top) © Patrick Lienin | Dreamstime.com, (bottom left) © Ryan Jones, (bottom right) © Dreamstime.com; page 13 © Scott Griessel | Dreamstime.com; page 19 © Laina Babb; page 20 (top) © Dreamstime.com, (bottom) © Chon Kit Leong | Dreamstime.com; page 96 © Laina Babb; page 97 © Lunamarina | Dreamstime.com; page 103 © Ryan Jones; page 124 © Laina Babb; page 125 © Ryan Jones; page 141 © Ryan Jones; page 148 © Jimkresge | Dreamstime.com; page 154 © Laina Babb; page 163 © Jimkresge | Dreamstime.com

Also Available

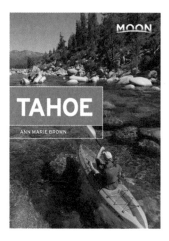

MAP SYMBOLS

≈≈≈	Expressway	○	City/Town	✈	Airport	⌐	Golf Course
━━━	Primary Road	⊙	State Capital	✈	Airfield	P	Parking Area
━━━	Secondary Road	⊛	National Capital	▲	Mountain	≜	Archaeological Site
⋯⋯	Unpaved Road	★	Point of Interest	✛	Unique Natural Feature	▮	Church
━━━	Feature Trail	•	Accommodation			▯	Gas Station
------	Other Trail	▼	Restaurant/Bar	⟆	Waterfall	⬠	Glacier
⋯⋯⋯	Ferry	■	Other Location	▲	Park	▦	Mangrove
≈≈≈	Pedestrian Walkway			▯	Trailhead	≋	Reef
▥▥▥	Stairs	Λ	Campground	⚡	Skiing Area	▤	Swamp

CONVERSION TABLES

°C = (°F − 32) / 1.8
°F = (°C x 1.8) + 32
1 inch = 2.54 centimeters (cm)
1 foot = 0.304 meters (m)
1 yard = 0.914 meters
1 mile = 1.6093 kilometers (km)
1 km = 0.6214 miles
1 fathom = 1.8288 m
1 chain = 20.1168 m
1 furlong = 201.168 m
1 acre = 0.4047 hectares
1 sq km = 100 hectares
1 sq mile = 2.59 square km
1 ounce = 28.35 grams
1 pound = 0.4536 kilograms
1 short ton = 0.90718 metric ton
1 short ton = 2,000 pounds
1 long ton = 1.016 metric tons
1 long ton = 2,240 pounds
1 metric ton = 1,000 kilograms
1 quart = 0.94635 liters
1 US gallon = 3.7854 liters
1 Imperial gallon = 4.5459 liters
1 nautical mile = 1.852 km

MOON PALM SPRINGS & JOSHUA TREE

Avalon Travel
An imprint of Perseus Books
A Hachette Book Group company
1700 Fourth Street
Berkeley, CA 94710, USA
www.moon.com

Editor: Sabrina Young
Series Manager: Kathryn Ettinger
Copy Editor: Ashley Benning
Production and Graphics Coordinator: Darren Alessi
Cover Design: Faceout Studios, Charles Brock
Moon Logo: Tim McGrath
Map Editor: Kat Bennett
Cartographers: Lohnes & Wright
Proofreader: Alissa Cyphers
Indexer: Greg Jewett

ISBN-13: 978-1-63121-393-9
ISSN: 2471-5530

Printing History
1st Edition — October 2016
5 4 3 2 1

Text © 2016 by Jenna Blough.
Maps © 2016 by Avalon Travel.
All rights reserved.

Some photos and illustrations are used by permission and are the property of the original copyright owners.

Front cover photo: Palm Canyon, Indian Canyons, Palm Springs © Dennis Frates / Alamy Stock Photo
Back cover photo: Yucca plants and sunset, Joshua Tree National Park © Biolifepics | Dreamstime.com

Printed in Canada by Friesens

Moon Handbooks and the Moon logo are the property of Avalon Travel. All other marks and logos depicted are the property of the original owners. All rights reserved. No part of this book may be translated or reproduced in any form, except brief extracts by a reviewer for the purpose of a review, without written permission of the copyright owner.

All recommendations, including those for sights, activities, hotels, restaurants, and shops, are based on each author's individual judgment. We do not accept payment for inclusion in our travel guides, and our authors don't accept free goods or services in exchange for positive coverage.

Although every effort was made to ensure that the information was correct at the time of going to press, the author and publisher do not assume and hereby disclaim any liability to any party for any loss or damage caused by errors, omissions, or any potential travel disruption due to labor or financial difficulty, whether such errors or omissions result from negligence, accident, or any other cause.